Heinemann **IT** Professional

ICT Systems Support

For the e-Quals IT Practitioner Diploma – Level 2

Andrew Smith, Monique Heery and Jenny Lawson

Series Editor – Jenny Lawson

Endorsed by
City&
Guilds

www.heinemann.co.uk
✓ Free online support
✓ Useful weblinks
✓ 24 hour online ordering

01865 888058

Heinemann
Inspiring generations

Heinemann Educational Publishers
Halley Court, Jordan Hill, Oxford OX2 8EJ
Part of Harcourt Education

Heinemann is the registered trademark of
Harcourt Education Limited

First published 2004

09 08 07 06 05 04
10 9 8 7 6 5 4 3 2 1

British Library Cataloguing in Publication Data is available from
the British Library on request.

ISBN 0 435 471511

Designed by The Wooden Ark Studio
Typeset by 🝔 Tek-Art, Croydon, Surrey

Original illustrations © Harcourt Education Limited, 2004
All photographs by Gareth Boden
Printed in the UK by Scotprint

Cover photo: ©

Acknowledgements

Every effort has been made to contact copyright holders of material reproduced
in this book. Any omissions will be rectified in subsequent printings if notice is
given to the publishers.

Websites

There are links to relevant websites in this book. In order to ensure that the
links work, and that the sites are not inadvertently linked to sites that could
be considered offensive, we have made the links available on the Heinemann
website at www.heinemann.co.uk/hotlinks. When you access the site, the
express code is 151IP.

Contents

Unit 402: Customer support

Unit 403/4: Install and configure equipment, operating systems and software

Unit 401

Maintain equipment and systems

Introduction

Since computers became part of commercial life in the 1950s, people have been employed to maintain, upgrade and fix these systems. Now that computers have become a part of everyday life, and they can be found in the home, at school and on nearly every desk in the work place, the need for trained professionals like you has become increasingly important.

In reading this unit, you will explore the main roles involved in maintaining a computer system, with the emphasis being on personal computer systems and how you can best support the user.

This unit is divided into seven sections, each looking at important aspects involved with maintaining computer systems:

- Why is maintenance important?
- What is 'health and safety' and why is it important?
- The challenges of electrostatic discharge (ESD).
- What is preventive maintenance?
- Successful fault-finding.
- Fixing the system.
- Tips for passing the module.

This qualification is primarily practical and you will be set a series of specific tasks as part of your assessment. This is supported by a multiple choice examination that you will complete when you have done all class-set assignments.

1

1 Why is maintenance important?

It's happened to you, it's happened to someone you know… you are busy working on the computer, typing that important assignment, emailing your best friend, defeating the evil alien in your game… then the computer freezes, bangs, blue screens or eats your hard drive as if you forgot to feed it.

While computers are prone to failure due to the nature of the technology, many problems can be prevented by simple routine maintenance.

What does it mean?

Blue screen: Comes from the term 'the blue screen of death' which was Microsoft's way of displaying serious errors with its earlier Windows operating systems.

Cars run well when maintained, and it is an accepted part of car ownership that you will have:

◆ changed the oil regularly
◆ ensured that the radiator has anti-freeze in the winter
◆ made sure that the tyres have a legal tread and are fully inflated
◆ sent the car for an annual check
◆ ensured that the car has passed its MOT
◆ checked that there are no cracks and chips in the windscreen
◆ ensured the CD auto-changer and speaker system is working properly!

Some of the above points are legal obligations for the safety of yourself and others on the road; others are sensible precautions.

While maintaining a computer is different from the responsibility of maintaining a car, the damage that can be caused by a computer failing can affect the lives of many. In a society where we depend on computer systems for many of our routine tasks, a computer failing during the payroll run at the end of the month could:

◆ affect your income for that month, and
◆ make you the most unpopular person in your company as it will affect everyone.

Therefore, there are recognised practices in the computer industry to prevent failures from happening, or if they do (remember that the technology is unreliable) then a rapid solution or replacement can be implemented.

Maintenance of a computer system often involves:

◆ checking that the technology is adequate for the task
◆ regularly backing up the data

- maintaining quality and quantity of the storage
- ensuring that there is a regular stock of consumables
- running diagnostic programs
- portable appliance testing (PAT)
- checking the system for viruses/Trojans/worms, etc.
- applying critical software updates
- ensuring that you keep an open dialogue with the user, if only because they may notice a fault long before you do.

What does it mean?

*A personal computer and its peripherals are classed as **portable** (anything that is not fixed to the desk).*

***PAT (portable appliance testing)** is a legal requirement to test the electrical safety of all portable electrical equipment to prevent electric shocks.*

Check your understanding

Look at the computers at your centre. Some may have a small sticker on the plug, monitor or base unit, showing when they were last PAT tested. Go to www.heinemann.co.uk/hotlinks and follow the links to discover what UK legislation covers the legal duty to carry out PAT testing.

2 What is health and safety and why is it important?

Working with computers still means that you have to comply with and be aware of legal and safety constraints. In this section you will explore the legislation, look at some of the practical requirements and develop an understanding of how this involves you.

2.1 The legislation and your responsibility

Everything done in the workplace is governed by the **Health and Safety at Work Act 1974**. This Act is a combination of many Acts of law and is supported by a wide array of legislation to ensure that employees can work safely. The Act is criminal legislation; this means you or others can serve a prison sentence for serious breaches of the law.

All employees are responsible for their own personal health and safety as well as that of everyone else working around them. As a computer maintenance professional this law will apply to you.

Another law that affects you directly as a computer maintenance professional is the **Control of Substances Hazardous to Health (COSHH) Regulations**. The foam that you may use to clean monitors, printers and computer base units and toner for laser printers are controlled under this legislation.

◆ Under the Health and Safety at Work Act you have four main responsibilities:

1 To work safely.

2 To cooperate with your employer in any work safety systems.

3 To report any hazardous conditions.

4 Not to interfere with safety systems for any reason.

◆ You also have 'other' legal responsibilities:

1 To be aware of fire procedures and evacuation.

2 To carry out accident reporting procedures.

3 To be aware of any special safety features in your workplace (this may be especially important if you work for a manufacturing organisation).

4 To know actions that are to be taken in an emergency.

Check your understanding

1 Your centre should have clearly displayed evacuation procedures. Find them and discover the location of your nearest evacuation point.

2 Identify the unique hazards that your centre has and list them.

3 Who is responsible for managing health and safety at your centre?

4 Where is the accident book kept?

2.2 Hazards and risks

Some **hazards** are unique to working with computer systems:

◆ electric shock from the computer chassis or monitor

◆ some computer cases posing a 'cutting' hazard where the metal has not be turned properly

◆ manual handling or lifting hazards

◆ chemical hazards, especially from laser printer toner.

However, the biggest hazard in any workplace is you! Most accidents occur due to negligence or foolish behaviour.

All hazards can be avoided through 'common sense' or safe practices. Often, being aware that some elements of computer systems are hazardous is enough to prevent an accident from occurring.

A **risk** is an activity or venture that may lead to danger. The difference between a hazard and a risk is …

- A mountain is a **hazard**: people may climb up it successfully, and some people may die from doing so.
- Mountain climbers take a **risk** by climbing the mountain. They know that it is a hazard and they are aware they may (or may not) die in the attempt.

When you open a computer that is still connected to the electricity supply, you take a risk because there is an obvious hazard. You can reduce the risk by disconnecting the computer from the electrical outlet. Naturally, it is essential that you make every reasonable effort to minimise or remove the risks that you are taking when carrying out any computer maintenance task.

In working with computer systems, it is important that you are aware of common hazards and risks.

- You need to take care in your use and maintenance of equipment such as printers, monitors and computer base units.
- The clothing or jewellery that you choose to wear may pose risks.
  - Ties should be clipped or tucked into your shirt so that they cannot be trapped in the roller assembly of a printer.

- Dangling metal jewellery is an electrical safety hazard.
- Your hair may also be a hazard if it is long and is not tied appropriately.
- Flowing garments are generally unsafe.

◆ Your use of materials or substances has to be carefully managed. For example, the toner in a laser printer cartridge is a known carcinogen.

What does it mean?

Carcinogen: A hazardous substance that through prolonged unsafe and unprotected exposure, may lead to the development of cancer.

◆ All working practices and behaviour must conform to the employer's health and safety procedures.

◆ Accidental breakages and spillages must be cleaned up in a safe and effective manner.

◆ Considering environmental factors, you must make safe the storage of equipment and resources on shelves, and ensure the safe laying of power and data cables.

◆ All computer power supplies handle an input hazardous voltage of 240 volts, and monitors and laser printers can operate at a range of over 1000 volts.

Reporting and managing hazards

You are legally obliged to report any hazards in the workplace; this is equally applicable to students at your centre as well as employees of any organisation.

All organisations must appoint a suitably trained member of staff as a Health and Safety Officer. Some are in a full-time capacity, others may do this as part of their main duties. If you become aware of, or are involved with, creating a potential hazard, you must report it immediately to the Health and Safety Officer or to your tutor or manager.

You must not assume that someone else may do it or that it's not your job to do so. It is normal practice to inform someone in writing by a memo or an email.

Check your understanding

With the permission of your tutor, tour your centre (or classrooms that you use) and list all potential hazards.

◆ What are they?
◆ What risk do they pose?
◆ What must be done to remove the risk?

2.3 Manual handling

There is a right way and a wrong way to lift a heavy object. In a computer maintenance and support role, you will often lift computer base units and monitors. Do this the wrong way too often and you could damage yourself and suffer long-term back problems.

Wrong way
If you do not bend your legs and lift straight upwards, you can injure your back

Right way
You need to bend your legs and lift from the ground upwards

Figure 1 Manual handling

To lift something safely, bend your knees and lift the object in a straight upwards direction. If the object is too big, ask for help. A trolley or other type of wheeled carrier should be used to move the equipment any distance.

PRACTICAL TASK

Weight lifting for beginners!

For this task you will need:

◆ a computer base unit

◆ a 17 inch monitor

◆ a 15 inch monitor.

Using each of the items you have collected, discover which is the safest way to pick them up and carry them 100 metres (yes, 100 metres, as by the time you cover this distance your arms or back will ache if you have not lifted the object correctly).

2.4 Fuse ratings

The fuse in the plug which connects to the wall socket is not there to protect the computer, but to protect the mains cable. Sometimes through a fault on the device, the electrical mains cable may get a surge in electricity. The job of the fuse is to protect the cable by 'blowing' when too much electricity is being passed through it.

How to calculate a fuse rating

To calculate a fuse rating you must first understand how a plug is wired (see Figure 2).

All plugs in the United Kingdom have at least two wires:

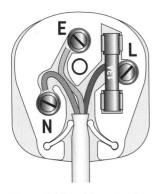

Figure 2 The wiring of a plug

◆ brown (the live cable which is always to the right and is connected to the fuse)

◆ blue (the neutral cable always to the left).

Higher voltage devices will have a third cable, the earth, which is green and yellow. The purpose of this cable is to send any excess voltage or manageable surges back into the main circuitry of your home, college or workplace and to lead it directly into the ground of the property.

All mains-powered equipment is sold with a rating plate or sticker on it (this may be on the back or underneath) showing all the relevant information required to calculate the correct fuse rating for the plug.

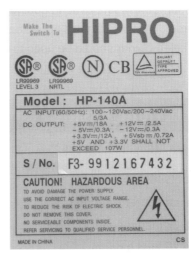

Rotating plate

The two pieces of information required are:

1 Voltage (240 volts in the United Kingdom).

2 The maximum power consumption – watts (which will be different for nearly every appliance).

Simply divide the maximum wattage by the voltage to indicate the total current flow, e.g., the rating plate on a computer base unit indicates that it consumes a maximum of 800 watts and requires 240 volts.

800 divided by 240 = 3.33 amps

Fuses with this precise rating are not available, so the nearest standard rating ABOVE the calculated figure must be chosen – in this case 5 amps. If you put a fuse with a lesser rating into the plug, you will find that the fuse will fail repeatedly.

If unsure a good rule of thumb that you may wish to use is:

◆ below 750 watts – fit a 3 amp fuse

◆ 750–1250 watts – fit a 5 amp fuse

◆ above 1250 watts – fit a 13 amp fuse.

Check your understanding

This exercise may appear in tests set by your awarding body.

Calculate fuse ratings for these items of equipment:

◆ A monitor.

◆ A computer base unit.

◆ A printer.

◆ A scanner.

◆ A soldering iron.

Surge protection and testing

Electricity is notoriously unreliable, and your supply to home, work or college is never the same. In the United Kingdom the voltage supplied is 240 volts, but this can be as low as 22 volts and as high as 260 volts (in some rare instances). Whilst conventional technology such as a toaster can cope with these radical changes in voltage, sensitive technology, such as your computer system, cannot cope and a surge of a few volts can turn your processor to toast.

To clarify how vulnerable the technology is, it is important to appreciate how long the electrical current has to be high before damage takes place.

◆ When the increase lasts three nanoseconds (billions of a second) or more, it's called a **surge**.

◆ When it only lasts for one or two nanoseconds, it's called a **spike**.

A surge protector passes the electrical current from the wall socket to a number of devices to which it is connected. If the voltage from the outlet surges or spikes, the surge protector diverts the extra electricity back into the wall socket's earth. This is achieved by a component called a metal oxide varistor (MOV) which diverts the extra voltage. The MOV forms a connection between the live power (the brown cable in Figure 2) and the earth.

A MOV has three parts: *A piece of metal oxide material in the middle (1), joined to the live power and earth by two semiconductors (2 and 3).*

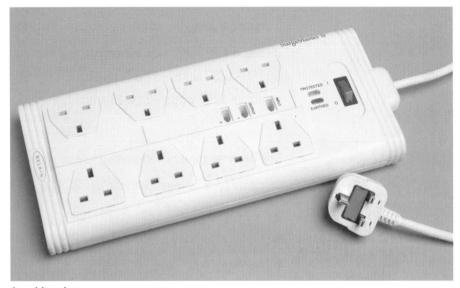

A multi-socket surge suppressor

To ensure that your computer system is 'safe!', you, your place of study or your employer may invest in a variety of surge protection systems. These could be:

◆ a plug that is connected to your wall socket, which your computer may be plugged into

◆ a power block, on which there can be up to 10 sockets to support a variety of devices.

2.5 What is PAT testing?

PAT testing is covered by five Acts of Parliament:

1 **Health and Safety at Work Act 1974**

2 **Management of Health and Safety at Work Regulations 1999**

3 **Electricity at Work Regulations 1989**

4 **Workplace (Health, Safety and Welfare) Regulations 1992**

5 **Provision and Use of Work Equipment Regulations 1998.**

This is to ensure that all portable equipment – printers, cooling fans, computer base units, photocopiers, drills, microwaves, etc. – is safe to use. The Health and Safety Executive are quoted as saying *'25% of workplace accidents occur because of unsafe electrical equipment'*. The legislation states that *'we have to regularly test all portable electrical equipment'*, but does not define how often 'regular' is.

Common, good practice presumes that regular testing is done once a year, and no less than three years apart for any given piece of equipment. This may vary considerably at each organisation, but since it is assumed that all computers become dated after three years, they must be tested at least once in their lifecycle.

The PAT testing must be done by someone 'competent' to do so. The tester must be trained accordingly. So, unless you have the City and Guilds certification, you must hire a professional to check your company's equipment and to give you a record of all devices that have been checked and their safety status. If any device fails the test, it must be repaired, checked and passed; otherwise, it must be disposed of.

If a computer or other portable device has been tested it will be labelled as such, showing date, time and the tester's initials. All labels will contain a serial or unique reference number, and this is recorded in a PAT testing log book which should be kept with the original tester and the manager in charge of information technology (in some companies an appointed Health and Safety Officer will also retain a copy). This is to provide a solution if the testing label goes missing (it falls off or someone removes it).

2.6 Fire extinguishers

Reading this section will not make you a competent fire officer; for this you must be suitably trained. The information supplied here is only intended as a guide.

A fire extinguisher is a lifesaver and is designed to combat small fires. If the fire is a large one or you believe that it is too big for you to tackle, then raise the alarm, retreat to safety and ensure that others around you are also safe.

There are four classifications of fire and an extinguisher for each, only three of which (B, C, D) can be used if a computer or monitor is on fire:

◆ **Class A** extinguishers are for fires in ordinary combustible materials such as paper, wood, cardboard, and most plastics. The number on class A extinguishers shows the amount of water it holds and the amount of fire it can put out.

◆ **Class B** extinguishers are for fires in flammable or combustible liquids such as petrol, kerosene, grease and oil. The number on class B extinguishers shows roughly how many square feet of fire it can put out.

- **Class C** extinguishers are for fires in electrical equipment, such as appliances, wiring, circuit breakers and outlets. Never use water to put out a class C fire. The risk of electrical shock is far too great. There is no number on a class C extinguisher. The class C means the extinguishing agent does not conduct electricity.
- **Class D** extinguishers are commonly found in a chemical laboratory. They are for fires that involve combustible metals, such as magnesium, titanium, potassium and sodium. There is no number on a class D extinguisher. They do not have a multi-purpose rating. They are meant for class D fires only.

Some fires may involve a combination of these classifications. Fire extinguishers should have ABC ratings on them. These are some of the most common types of fire extinguisher:

- **Water extinguishers** or air-pressurised water (APW) extinguishers are suitable for class A fires only. They must never be used on grease fires, electrical fires or class D fires. This is because the flames will spread and make the fire bigger. Water extinguishers are filled with water and pressurised with oxygen. They should only be used to fight a fire when you are certain it contains ordinary combustible materials only.
- **Dry chemical** extinguishers come in a variety of types. They are suitable for a combination of class A, B and C fires. They are filled with foam or powder and pressurized with nitrogen. Dry chemical extinguishers have an advantage over CO_2 extinguishers since they leave a non-flammable substance on the extinguished material, reducing the likelihood of re-ignition.
  - **BC** – This is the normal type of dry chemical extinguisher. It is filled with sodium bicarbonate or potassium bicarbonate. The BC variety leaves a mildly corrosive residue. This must be cleaned at once to prevent any damage to materials.
  - **ABC** – This is the multipurpose dry chemical extinguisher. The ABC type is filled with mono-ammonium phosphate. This is a yellow powder that leaves a sticky residue. This may be damaging to electrical appliances such as a computer.
- **Carbon dioxide (CO_2) extinguishers** are used for class B and C fires. CO_2 extinguishers contain carbon dioxide, a non-flammable gas. They are highly pressurised. The pressure is so great that it is not uncommon for bits of dry ice to shoot out of the nozzle. They do not work very well on class A fires because they may not be able to displace enough oxygen to put the fire out. This causes the fire to re-ignite. CO_2 extinguishers have an advantage over dry chemical extinguishers in that they do not leave a harmful residue. This means that they are a good choice for an electrical fire on a computer or other electronic device.

If you encounter a fire, you must aim the extinguisher at the base of the fire and ensure that you use the correct fire extinguisher.

Figure 3 The safe use of a fire extinguisher

PRACTICAL TASK

Take the time to walk around your centre and take a note of all the fire extinguishers that are available.

◆ What types are in use?

◆ How many of each type is there?

◆ What is important about their location?

3 The challenges of electrostatic discharge (ESD)

Static electricity is caused by a physical process called **triboelectrification**. All atoms have electrically charged elements called electrons that will jump from one atom to another. Static electricity builds up when electrons jump back and forth between these atoms, and the result is **static electricity**.

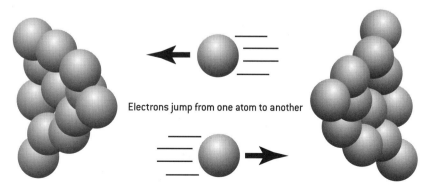

Electrons jump from one atom to another

Figure 4 Triboelectrification

It takes a static electricity charge of over 1000 volts before our hair stands on end or a small spark jumps from an object to ourselves. Static electricity is harmless – you can endure discharges of over 10,000 volts.

Computer processors, motherboards and associated circuitry will normally operate at a maximum of ±5 volts. So, an ESD of 1000 volts will wipe or blow many of the sensitive components and a touch from you could be the kiss of death for your motherboard!

What does it mean?

Motherboard: A complex array or circuits and microprocessor that supports your personal computer system and all its components.

Figure 5   An ESD warning sign

If a computer component has been subjected to ESD it is beyond economic repair. In most circumstances, it is less costly to replace the component with one that is undamaged.

A motherboard costs £25–£200, and any ESD damage can void any warranty agreement between yourself and the supplier. So, any damage is a costly problem, and you, your company or customer will be out of pocket.

What does it mean?

Warranty: A legal agreement whereby a supplier or manufacturer will replace any faulty goods within a given period (normally one year unless you purchase or negotiate an extended period).

3.1 How to prevent ESD

A range of ESD protective devices can be used to protect the computer from you. These are *not* to protect you.

Table 1 *Electrostatic discharge protective devices*

Device	Purpose
Wrist strap	This is an elasticated wristband with a metal pad that will fit next to the skin. The cable runs to a ground connector which may fit into a plug that connects to the earth in the mains. Or, it will connect to a specially fitted earth circuit.
Anti-static mat	A large rubber mat, usually one metre square in size, this will fit into a plug that connects to the earth in the mains. You may also be able to connect your wristband to the mat. This provides a safe area large enough to work on your open computer base unit.
Anti-static bag	Used to transport and protect all computer components, an anti-static bag is often included when you purchase new items. Any component that is not in the chassis of the computer must be kept in one of these bags.

When you are working inside a computer, you must always connect yourself to an **electrostatic wristband** and ensure that it is **earthed,** by connecting it to an **ESD plug** that is connected to an electrical outlet; or ensure that it is connected to an **anti-static mat** that is connected to an electrical outlet. This is also true when handling all computer components when they are *not* connected to the computer.

What does it mean?

Earth: In all electrical circuits, there needs to be somewhere for the excess current to go. A building will have a copper strip or rod that is driven into the ground, to which every plug is connected.

When you are not using any 'spare' components ensure that they are kept in an **anti-static bag**. This will protect them from misuse by others and often protect the delicate equipment from damage.

Good practice tip: Always connect yourself to an ESD band when working on all computer equipment to protect it from yourself.

When does ESD become dangerous?

ESD can be very harmful to the computer. In three specific situations, wearing an ESD wristband can also be very harmful to you, and may well lead to your death.

◆ When working on a computer chassis that is connected to the mains or the power supply, the power supply converts from 240 volts to less than 12 volts. The capacitors used to do this store a large quantity of electricity, which, if discharged, would cause you serious harm.

◆ A monitor converts (or steps up) the mains voltage from 240 volts to 2000 volts to charge the cathode ray tube (the screen). It is very unlikely that you would survive any shock received from this.

◆ A laser printer also uses a charge of over 2000 volts to attract the toner. This is a static charge, and concentrating it to the ESD wrist strap uses you as the earth and this is, therefore, potentially dangerous.

So, unless you are working on a computer chassis and the computer is disconnected from the mains, any repair activity using an ESD strap is too dangerous.

Why should we test ESD protection devices?

Ensuring that an ESD device is effective is more important than your wearing it. What is the point of having a wrist strap that you believe protects the computer from electrostatic discharge if it is ineffective? You may as well not be wearing it!

To test your ESD wrist strap, connect an ordinary multi-meter to the strap while it is connected to the ground. If the multi-meter shows that the ground is 'active', then the strap is working.

Good practice requires you to:

◆ complete the testing of ESD devices periodically

◆ keep a record of the testing and log success or failure and what has been done with the anti-static devices that have failed (disposed of, as they are not serviceable).

This can be done once a month to ensure that you have adequately protected your computer equipment.

PRACTICAL TASK

It essential that you keep records of the testing of ESD devices.

Task one

Devise a testing record card:

1 Include a section that shows the serial number of the ESD device, as well as a description of the equipment.

2 Create a table that shows date, time and who tested the device (include name and signature). Include whether the device has passed or failed, and if the device has failed what was done with it.

3 Include space for the counter signature and name of a supervisor (who may be your tutor) as part of a quality control system.

Task two

Over a period of three months, use the test sheet you have devised to carry out regular tests on three separate ESD devices.

4 What is preventive maintenance?

Preventive maintenance is the process of employing others to inspect equipment to reduce the likelihood of it failing. With the computer system being a complex interaction of many other smaller systems, each has its own need for preventive maintenance.

Why do we need preventive maintenance?

With technology being a major part of our lives, we depend on it for our livelihood and often our personal safety, so preventive maintenance is essential.

Preventive maintenance is carried out in many areas. You may do it on your car, bike or motorcycle.

◆ Paying a garage to carry out the MOT on your car or motor.

◆ Ensuring that the tyres on your bike are fully inflated.

◆ Paying a central heating engineer to check your home's system before the onset of winter.

◆ Regularly running disk maintenance programs on your computer.

◆ Testing the theme park ride daily to ensure that it is safe.

4.1 Preventive maintenance in the computer industry

Preventive maintenance covers a multitude of areas within computing as summarised in Figure 6.

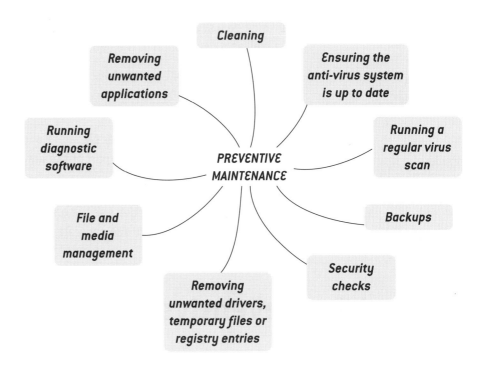

Figure 6 Preventive maintenance

Preventive maintenance involves a wide-ranging skill set. You must:

◆ **Follow procedures** that are predefined by your employer or the manufacturer of the technology. In most cases this means that you have to read the manual. For most companies preventive maintenance is part of a routine support process, which is recorded in standard organisation documentation. Keep records of all the preventive maintenance that you have done and report any problems.

◆ **Liaise with the user** or an appropriate supervisor before preventive maintenance can be carried out. Most preventive maintenance will be part of a prearranged schedule. Nevertheless, turning up unannounced and working on any computer will incur the displeasure of most users. So ensure that the time is convenient in advance.

◆ Clearly **identify the resources** you need to carry out any preventive maintenance tasks, make sure you have the right tools, spares etc.

◆ You need to know what to do if you encounter **faulty equipment or systems**. This chapter offers you the opportunity to discover all the possible reasonable outcomes by completing diagnostic routines to identify what the issue may be.

4.2 Cleaning equipment

In the use and management of computer systems, many components are prone to failure due to dust or dirt.

◆ Input devices, such as scanners, keyboards and mice.

◆ Output devices, especially inkjet and laser printers.

◆ The insides of computer base units.

◆ External surfaces of cases and monitor screens.

This section explains how to clean each component and why it is important to do so.

Cleaning scanners

A **scanner** is a digital device that can convert a printed picture or photo to a computer stored digital image. With appropriate software it can read printed text and convert it to a format understood by Microsoft Word.

All flatbed scanners have a glass plate on which to lay the document or image. Through time, this plate will collect dust, paper fragments and finger prints. This will impair the quality of the image and may corrupt any text that is being read in to a Microsoft Word document.

Ordinary window (glass) cleaner will solve this (the same product kept in the kitchen at home), but you must use a lint-free cloth.

To clean the scanner, make sure that you apply a very small quantity of the window cleaner, and gently rub the glass, ensuring that there are no smears.

For home and ordinary office use, this will need to be done infrequently; in a publishing/graphics environment, this may need to be done monthly.

Check your understanding

Cleaning materials for computer resources can be obtained via many websites. Using Google or another suitable search engine find at least five prices for lint-free cloth (may also be called computer cloth or computer wipes) and compare each for value.

Cleaning keyboards

Keyboards are well-known collectors of dirt from:

- hands that are not clean
- dust
- tea/coffee/soft drinks being spilled
- food crumbs.

Through time, this may affect the performance of the keyboard.

Cleaning the keyboard is often considered the job for the new recruit in many companies due to its boring but essential nature.

Keyboard cleaning is two separate tasks: removing surface dirt and cleaning inside.

To remove surface dirt, use a product called **anti-static cleaning foam** costing £8–£25 a canister. This is to be done when the keyboard is disconnected from the computer.

- Spray a small quantity of the foam on a lint-free cloth.
- Scrub the keyboard keys aggressively with the cloth.
- Keep adding small quantities of foam until the keyboard is clean.

Cleaning inside may be necessary when a colleague comes to you and says 'I've spilt my coffee on my keyboard' or when you turn the keyboard upside down and crumbs fall from between the keys. Whatever you do, do not attempt to lever out the keys with a screwdriver.

- Disconnect the keyboard from the computer.
- Open the back of the keyboard by removing the screws (some low cost keyboards have snap tight lugs).
- Carefully extract the keyboard membrane.
- Spray a small quantity of the foam on a lint-free cloth.
- Clean the membrane gently.
- If required, use a compressed air canister to 'blow away' any dust.
- Replace the membrane.
- Replace the back of the keyboard.
- Reconnect the keyboard to the computer.

Cleaning mice

There are two types of mice in common use: optical and opto-mechanical.

What does it mean?

Opto-mechanical uses light in a mechanical process. See Unit 403, page 122 for a more detailed explanation.

Optical mice are easy to clean because there are no moving parts; on the underside of the mouse are a small LED (light emitting diode) and a light sensor. Cleaning can be done with a single cotton bud to remove any collected dust or dirt.

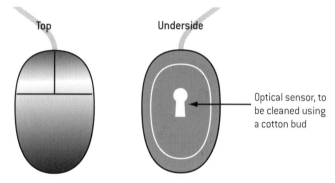

Top   Underside

Optical sensor, to be cleaned using a cotton bud

Figure 7 Cleaning an optical mouse

Opto-mechanical mice are commonplace, being the standard in mouse technology for over ten years. Because the mechanical process (see Figure 8) relies on the mouse using rollers to connect to the ball that rolls across your desk, the system is very prone to collecting dust, dirt and hair.

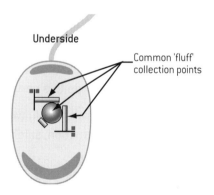

Underside

Common 'fluff' collection points

Figure 8 Cleaning an opto-mechanical mouse

Cleaning an opto-mechanical mouse is slightly more complicated:

◆ remove the mouse ball cover and extract the ball
◆ clean the ball with a lint-free cloth
◆ clean the three rollers with a cotton bud

- if the 'fluff' is solid, you may need to use a small craft knife to cut way the debris
- replace the ball
- replace the mouse ball cover.

It's worth noting that mice are now very low cost items. A new opto-mechanical mouse can be purchased for as little as 69p.

Cleaning printers

The process for cleaning printers differs according to the type and model. Not only do you have the toner or ink, you may need to move paper from the roller assembly.

An **inkjet printer** operates using disposable/refillable printer heads. The need for cleaning varies according to manufacturer and the quantity of the cartridges. The main reason for cleaning is if too much ink has been discharged (printing large quantities of one colour may cause this) or the printer has been left unused for some time.

Some printer manufacturers will include a head cleaning routine with their printer software. Using this will often consume excessive quantities of ink.

To clean an inkjet cartridge:

- Remove the cartridge from the printer.
- Wipe the head with a tissue, until some ink appears.
- Replace the cartridge.

Laser printers conduct high voltages while in operation.

STOP! This is dangerous and is fraught with issues. So complete cleaning of any assembly must be done by qualified professionals. Normally, the manufacturer will be able to recommend recognised companies that can provide this service.

There are only two areas that you may clean successfully and, with instruction, safely.

- Cleaning the toner can be done with a make-up brush; most printers will have a small brush in the kit on purchase. This is only to be used if any toner was spilt from the cartridge on insertion or removal. Laser printer toner is a carcinogen, which through prolonged exposure may cause lung cancer.
- It is now uncommon for manufacturers to make a printer without easy access to its roller assemblies. So you can easily remove paper that is trapped from most models of laser printer.

Cleaning computer base units

As the main part of the system, cleaning computer base units is an essential task.

Go out and try!

With the permission of your employer, tutor, or the person that owns the computer at home, open the base unit and discover how much dust and fluff has collected.

Thirty years ago, computers were normally large-scale systems that were kept in dust free, air conditioned environments. Unfortunately, today, most offices – and especially your bedroom – cannot be classified as such.

Through time, the power supply and processor fans will work together to suck into the computer case a large quantity of dust and fluff. Left unchecked, this will cause the motherboard to heat up and will, in turn, degrade the performance of the computer system. Also, dust will collect in the various ports which, if any additional cards are added, may cause the connection to the device to fail.

Removing the dust from inside the base unit must be done carefully because you can easily damage the components.

- Ensure that the base unit is disconnected from the mains and any other devices.
- Connect yourself to an ESD wristband and ensure that it is connected to an appropriate earth.
- Unscrew the lid of the base unit.
- Remove the surface dust with a compressed air canister.
- Remove the dust from any fans using a make-up brush.
- Replace the lid and ensure that it is screwed in correctly.
- Correctly reconnect the base unit to the mains and any other devices.

Check your understanding

Compressed air canisters that are used for cleaning computers can be obtained via many websites. Using Google or another suitable search engine, find at least five prices and compare each product for value.

Cleaning the monitor

Under no circumstances will you need to open a monitor.

Cleaning computer monitors is no longer a straightforward process as we have laptop/TFT monitors as well as CRT (cathode ray tube) systems. The process for cleaning each is very different.

For cleaning a laptop/TFT, you are often advised to use a dry lint-free cloth. It is important that you clean off the dust and marks without applying too much pressure. If you do, you will cause damage to the LCD (liquid crystal display).

Cleaning a CRT monitor must be completed in two separate stages.

◆ Spray some glass cleaner onto a lint-free cloth and clean the screen thoroughly.

◆ Use a separate, dry lint-free cloth to clean the rest of the case. Try to squeeze the cloth into the gaps for the rear ventilation.

Note: If the monitor has an anti-glare mesh on the screen, it will be impossible to clean.

PRACTICAL TASK

While unexciting, cleaning computers and their associated components is an essential role of any computer support specialist.

To complete this task, you will need these items:

◆ supply of lint-free cloth
◆ tissues
◆ screwdriver
◆ compressed air canister
◆ glass cleaners
◆ cotton buds
◆ small craft knife or similar tool
◆ ESD wristband.

If you are doing this task for the first time, ensure that you have suitable permission before you start.

Following the guidelines listed above, clean these items of equipment:

◆ monitor
◆ keyboard
◆ mouse
◆ inkjet printer (or a laser printer if one is available)
◆ computer base unit.

Once you have completed the above, complete these additional tasks:

◆ Create a schedule to show where you have taken responsibility for cleaning the computers in your classroom or work area. Keep a log of all the work you have done; include date, time, task and resources used.

◆ Create a simple preventive maintenance procedure for cleaning a mouse, keyboard and a computer base unit.

4.2.1 Anti-virus software

Every computer must have suitable anti-virus software; every organisation must have a procedure to deal with viruses and the protection of the computer system.

What does it mean?

Virus: *Malicious software designed to cause havoc on your computers. Viruses are associated with other malicious programs called Trojans or worms, all of which can damage data, the operating system or, in some extreme cases, your hardware.*

To operate successfully, the anti-virus software runs as a small background program called a **service** on your computer. It has a database of all current threats and this needs to be updated daily on every computer that uses:

- email
- Internet chat
- Internet web access
- CD-ROM
- DVD-ROM
- zip/tape drives
- floppy disks
- removable storage such as memory sticks.

Every medium is a potential virus carrier; it only takes one file to infect a computer and, eventually, an entire network. As virus writers are continuously working on their craft, new viruses appear every day. Often, viruses that were popular months ago are re-written to evade new defences.

What does it mean?

Medium: *A method for carrying information. Television is a popular medium for transmitting visual information.*

Go out and try!

Visit www.heinemann.co.uk/hotlinks and follow the links to the website of the organisation which created the McAffee anti-virus application. The website has the AVERT anti-virus database. Review the latest alerts and discover how many viruses the AVERT database contains.

PRACTICAL TASK

Installing anti-virus software

If you do not have anti-virus software installed, it is essential that it is done as soon as possible. With the permission of the person that owns the computer you are working on, go to www.heinemann.co.uk/hotlinks and follow the links to the Grisoft website, where you can download the free version of their popular *AVG anti-virus*.

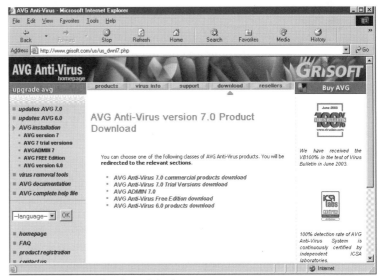

Figure 9 Downloading from Grisoft

You must register your email address with Grisoft so that they can send you a registration number that will be used during installation (as seen in Figure 10). If you do not have an email address, create one by setting up a Hotmail account.

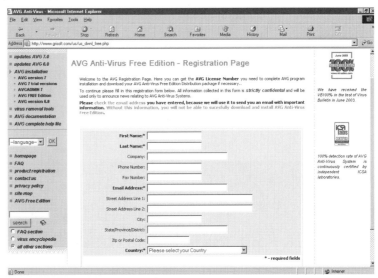

Figure 10 Registering your software

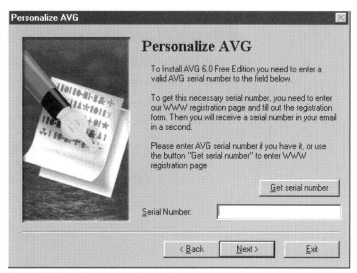

Figure 11 Entering the serial number

During installation, you are presented with a series of options. Unless you are an expert user, click/check Yes for all of them. Once installation is complete, you will be asked to restart your computer.

Anti-virus software operates at a variety of levels and it will check that the following are free from viruses, Trojans and worms:

◆ the boot sector of the hard drive or bootable CD-ROM

◆ the computer's memory

◆ files that you access on your hard drive or any other media

◆ any emails that you receive

◆ any websites that you visit which may have malicious JavaScript, VBScript or ActiveX code.

To successfully complete this, it will check your hard drive's boot sector when your computer is restarted and load itself into memory once the operating system has loaded. As viruses are constantly being written and re-written, to ensure that your computer is under constant protection, you must regularly configure the anti-virus software to:

◆ scan the entire hard drive for any new viruses or other threats

◆ update its database of viruses from the software manufacturer.

Once you have successfully installed your anti-virus application, you need to configure the software:

◆ using the **scheduler**, so that the anti-virus software can frequently check your hard drive

◆ ensuring that the anti-virus software is aggressive

◆ using the **update manager** so that the database is kept current.

PRACTICAL TASK

Configuring anti-virus software

Step 1: Enable the scheduler

If this is the first time that you have started the anti-virus software, and you are using the downloaded AVG application, activate the control centre.

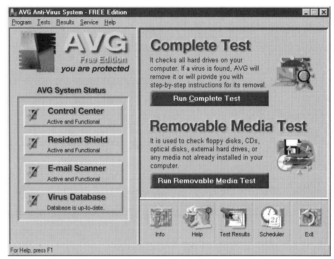

Figure 12   The AVG console

Once that has been successfully completed, click on the scheduler option to see at what time the anti-virus check is set to run automatically.

The scheduler is set, by default, to run a complete virus scan every 24 hours; this is considered a normal time period in the computer industry. If you delay scanning too long (for example doing a scan once a week), a virus is almost guaranteed to infect your system. It is worthwhile setting the scan for a time when your computer is unused because it takes time. 10 Gb of data can take half an hour to scan and the scan can slow down your computer because the hard drive is busy.

Figure 13 shows setting the time for the virus check to the middle of the night. This means that your computer is available during the day. If you have a network of 100 computers, you must do this scheduling for every computer on the network.

Figure 13 The scheduler

PRACTICAL TASK

Configuring anti-virus software
Step 2: Let's get aggressive

The world of virus writers is one of stealth and aggression, so ensure that your software can manage this. Start the control centre by right-clicking on the icon in the bottom right-hand corner of your computer's screen (see Figure 14).

Figure 14 The anti-virus console icon

The screen shown in Figure 15 will then appear.

Figure 15 The anti-virus console

The resident shield is the part of the system that is constantly running. One of the options is **heuristic analysis**. This enables the anti-virus software to check files for the footprint of a potential virus that has not yet made it to the database provided by the software company.

What does it mean?

Heuristic: To use many methods to reach a solution.

You must set the software so that it goes to the manufacturer's website and downloads the latest database frequently. Figure 16 shows that the update is scheduled for late at night so that it can update the database before the computer completes the scheduled scan of the hard drive (see Step 1).

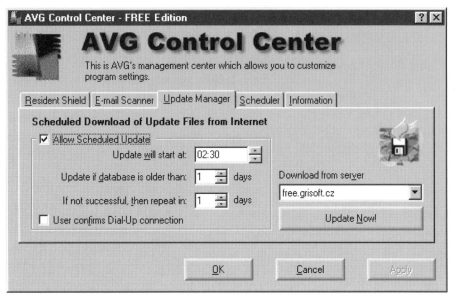

Figure 16 Update Manager

Go out and try!

First, make sure that you have the permission of the person that owns the computer you are using. Then check the settings of the anti-virus software that may be installed. Look for an equivalent of the update manager and the scheduler and identify if heuristic scanning is used.

Once you have your computer protected from viruses all should be well, but there are new threats against your system all the time. Some, you will be protected from; others may catch you unawares.

On large systems, it is likely that some computers may be infected from viruses from time to time; this is accepted as normal. What is done next is critical because it can prevent the spread of the virus (or worm or Trojan) as it attempts to infect other systems.

To ensure that one infected computer does not become one thousand, you will need to follow these procedures.

◆ Immediately disconnect the computer from any external network or Internet connection. This will prevent any other malicious attacks from infecting your computer as well as stopping your computer from infecting any others.

◆ Using another computer that has the latest database, is not connected and has been checked not to be infected (i.e. by running the virus scanner), create a 'rescue disk' (you may need one or more floppy disks for this).

◆ Re-boot the infected computer using the rescue disk. This will check the boot sector and run a comprehensive scan of the entire hard drive. As the operating system is not resident it will not load or run the virus. The rescue disk will eventually find the virus and remove it from the infected file.

- If the user has created any floppy disks or CD/DVD ROMS, disconnect another computer from the network (this machine is referred to as a **sheep dip**) and scan all media.
- Re-boot the computer and scan again.
- If the scan shows that there are no viruses, remove the rescue disk and restart the computer.
- If you are on a network, it is worthwhile running a check on all computers and warning staff, customers and suppliers about the infection.
- Once all of this is done, then you may reconnect the previously infected computer to the Internet/network to make sure that the virus database is up to date and to re-scan the hard drive once again.

The previous techniques are thorough, but not fool proof. Virus writers use a variety of tactics to hide and propagate their wares. Ensure that you have the latest updates for your operating system and scan your system, incoming data and media regularly. You may be lucky enough never to be hit by a virus; unfortunately, this is rarely the case.

Check your understanding

You have already visited the AVERT website. Now visit the Microsoft, Novell, Linux and Apple websites and compare the operating systems with respect to their critical updates. You can access these websites by following the links from www.heinemann.co.uk/hotlinks.

What does it mean?

Critical update is a solution to known virus/worm/Trojan vulnerability.

PRACTICAL TASK

- Create a schedule to show you have taken responsibility for scheduling anti-virus software on the computers in your classroom or work area. Keep a log of all the work you have done; include date, time, task and resources used.
- Create a simple preventive maintenance procedure for installing anti-virus software and ensuring that it is up to date.

4.2.2 Backups

Backups are used as a technique to store important data safely so that it can be recovered at a later date.

Ever since the advent of computers, industry, commerce, government organisations and society have become increasingly dependent on their use and the data/information that is stored on them. If a company like Amazon were to lose access to their data for a short period of time, they could lose hundreds of thousands of pounds in potential income.

With the development of suitable storage systems, all professional computer users, developers and managers should take regular backups of their systems to protect the company or organisation from potential disaster.

While unexciting, being able successfully to back up and recover organisational data is an essential skill. This section looks at:

◆ the terminology used
◆ the equipment and media used
◆ common backup procedures
◆ using backup software
◆ successful recovery of a backup.

Jargon is rife in the computer industry. The industry sector that provides backup software is no different in its use of backup terminology.

Table 2 **Backup terminology**	
Term	**Meaning**
Archive	Another term for a backup (an archive is a room or building where old records are kept)
Compression	The compact storage of data by removing all unrequired binary 0s
Zip	Either a method of compression or a type of storage media developed by Iomega
DAT	Digital audio tape, used in both the music and computer industries
Recover	To restore data from a prior backup
Mirroring	To have two systems or storage devices with the same information

The technology used to back up data has improved radically over the last 15 years. At one time, it was commonplace to use only tape-based systems to create backups of essential data. Nowadays there is a variety of solutions that can be used.

Even while you are reading this section, new and faster technologies are being released or developed. This section looks at common systems that are being used.

- RAID.
- Tape drives.
- Optical media.
- Zip drives.

RAID

What does it mean?

RAID: Redundant array of independent disks.

RAID is a way of storing the same data in different places (thus, redundantly) on multiple hard drive systems.

- Storing the same data on multiple disks can improve system performance by providing overlapping read and write operations.
- Using multiple disks reduces the failure rate.
- Storing data redundantly increases fault-tolerance.

A RAID system is seen by the operating system as a single logical hard disk. You may be using a computer without knowing that inside is a RAID array.

RAID employs a technique called **striping** (Figure 17), which involves dividing (called partitioning) each drive's space into smaller units ranging from a sector (512 bytes) up to several megabytes.

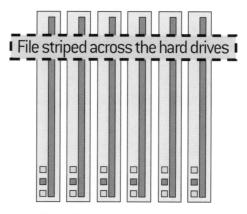

Figure 17 An example of striping

In a single-user system where large records, such as movies or other media, are stored the stripes are typically set up to be small (perhaps 512 bytes) so that a single record spans all disks and can be accessed quickly by reading all disks at the same time.

In a multi-user, network based system, better performance requires establishing a stripe wide enough to hold the typical or maximum size record. This allows overlapped disk input/output across drives.

There are at least ten types of RAID currently available:

◆ **RAID-0** has striping but no redundancy of data.

◆ **RAID-1** is also known as **disk mirroring** and consists of at least two drives that duplicate the storage of data. There is no striping. Disk read performance is improved since either disk can be read at the same time. Write performance is the same as for single disk storage.

◆ **RAID-2** uses striping across disks with some disks storing error checking and correcting information.

◆ **RAID-3** uses striping and dedicates one drive to storing parity information. The system also uses logical mathematic computations to complete the recovery of data in the case of failure.

◆ **RAID-4** uses large stripes, which means you can read records from any single drive.

◆ **RAID-5** includes a rotating parity array, solving some limitations in RAIDs 2, 3 and 4. RAID-5 requires at least three and usually five disks for the array. It's best for multi-user systems in which performance is not critical.

◆ **RAID-6** is similar to RAID-5 but includes a second parity scheme that is distributed across different drives and is very fault and drive-failure tolerant.

◆ **RAID-7** includes an embedded operating system as a controller. This is a specific system offered by one manufacturer.

◆ **RAID-10** is an array of stripes in which each stripe is a RAID-1 array of drives.

◆ **RAID-53** is an array of stripes in which each stripe is a RAID-3 array of disks.

Go out and try!

It is likely that your school, college or workplace has a RAID array in operation on a server. With the permission of your tutor or someone in authority find out what version of RAID is in use.

Tape drives

Tape drives have been in use since the development of magnetic storage media in the 1960s.

A tape drive is a sequential storage system where one piece of data is written after another along the run of the tape. Tape is a slow storage medium, but is perfect for the long-term storage of large quantities of data.

Figure 18 Sequential tape

Most servers will have a tape drive included so that you can back-up current system data. The tape drive relates to the type of tape media that you are going to use where there are differences in speed and quantity of data that can be held on any tape. Common tape systems include: DAT (digital audio tape), SuperDLT (digital linear tape) and LTO (linear tape open).

CD/DVD rewritable drives

Optical media has been available since the 1980s and the recent development of DVDs (digital versatile discs) has increased the quantity of data that can be stored on the media.

Both CD and DVD drives operate by scanning a Class 1 laser over the disc, and the device calculates the time taken for the reflection to come back to interpret the binary data.

The cost of CD and DVD rewriters has dramatically dropped making them a very accessible backup device for the home user or the small company. At the time of writing you could obtain a CD rewriter for less than £40 and DVD rewriters could be obtained for under £99.

Rewriteable CDs can store up to 800 Mb and rewritable DVDs have the potential of storing 17 Gb of data though, currently, 8 Gb is the best available.

ZIP drives

A variation on the floppy drive, the zip drive is popular amongst Apple computer users and is a low-cost, high-speed, backup storage system. Capable of storing up to 250 Mb of data it is useful for 'critical' data and offsite storage.

Common backup procedures

The successful completion of a backup may be the most critical part of your job; any failures may result in immeasurable loss of income to your employer. Some computer professionals have been known to lose their jobs over failed backups.

To ensure that the backups are successfully managed, you need to complete two important procedures:

1 Successful completion of a selected backup technique.

2 Safe storage of the completed backup media.

There are three commonly used backup techniques: full, incremental and differential. Table 3 shows how each technique offers different advantages to the organisation that implements them.

Table 3 *Backup techniques*

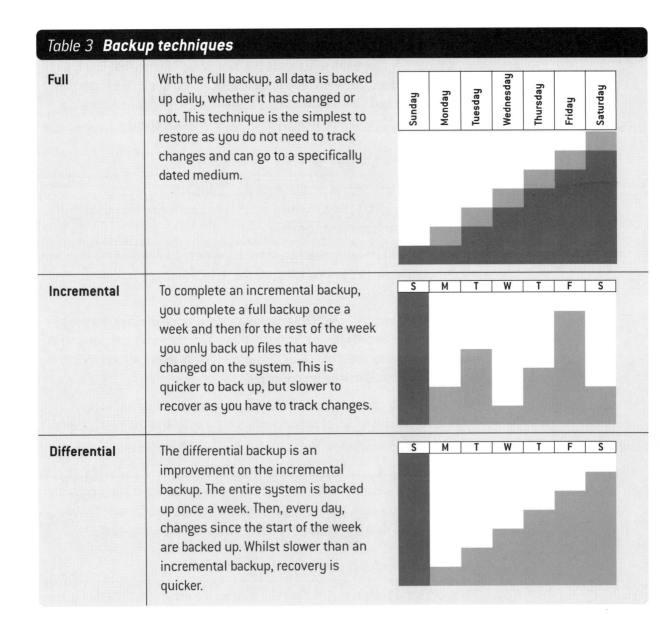

Full	With the full backup, all data is backed up daily, whether it has changed or not. This technique is the simplest to restore as you do not need to track changes and can go to a specifically dated medium.
Incremental	To complete an incremental backup, you complete a full backup once a week and then for the rest of the week you only back up files that have changed on the system. This is quicker to back up, but slower to recover as you have to track changes.
Differential	The differential backup is an improvement on the incremental backup. The entire system is backed up once a week. Then, every day, changes since the start of the week are backed up. Whilst slower than an incremental backup, recovery is quicker.

Safe storage of backup media

Once you have successfully obtained a backup of your employer's critical data, what should do you do with it?

Storage and management of data are equally as important as creating the backup in the first instance. This will depend on the size, quantity and type of media that are being used. In most organisations, it is common practice to do all (or some) of the following:

◆ *Storage of the media in a local **fireproof safe***
If the data is corrupted or disaster befalls the organisation then the data is accessible and, hopefully, is safe.

◆ *Storage of the media in an off-site, remote location*
Many organisations have multiple sites and it is common practice for a weekly or monthly backup to be placed in a fireproof safe elsewhere. If the data backed up is considered exceptionally critical to the organisation, this may become a daily occurrence. Some companies will maintain a contract with a third party security storage company that will hold copies of their media.

Backup software

Many backup software applications are available for commercial and home use. Some are designed for small backups of local data while others, like Arcserve, will back up multiple servers. A small application called *ZipGenius* is a backup and file compression utility that allows you to store your important files in a remote location, while taking up as little hard drive space as possible. It can be downloaded for free: follow the instructions at www.heinemann.co.uk/hotlinks. ZipGenius is an easy website to navigate; you will find the application in the Downloads section.

ZipGenius like many other applications used for backup and data storage will compress (or zip!) the files into one archive file. There are two levels of **compression** that you need to use.

◆ High compression uses less storage space but takes longer to complete.

◆ Medium to low compression uses more storage space (but less than that of the original files) and is quicker to complete.

PRACTICAL TASK

In this task, you will create a backup of essential files on your computer.

1 First ensure that you have appropriate permission to download and install ZipGenius.

2 Open ZipGenius, so that you are presented with the screen shown in Figure 19.

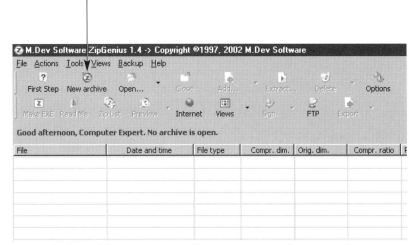

Figure 19 ZipGenius

3 Create an archive by clicking on the New archive icon (top left on Figure 19).

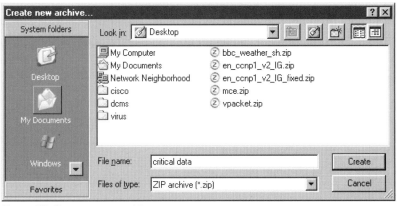

Figure 20 Create a new archive

4 Save the archive in a suitable location on your system. Then add appropriate files to the archive. This could be the contents of your My Documents folder or a selection of files on the network at your college/workplace.

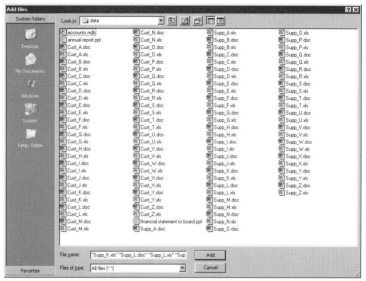

Figure 21 Select files to archive

5 Click on the Add option. Choose files or folders; this depends on the data that you have selected to archive.

6 Choose the medium compression option.

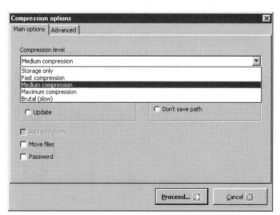

Figure 22 Compression options

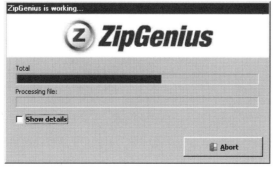

Figure 23 Successful compression

7 When the archive/compression process is complete, you will see a summary of all the files, their original size and their new compressed size.

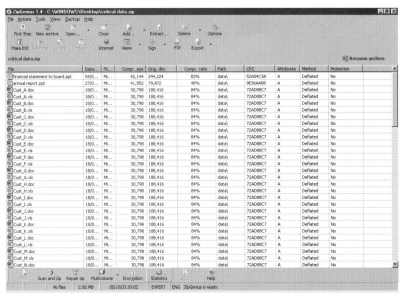

Figure 24 Summary of all compressed/archived files

8 Click on the Statistics option at the bottom of the screen and you will see a comparison of the original size of the files to their current compressed size.

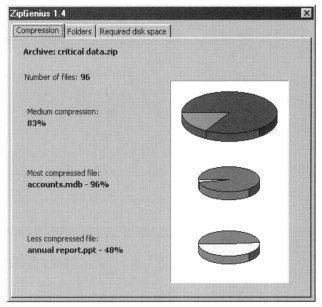

Figure 25 Compression statistics

9 The compressed file can now be saved to a tape system, CD-ROM or uploaded across the Internet to another location.

Go out and try!

ZipGenius has many other features that are very useful in backing up data. Ensure that you are working on a copy of files/data that is not important and try the following:

1 Use the backup menu illustrated in Figure 26 to back up critical system data.

2 Use the Encryption option to protect your data.

3 Use the Make EXE option to save your archive as a self-extracting file. This is very useful for programmers, games designers and web developers.

4 Explore the multi-volume option.

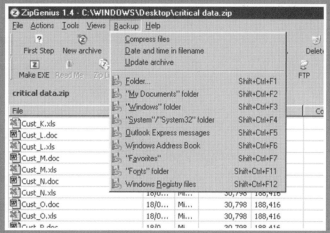

Figure 26 Backup alternatives

Recovering data from a backup

Recovering data that you have archived can be relatively painless. In most situations you simply need to identify the correct backup run before opening and recovering the file. However, reinstating the old version of a file can be damaging.

There are two areas where you have to be cautious in the recovery of data:

1 The recovery of system specific information, if replacing the current data, may set the system back hours, days or weeks and remove any changes that have occurred. Even more critically, this may cause a lack of synchronisation in the system and initiate a failure.

2 The recovery of company specific data that is too old will affect the daily operation of the company and its financial status. Suppose for example, that a web server that handled online shopping crashed and you were only able to recover data from 23 hours ago. Apart from the considerable financial loss, there are implications for the company regarding its legal obligation to its customers and the potential loss of good faith as word travels about the failure.

PRACTICAL TASK

In this task, you will recover files from the backup you have created in the practical task on page 38.

1 Open the My Computer icon on your computer and select the C: drive. Right-click on this to create a new folder and name it Restore.

2 Start ZipGenius and open the Critical Data archive.

Figure 27 Extracting an archived file

3 Right-click on a file of choice as shown in Figure 27 and select the extract option. Select the Restore folder and then click on the extract option.

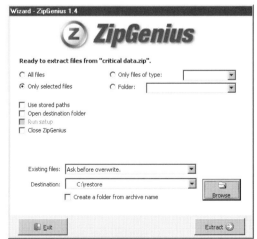

Figure 28 File restoration

4 Open the Restore folder, and check that original file is intact.

Figure 29 A recovered file

1 Why is it unwise to recover an older file over a newer version?

2 What will happen to a computer if you recover and overwrite system files?

3 What is the common frequency for backups in most organisations?

Go out and try!

Backup and archiving are boring but good habits to form. You never know when you may need a file that may have been lost to system issues, virus destruction or user error.

Establish the same habits with your college work at home. Create a simple system where you back up your work on a weekly basis.

PRACTICAL TASK

◆ Create a schedule to show that you have taken responsibility for completing backups on the computers in your class room or work area. Keep a log of all the work you have done; include date, time, task and resources used.

◆ Create a simple preventive maintenance procedure for carrying out backups.

4.2.3 Security checks

Since the development of network technology in the 1960s, there has also been the issue of computer security. A variety of systems are vulnerable to a multitude of negative external influences. Since the boom of Internet use, this issue has become more prevalent for colleges, companies and home users. This section does not attempt to turn you into a computer security expert, but does introduce some relevant issues:

- managing Internet use
- hiding files and folders
- common attacks
- protecting the computer
- what is a firewall?

4.2.3.1 Managing Internet use

The Internet gives everyone the freedom to communicate, exchange ideas, express opinions and carry out free trade. Like every freedom in society, there are some activities that are either undesirable or non-essential.

Most organisations are happy to allow access to the Internet for their employees so long as they do not visit undesirable websites:

- those that promote undesirable images or videos
- sites which provide content that is bigoted in any way
- any sites that infringe copyright law
- sites which incite behaviour to break any countries' laws.

To restrict access to such sites, organisations may use 'Nanny' systems which will control the user's access to websites.

Go out and try!

Visit www.heinemann.co.uk/hotlinks and follow the links to the Net Nanny and Websense sites.

Compare the two products and identify the web content management services that they offer.

Unfortunately, the disreputable websites are constantly on the move. They are constantly changing their web addresses, so it is almost impossible to block the content of such websites. To keep a track of this and to make sure that employees are not abusing the Internet connection, a good systems manager needs to develop a forensic attitude to discover any abuse.

What does it mean?

Forensic: A scientific and systematic approach to gathering evidence for potential legal proceedings.

It is easy to discover on any computer where various users have been on their Internet travels. Windows keeps three sets of information that can be interrogated:

1 A **history** of websites visited.
2 A **cache** of all the pages, scripts, images and applets downloaded.
3 A store of all **cookies** that have been submitted by the websites.

What does it mean?

Cache: *Short-term/temporary storage area.*

Cookie: *A tasty and sweet baked product or a small file left on your computer to record what you last did on a website.*

In Windows 98, the History/Cache/Cookies can be found in C:\windows\ (Figure 30).

In Windows ME/2000/XP, the History/Cache/Cookies folders are found in two locations: C:\documents and Settings\<username> (where the username will depend on whose computer you are using and their profile on the system). Here you will find that the Cookies folder and the cache/history are held in the local settings folder (Figure 31).

Figure 30 History/ Cache/Cookies folder for Windows 98

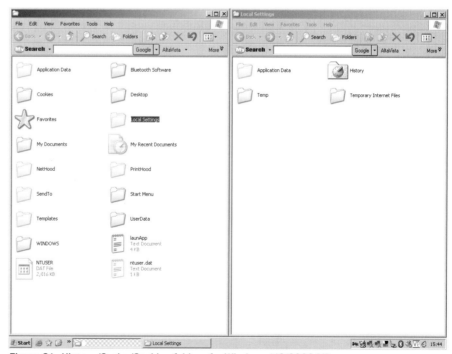

Figure 31 History/Cache/Cookies folders for Windows ME/2000/XP

The **History folder** contains a log of all websites that have been visited by the user in time and date order. From this, the surfing habits of the user can be identified: a list of each page that they have visited on that website and at what time. So long as the system clock is correct, companies have the option to discipline or sack staff for gross misconduct based on their Internet use.

Figure 32 Websites visited

Go out and try!

Viewing other people's computer files without permission can have legal implications. So, using your computer only, look for the History folder and identify your web surfing history for the last 30 days.

The **cache** contains all files, web pages, images, scripts and applets downloaded. The purpose of the cache is to speed up Internet access; storing frequently visited pages locally after the first download reduces the amount of time required for downloading them. However, unless you configure your computer to manage your cache, the content of sites that you have visited remains indefinitely and may eventually 'eat away' at your hard drive space.

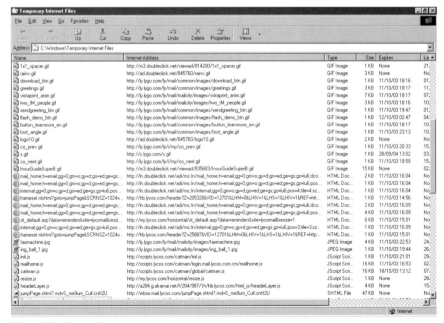

Figure 33 The cache

Remember! Viewing other people's computer files without permission can have legal implications. Look for the Temporary Internet Files folder and identify your web surfing history for the last 30 days.

Note how many files have been downloaded, the size of the folder and the types of files contained. Attempt to copy and open the copied file.

The **Cookies folder** allows websites to track your web behaviour. For example, if you regularly visit a reputable shopping website, the retailer will use a cookie to keep a track of you and to automatically log you in when you next visit the site.

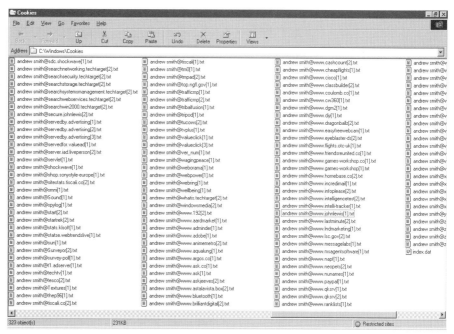

Figure 34 Cookies

Cookies may also give away the behaviour of a user. This can be as useful for less than favourable websites (hacking, pornography, etc.) as for those that are reputable. However, you can control the behaviour of the History/Cache/Cookies folders on any Windows system by configuring the Internet settings option provided in Internet *Explorer*.

PRACTICAL TASK

In this task you will configure the History/Cache/Cookies folders for your computer.

1 Open Internet *Explorer*, select the Tools menu and open Internet Options. Take care … Don't get over-excited and start playing with this feature as you can easily disable Internet access for your computer.

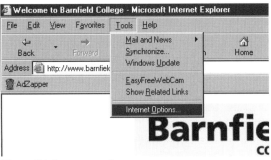

Figure 35 Internet options

2 Using the General tab, clear the cookies held on your computer along with the contents of the cache and the history.

3 Change the setting of the history to zero days, which means that it will only hold files for 'today' and no other day.

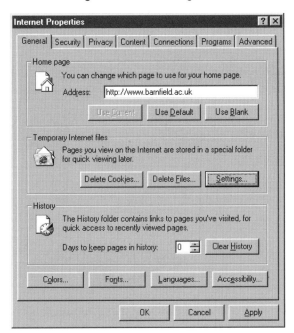

Figure 36 Internet properties

4 Click on the Settings option to limit the size of the cache to 1 Mb. This will reduce the number of files held on your computer and the length of time that files are stored.

◆ Create a schedule to show that you have taken responsibility for clearing all cache items on the computers in your classroom or work area. Keep a log of all the work you have done; include date, time, task and resources used.

◆ Create a simple preventive maintenance procedure for clearing all cache items.

Go out and try!

Power users can configure the way that their computer handles cookies, following on from the practical task on page 47.

1 In Internet properties, click on the Privacy tab and configure the cookie settings. Set it to be very restrictive so that your computer will warn you every time a website attempts to leave a cookie on your computer.

2 Then switch the option off, allowing all cookies from all good and bad websites on your computer.

4.2.3.2 Hiding files and folders

Originally designed as a feature for protecting system files and folders, the practice of hiding files and folders can be abused. In this section you will learn about:

◆ using system resources to discover hidden file and folders

◆ discovering other concealed files.

To hide any file is simple. All you need to do is to tell the disk operating system that the file is not to be displayed using *Explorer* or a directory command. Since the advent of MS-DOS you could hide and reveal files and folders using the ATTRIB command.

PRACTICAL TASK

In this task you will hide an ordinary file. Before you do this, you will need to choose a *Word* document that is not important, copy it to the C: drive and rename it as hideme.

1 Click on the Start menu, select Run and type Command. This will work for all versions of Windows up to XP/2003.

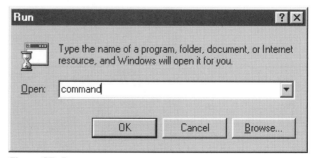

Figure 37 Run

2 You will now be in the **Command prompt** which will give you access to some underlying operating system commands and applications.

Figure 38 Hiding a file

Following the example given in Figure 38, use the following commands to hide the file hideme.doc.

◆ CD\ will send you to the top of the C: drive (called the root).

◆ DIR hideme.* will list all files with the name hideme.

◆ ATTRIB hideme.doc + H will add the hidden flag to the file hideme.doc.

◆ DIR hideme.doc proves that the file is now hidden.

◆ To find any files that have been hidden you can use the ATTRIB command to display all files and folders.

◆ Use ATTRIB *.* and you will see hideme.doc.

Figure 39 File attributes

Another technique for finding hidden files is available through all versions of Windows. By using My Computer, you can select the View menu and open Folder Options (see Figure 40). Once you have opened the Folder Options window, select the View tab (see Figure 41); in here, you can see the Show All Files option. This will display every type of file and folder on your system, including those hidden by Windows or the user.

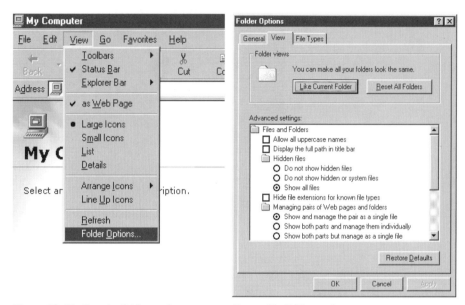

Figure 40 Finding the folder options   Figure 41 Folder options

While it may be the fiction of James Bond and his work for Universal Imports, **industrial espionage** is commonplace where employees have been known to trade corporate secrets with the opposition.

Sending an email to a friend with a seemingly innocent photo attachment will go unnoticed, unless individuals take the time to check the system.

Look again at Figure 41. There is an option called 'Hide file extensions for known file types'. If this is not checked, a *Word* document such as Fiscal Report will be displayed as 'fiscal_report.doc'.

Go out and try!

Using the file that you created in the practical task on page 49, click on the file name once. Windows will let you edit the full name of the file; rename it as sunset.jpg.

What will Windows do to the icon? Can you open the file? What happens if you try to open it in *Word*?

It is also possible to rename files in the underlying operating system (Figure 42).

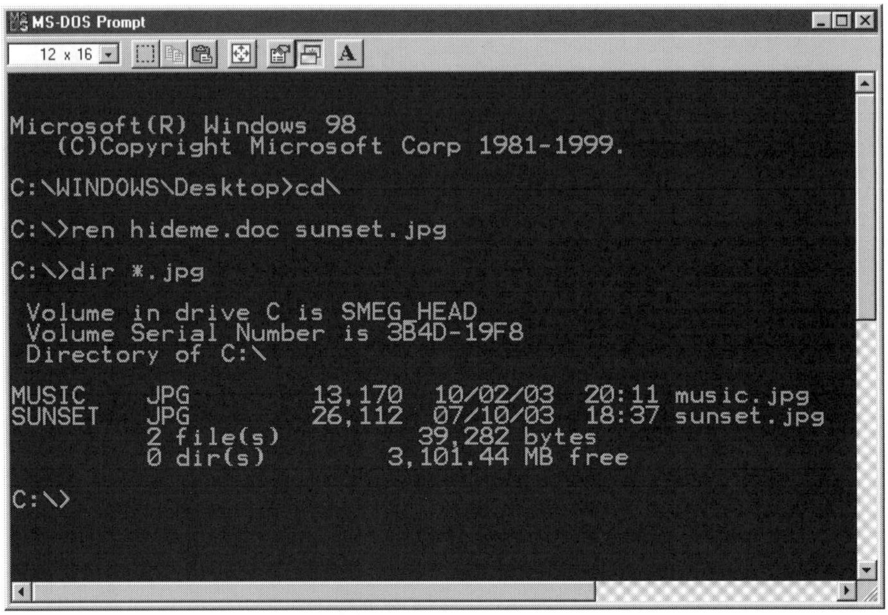

Figure 42 Renaming files

Go out and try!

Using the skills learnt in the practical task on page 49, start the Command prompt. Following the example given in Figure 42, use the system command REN to rename hideme.doc as sunset.jpg.

4.2.3.3 Common attacks

While this book is not about networking, it is prudent that you have the opportunity to appreciate some of the issues involved. This may affect the way you manage your computer and those that belong to other users.

Every day new attacks are being devised; it is often a challenge to keep up with current attacks.

◆ Viruses, Trojans and worms.

◆ Your operating system being exploited.

◆ A denial of service attack.

◆ Your computer being scanned and entered.

Anti-virus systems are described in detail on page 25; it is worth rereading that section now. As part of the virus threat we also have to endure **Trojans** and worms. The name Trojan comes from an ancient classic book called the

Iliad by Homer. He writes of how an invading army leaves a wooden horse outside the gates of the city of Troy. Thinking that the horse is a gift from the Gods, the residents of the city (the Trojans) bring the horse in and have a party to celebrate. While they are sleeping, invading soldiers who were hidden inside the horse leave and cause havoc in the city, before opening the gates to allow the rest of the army to enter and take control.

A common example of a Trojan is Sub7 which can be hidden in a fun screen saver. Once loaded, Sub7 will allow the sender to take complete control of your computer.

What does it mean?

*A **Trojan** is a computer program that, through deceit, will install itself on your system and then allow the sender to obtain access at a later date.*

Check your understanding

Visit the McAfee Security site by following the links from www.heinemann.co.uk/hotlinks and look up in the AVERT database for the most common Trojans.

Worms either move across networks such as the Internet by scanning and finding computers that are willing to talk to them or can pass themselves via the email system, using various users' address books as a method for reproduction.

What does it mean?

*A **worm** is a self-reproducing program that can move itself from one computer to another, leaving a damaging payload in its wake.*

Your operating system is a complex system using a variety of protocols, technologies and applications. Due to its complexity, it is potentially easy to exploit; unscrupulous parties can use flaws in your computer's operating system to cause damage, take control or exploit your system.

You can manually update your operating system (which will work for Windows 98 as well as later operating systems), www.heinemann.co.uk/hotlinks and following the links.

With later systems, such as Windows 2000 and XP, you can configure your computer to automatically go onto the Internet and download the latest update, and this should reduce the chances of your computer being exploited.

PRACTICAL TASK

(This task can only be completed on a computer with Windows 2000/XP installed.)

1   Find the Automatic Updates feature on your computer. For Windows 2000, you will find it as an icon in the Control Panel; for Windows XP, it is a tab in the System icon in Control Panel.

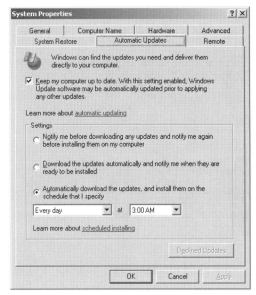

Figure 43 Automatic updates

2   Configure this feature to take a daily visit to the Microsoft web server, so that it can check for and download any new features for your operating system.

◆ Create a schedule to show that you have taken responsibility for ensuring that the computers in your classroom or work area are kept up to date by Microsoft. Keep a log of all the work you have done; include date, time, task and resources used.

◆ Create a simple preventive maintenance procedure for configuring automatic updates.

A **denial of service attack** is an aggressive technique, where an assailant (or in this case a group of assailants) will bombard your computer with so much network traffic that it is unable to communicate with the main system.

Users realise that this is happening when their computer cannot use the Internet or email, or (as in many cases involving Windows) the system keeps crashing.

A denial of service attack is a criminal offence under the remit of the Computer Misuse Act 1990.

PRACTICAL TASK

Note: The technique that you will apply is harmless and will only cause problems for your computer.

1 Start the underlying system as shown in the practical task on page 49.

2 Enter PING 127.0.0.1 –t –l 65000.

3 Return to Step 1.

4 Keep repeating Steps 1–3, until your screen is similar to that shown in Figure 44.

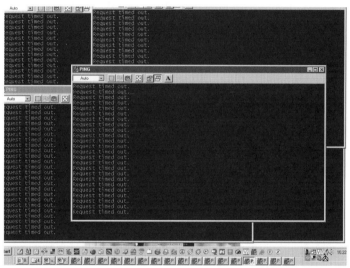

Figure 44 Request timed out

If you suspect that your computer or one that you have been working on has been the victim of a denial of service attack, you can discover who has been 'attacking' your system:

◆ Unplug the network/Internet connection.

◆ Run the command 'ARP –a' in the underlying operating system.

```
Microsoft(R) Windows 98
    (C)Copyright Microsoft Corp 1981-1999.

C:\WINDOWS\Desktop>arp -a

Interface: 172.16.0.1 on Interface 0x2000003
    Internet Address        Physical Address        Type
    172.16.255.254          00-40-96-3a-4a-90       dynamic

C:\WINDOWS\Desktop>_
```

Figure 45 ARP

What does it mean?

ARP (address resolution protocol) is a technology used to match Internet addresses to a unique ID that is held in the network card which is part of your computer.

The ARP command lists the addresses of any computer that has been used to communicate with your computer. By running this command, you can identify anyone who has completed a denial of service against your computer. This can be used by the police in the pursuit of the Computer Misuse Act.

If a denial of service attack is not bad enough, assailants can also **scan your computer remotely** and attempt to gain entry. Available on the Internet are many 'scanners' that will check if computers are switched on. They will also identify those offering open shares, and can then access your hard drives and other media.

4.2.3.4 Protecting the computer

Protecting the computer is a task that is often reserved for experienced system administrators and network security experts. As a trainee expert, you are only expected to have an understanding of what is potentially vulnerable on a computer. To summarise then, most computer systems can be exploited is any of these ways:

◆ sending viruses to corrupt or damage the system

◆ sending Trojans to obtain covert access into the computer systems

◆ scanning the computer to find any vulnerabilities

◆ exploiting any shared files, folders or printers.

To protect the computer, you must ensure that you have installed adequate virus scanning software, regularly updated the operating system using the automatic updates facility and installed a **firewall** to protect the system from remote attack.

4.2.3.5 What is a firewall?

A firewall is a specialist application or hardware device whose sole purpose is to protect the system from unwanted attention or attack; it does this by monitoring all incoming and outgoing traffic from your computer/network and denying access as appropriate.

The firewall can be configured to permit or deny a variety of incoming or outgoing applications or communications channels:

◆ email

◆ chat

◆ file sharing

◆ web browser access.

For example, a firewall can be used to allow outgoing traffic that will return to the system. However, it can prevent incoming traffic that did not originally come from your computer or network.

Network/Internet communication takes place using small units of data called **packets**. As each packet of data leaves or enters your computer, your system's firewall will look at the contents of the individual data packet and decide whether it is a safe or unsafe data packet. If the data packet is deemed safe, the firewall will let the packet through; otherwise, it will block the packet, preventing it from reaching its destination.

Each type of packet goes through a channel known as a **port**; systems that use the **TCP/IP protocol** have a total of 65,536 different ports. Your computer may only be using eight of them at any one moment, therefore making it vulnerable on over 65,500 other ports. This where the firewall steps in. By blocking all unused ports and watching the ports that are commonly used by your system, it acts like a security officer, ensuring all that exits or enters your system is legitimate.

What does it mean?

Protocol: A set of rules used in the exchange of information.

TCP/IP: Transmission control protocol/Internet protocol is the primary technology used in connecting systems across the Internet.

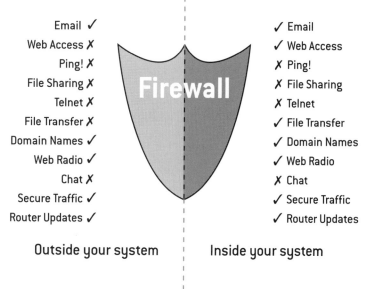

Controlling incoming and outgoing network traffic

Outside your system		Inside your system
Email ✓		✓ Email
Web Access ✗		✓ Web Access
Ping! ✗		✗ Ping!
File Sharing ✗	**Firewall**	✗ File Sharing
Telnet ✗		✗ Telnet
File Transfer ✗		✓ File Transfer
Domain Names ✓		✓ Domain Names
Web Radio ✓		✓ Web Radio
Chat ✗		✗ Chat
Secure Traffic ✓		✓ Secure Traffic
Router Updates ✓		✓ Router Updates

Figure 46 *How a firewall works*

Go out and try!

Visit www.heinemann.co.uk/hotlinks and follow the links to see a list of all current and common ports in use.

1   Look through the list to identify what ports are used for the World Wide Web, file transfer and simple mail transfer.
    Hint: they are near the beginning.

2   Then, carefully read through the list and identify the services commonly used by ports 23, 119, 139, 443, 666 and 7015.

Go out and try!

With the permission of your tutor, line manager or at home, visit www.heinemann.co.uk/hotlinks and follow the links to the Warriors of the Net website. Download the movie promoted on the website. The movie is no longer than twelve minutes and is an interesting description of data packets, firewalls and how networks transmit data across great distances.

Once you have watched the video, answer these questions:

1   What happens to the data at the source computer?
2   What types of traffic are there?
3   What is the role of the router?
4   What is the role of the firewall?
5   What ports did the firewall block?

Firewalls come in all shapes, sizes and technologies, costing from £20 to £10,000, and able to support 1 to 10,000 users. Some firewalls have advanced adaptive features. Others you can configure and some are so simple that you do not need to do anything.

Go out and try!

Carry out some research on the Internet to discover the many different types of firewall products available. Divide your research into four categories:

1   Hardware firewalls for under £200.
2   Hardware firewalls for over £200.
3   Software firewalls for under £50.
4   Software firewalls for over £50.

Look at the services and extra tools that are available for each application.

Configuring and installing a firewall are as challenging as the product you have chosen. With the explosion in home Broadband, the need for simple, effective, easy to configure firewalls has grown. There are many good, free firewalls available which can be used for personal (not commercial) use. In the practical task on page 59, you will download and install a software firewall from Kerio, as seen in Figure 47. First, follow the links to the website from www.heinemann.co.uk/hotlinks.

Figure 47 Finding the Kerio personal firewall

You will need to download this firewall from the products/downloads/personal firewall submenu. Installation of the Kerio firewall is very similar to any other application you may have installed. Once the installation is complete, you will need to restart your computer so that the firewall can start as a service on your computer.

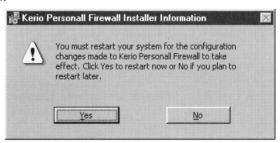

Figure 48 Restart your computer

PRACTICAL TASK

Installing a firewall

If the computer belongs to your centre of study, make sure that your tutor is aware that you are about to install a firewall, and that there is a 30-day approval period before the software must either be removed or steps taken to acquire an appropriate licence.

Once you have installed the firewall and successfully restarted your computer, the Kerio firewall will start the learning process. Set aside 10 minutes to make some checks.

◆ First, establish which network card is on a trusted network.

◆ When prompted, accept any system-related messages that may occur as these will normally be related to the operation of your computer.

◆ Run all applications that will need an Internet connection so that the firewall can learn about them. This will include *Word*, *Internet Explorer*, *Explorer*, *Outlook* and *Messenger*.

The messages will be in a format similar to that shown in Figure 49. You will be told where the data packet has come from or what application has initiated it. If you know that it is based on something that you have done on the computer, then click on the Create rule button and press Permit.

Figure 49 An outgoing connection

Occasionally a message will appear, with the firewall alerting you to an incoming connection. Unless you have knowingly installed an application that allows others to access your computer (a personal web server is a good example of this) then you will need to create a rule to deny the connection.

Figure 50 An incoming connection

Incoming connections are rarely innocent; it is most likely an unwanted inquisition of a potential hacker attempting to see if your computer is vulnerable.

Now that your firewall has learnt about the behaviour of your system and the traffic that it carries, it will successfully block all other unwanted traffic.

If you install any new applications, it will warn you about them and ask you to create a permit or deny rule as appropriate. Otherwise, the system will run as an icon in the system tray at the bottom right-hand corner of your computer, unnoticed.

You can manage the configuration of the firewall yourself and adapt some of its features as well as monitor any intrusions that it may have prevented.

The application window shows that there are options in how the firewall will operate.

◆ Current connections.

◆ Connection statistics.

◆ Network security.

◆ System security.

◆ Attempted intrusions.

◆ Web controls.

◆ Logs of all behaviour.

The **Network security** option lists all the rules that have been created by the firewall and yourself during the learning process. The **packet filter** option allows you to create specialised rules for some of the work that you may wish to do on your system.

The **System security** option lists all the applications that use network communication on your system and how the firewall wishes to manage them. You may have installed a free application that generates pop-up adverts, which your firewall has disabled.

With the **Intrusions** feature, you can prioritise how your firewall handles incoming and outgoing messages. You can effectively allow your firewall to ignore a variety of events.

The **Web** controls option will stop pop-up adverts (a pop under is a small window that will generate pop-up ads or other inappropriate content).

Figure 51 shows the content of the **Logs** option, and how the system has listed numerous ping attacks.

Figure 51 Intrusion log

Go out and try!

Managing the configuration of a firewall

To open the firewall, double-click on the shield icon in the bottom right-hand corner of the screen.

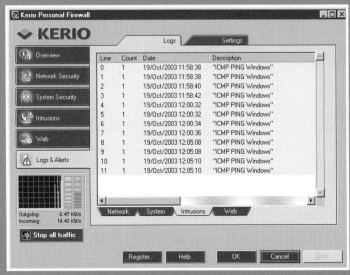

Figure 52 Firewall configuration

Explore the options to check what settings are in place, which applications are allowed access and which are not.

PRACTICAL TASK

◆ Create a schedule to show that you have taken responsibility for installing and configuring a firewall on the computers in your classroom or work area. Keep a log of all the work you have done; include date, time, task and resources used.

◆ Create a simple preventive maintenance procedure for installing and configuring a firewall.

4.2.4 Removal of temporary or unused files

During the normal operation of your operating system you will find that your system will slowly accumulate an unwanted collection of unused or out of date temporary files.

The system creates these files:

◆ during the installation of applications

◆ while you are using an application as a temporary storage facility

◆ when you browse the Internet.

On older systems this was an issue due to the limited hard drive space available. On newer systems this is rarely an issue unless you have already used over 80% of your hard drive for storing files and applications.

You may find your temporary files in more than one place. Common locations are C:\temp and C:\windows\temp.

Figure 53 Temporary files

You may be surprised when you look in your temp folder to see how many files there are and how big it has become. As you can see in Figure 53, a user has allowed their temp folder to accumulate over a period of time.

The solution is simple: delete these temporary files!

Making sure that the problem does not reoccur requires the application of common sense. All versions of Windows since 98 have a schedule agent and a disk cleanup wizard in the system tools menu (found in Programs/Accessories/System Tools).

PRACTICAL TASK

In this task you are going to configure your version of Windows to automatically clean unwanted files from your system.

Step one
Start Scheduled Tasks, which can be found in Programs/Accessories/System Tools.

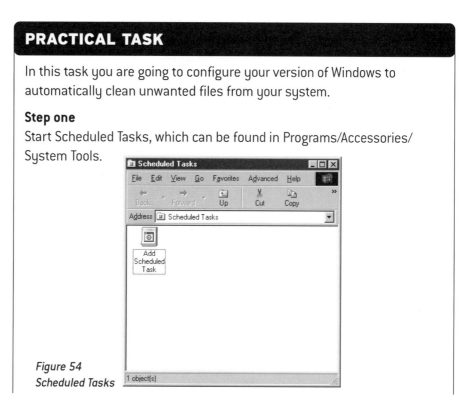

Figure 54
Scheduled Tasks

Step two

Double-click on the Add Scheduled Task icon. Work your way through the wizard to find the **Disk Cleanup** application.

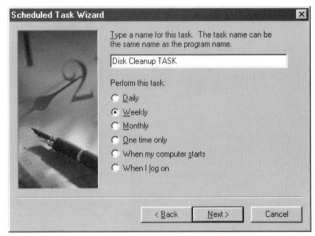

Figure 55 Scheduled Task Wizard

Step three

Set the frequency and time for the cleanup to take place. Unless your computer is exceptionally busy, you can set the system up for a weekly clean.

Figure 56 Schedule frequency

This task will faithfully carry out its role on the day, date and time that you have configured. You can choose to select advanced properties to add more factors to the frequency of the operation.

Go out and try!

The Task Scheduler can be used for a multitude of routine tasks. Spend time looking at how you could configure the Task Scheduler to run daily backups or open the web browser at a set time each day.

4.2.5 File and media management

Many operating systems such as Windows will place your work in common default locations, such as My Documents, and on multi-profile versions (Windows 2000/XP) you can have a My Documents folder for each user.

Many organisations expect staff to store work in common folders on networked servers. This means that everyone has to carry out common policies in saving and naming files so that each employee can successfully complete their work.

You may expect to see a file management structure similar to the one shown in Table 4.

Table 4 An example of a file management structure				
Drive	**Site**	**Department (folder)**	**Section (folder)**	**Team member (folder)**
P:	Cricklewood	Human Resources	Payroll	Mina Khan Tanya Wilson
		Finance	Credit control Budget management Payments Receipts Legal	Mary Kent Lynda Bains Tom Hardacre Jon Williams Adam Smith Terry Reid Mandy Simms
		Production		Peter Provost Gary Leeds Warren Earner Latif Qabal Delroy Wynter Tyrone O'Neill Yusuf Shah Amir Chaurdi
Q:	Hitchin	Sales	Accounts Telesales	Imran Hussin Asid Dad Maureen Layde Jane Sandler Andrew Smith Monique Heery Jenny Lawson Terry Pepper
		Marketing		Raymond Reed Chris Cain Aaron Moshe
		Computer Systems Support	Network and data management Workstation support	Sandy Kent Niall Keefe Kim Gilman Naomi Miller

4.2.6 Using diagnostic software

Looking after a computer often requires the computer professional to play close attention to the overall performance of the computer and its behaviour. To look after a computer successfully, you should use diagnostic software to carry out the task of monitoring the system for you.

Normally you will use diagnostic software in two situations:

◆ when there is an unexpected issue with a computer system
◆ as part of a routine maintenance programme, which may only be completed on an annual (or bi-annual basis).

It is essential that you keep records of the diagnostic routines you use:

◆ report any failures to the user as well as your supervisor so as to keep track of the fact that the fault may be part of a re-occurring issue with the user or the system involved
◆ organise for appropriate repairs or a replacement to take place (see the previous section).

You can use diagnostic software to check:

◆ your computer's software environment
◆ your computer's hardware system
◆ devices
◆ network systems
◆ snapshots of current system processes
◆ benchmarks.

This is done by the diagnostic software reading the computer BIOS, memory and system boards as well as the settings established in the Windows registry.

What is it?

Registry: In Windows technology, the registry is a database of all systems settings.

The software environment will contain a variety of information about the configuration of your operating system. If you are using a recent version of Windows you can expect to see information on:

◆ accessibility and appearance
◆ various software engines that may be running (the Kerio firewall described in the practical task on page 59 is a good example of a software engine)
◆ libraries of system and device drivers (used to control components such as the printer)

- features such as the underlying operating system and fonts that are available
- components that load on system start-up and applications that are installed on the computer (often the cause of many problems and can resolve any software licensing issues)
- how memory is managed
- the system and user profile.

The hardware system is a collection of information about the primary hardware components that are used and needed to run your computer system. In the hardware system you can expect to find information on:

- the CMOS and BIOS
- any buses and other system communication channels
- the motherboard
- ports and slots
- the processor.

You will find out more about how each of the above behaves in Units 403/404.

What does it mean?

CMOS: Complementary metal oxide semi-conductor is a rewriteable long-term memory that is used to maintain hardware settings on boot up as well as information for the system clock.

BIOS (basic input output system): a specialist chip found on your computer motherboard. Amongst its many roles it is involved in managing the way your computer boots up.

Your computer has many devices which, external to the main system, are used for input/output as well as for storing information. Diagnostic software will normally look at:

- hard drives or other storage media
- keyboards
- mice or other pointing devices
- display adapters (or graphic cards depending on the application)
- printers
- any other plug and play technology (automatically detected and installed technology).

The network systems components will vary dramatically depending on the configuration of your system. You would expect differing results for standalone, modem-based and directly connected systems.

In diagnosing your network systems you should be able to find information on:

◆ your Winsock library

◆ your Internet browser and email settings

◆ the behaviour of your web browser

◆ any direct network settings (such as local Internet address)

◆ any services your computer may be using across the network as well as sharing locally.

What does it mean?

Winsock: Short for Windows sockets, a collection of commands used for the management of communication session between your computer and an external network.

Taking a snapshot of current system processes is useful; you can see what is running, and what memory and processor resources are being used. This can be used to:

◆ diagnose any performance issues with the local computer

◆ identify Trojans or unwanted processes that require removal from the computer (Adware is a good example of an unwanted process).

Benchmarking is a term that comes from the measurement of software and systems against a known standard. A common practice in benchmarking comes from the automobile industry. Car manufacturers constantly benchmark their cars against the performance standard of similar models (often competitors') to measure and improve their systems. Often the result of automobile benchmarking is that the cars become faster, safer and more fuel efficient.

Benchmarking our computers at regular intervals is a useful task. If the computer was benchmarked when it was new, and then benchmarked at least once a year, you can identify any issues with the computer through a measured drop in the performance.

Common benchmarking tasks include:

◆ speed measurement of the processor

◆ display performance for the graphics card

◆ read/write access times for the hard drives (this can also include CD/DVD technology)

◆ read/write access times for the system memory

◆ measurement of access times for the network connection.

PRACTICAL TASK

In this task you will download and install a diagnostic application and use it to create a report on the profile of your computer.

With the permission of the computer's owner, go to www.heinemann.co.uk/hotlinks and follow the links to download and install the *FreshDiagnose* application. *FreshDiagnose* is easy to use and its simple menu system will let you access information and benchmarks on all major system components.

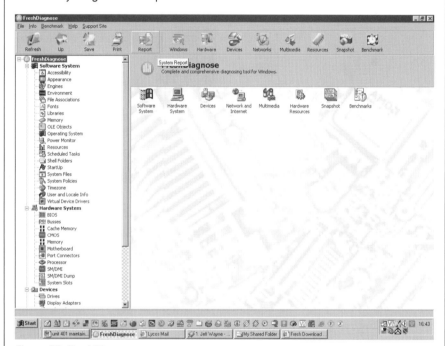

Figure 57 FreshDiagnose

If you click on the report button, you will have the opportunity to build a comprehensive report on all system features associated with your computer.

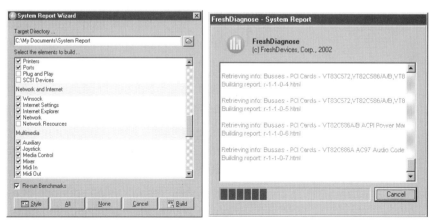

Figure 58 System report feature

Once compiled, *FreshDiagnose* will save your report as a web page. This can be retained and used as part of your employer's system management policies.

Figure 59 Completed system report

Go out and try!

There are many other commercial computer diagnostic systems. Using an appropriate search engine carry out some research into the popular brands of computer diagnostic applications that are available.

Once you have completed any diagnostic routines, you need to record the work you have done, keeping a note of:

◆ system performance

◆ any issues that have been identified.

4.2.7 Removing unwanted applications

Through time you will find that you may have installed applications on your computer system that you no longer need because they are out of date, no longer relevant or, more likely, you never needed them in the first place. Keeping unwanted applications on a computer in a corporate environment may cause problems.

◆ It prevents a more deserving user from having the software as you are needlessly sitting on a licensed use of the application.

◆ It takes up valuable hard drive storage space (this is true for all computer systems, and some applications such as games can consume large quantities of storage space).

◆ It uses system resources as your operating system has to manage a variety of drivers, memory allocation units or part of your application has loaded as a service on start-up.

Windows makes this process easy by keeping a log of all applications installed (review the practical task on page 69 as this is also a feature of *FreshDiagnose*). While the feature has the same overall outcome, there are differences in appearance and behaviour between Windows 98 and Windows 2000/XP.

PRACTICAL TASK

In this task you are going to review the applications installed on your computer and discover if you need to remove any that are unwanted. If you are attempting this task at your centre of study ensure that you have the permission of your tutor.

For the purposes of this task you will need a computer that has Windows 2000/XP.

To manage an application you need to open the Control Panel and double-click on the Add/Remove Programs option as shown in Figure 60.

Figure 60 Add/Remove Programs

As you can see from Figure 60, *Microsoft Flight Simulator 2000*, while an enjoyable application, has not been used for some considerable time. With its overhead of 1 Gb it is taking up valuable storage space. Therefore, it is worthwhile clicking on the Change/Remove option to remove this application.

Look carefully through the list that has been presented on your computer. Discuss with your tutor, or someone with experience, what might be a worthwhile application to remove. It may be the case that you need to keep all applications present on your system.

Go out and try!

Like all tasks that involve changing the configuration on any system, ensure that you have the permission of someone who is responsible for the computer that you are working on.

As you may have noticed when attempting the practical task on page 71, Figure 60 also had a button for Windows components. Click on the button and you will have a variety of options to Add/Remove integral Windows features. Explore this feature and take note of the fact that you can remove *Internet Explorer* and replace it with a third party browser.

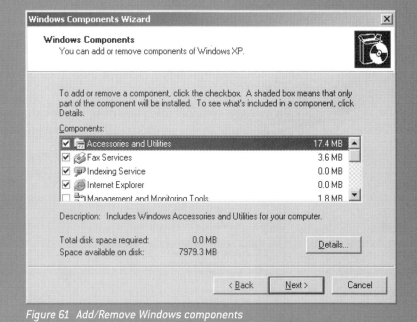

Figure 61 *Add/Remove Windows components*

4.3 Preventive maintenance and the customer

So far this section has looked in detail at the technical aspects of preventive maintenance and how it will affect you and the computer that you are maintaining.

The majority of computer systems support jobs involve working with a customer. The customer may be:

◆ a colleague in your department who needs your specialist skills to support a task that they are working on

◆ a member of another department who is looking for your support in solving a problem with their computer system

◆ a direct customer of your organisation, with whom you have a contract and a duty to support

◆ a supplier of your organisation, through whom your company is supported

◆ someone junior or subordinate in your company

◆ a senior manager or executive in your organisation.

The customer is a many-headed beast who will literally bite if you get it wrong. The job you complete may either involve direct contact with the customer, which implies a professional and courteous manner, or the task has a customer that you do not meet, but who will require an efficient and effective response.

Preventive maintenance and its involvement with customer support means you need to know the answers to these questions:

◆ What are the right customer support procedures?

◆ Why must you co-ordinate with the user?

◆ Who implements preventive maintenance?

◆ What resources are required to complete preventive maintenance?

◆ What do I do if I encounter problems?

4.3.1 What are the right customer support procedures?

Many organisations will interpret this section differently according to their business needs, but all will agree that getting it wrong will result in:

◆ loss of income

◆ loss of good faith

◆ loss of business

◆ a damaged reputation

◆ an opportunity to spend time fending off legal action.

Common customer support tasks will include:

◆ preventive maintenance

◆ fault-finding (see Section 401.5)

◆ upgrading systems

◆ systems replacement.

Preventive maintenance can be as exciting as cleaning your bedroom or changing the oil regularly in your car. Most organisations will arrange an annual health check for all their computer systems. If you are a customer of a well-known computer retailer you can pay for an annual systems check. This will normally be set at a date that is exactly 12 months from the day of installation or purchase. The tasks you are expected to complete include:

◆ **defragmentation** of the hard drive

◆ removal of any unwanted drivers

◆ removal of any temporary or cache files

◆ check of PC performance

◆ removal of any unwanted programs or services

◆ check for any viruses or Trojans and ensure that the virus scanner is current

◆ check of the systems security

◆ application of any software updates, if required.

All of which have been explored in Section 401.4.2.

Check your understanding

Many well-known computer manufacturers and retailers offer a PC support service. Follow the links to PC World, Watford Electronics and Tiny from www.heinemann.co.uk/hotlinks.

Now compare and contrast the support services they provide and attempt to identify the best that each provides.

Your computer can be out of date before you have purchased it. Top specification technology is normally 3 months out of date and entry level technology can be up to 18 months behind the latest technology. You never need to upgrade your computer, as you will never exceed its potential. Unfortunately this is never the case for many customers who, when complaining that their computer does not work effectively, are hoping to have their system upgraded.

It is considered wise in the computer industry to upgrade before the problem occurs, as such a problem can cause loss of business or effective work time.

Upgrades tend to be specific to the customer and what they are doing with their systems. It is likely that you may encounter the following common upgrade scenarios:

◆ the computer requires more memory

◆ the hard drive is near its capacity

◆ the operating system is out of date for the task required

◆ the software used is out of date.

Often the lowest cost solution is the addition of memory; if the motherboard has spare slots you can add new memory or replace existing cards. Additional memory will release the operating systems processes, so that it can carry out a greater variety of tasks. At the time of publication, the average minimum was 256 Mb of memory and you could upgrade to 512 Mb at a very low cost.

Memory used to be an expensive resource in a computer system, but since the late 1990s the price per unit has dropped dramatically. Most motherboards have three slots for memory.

Visit the ebuyer website by following the links from www.heinemann.co.uk/hotlinks and obtain the best price for 128 Mb, 256 Mb, 512 Mb and 1 Gb memory sticks.

How much memory could you fit into a three-slot motherboard, and how little could it cost?

If a hard drive is near its capacity, check with the customer; they may have saved resources on the hard drive that are best placed on a CD-ROM or DVD-ROM. If you are working for a retailer, you may get the commission for an extra sale out of this. It is also possible that you need to carry out a disk-cleaning exercise to remove a variety of temporary files from the system.

Replacement hard drives are easy to install, and they cost at least £40 for an entry level solution (40–60 Gb at the time of writing). You can add an additional hard drive into a computer, as there should be an additional IDE channel (see Unit 403). In this way you can move non-essential files over to the second hard drive.

When a customer purchases a computer, they often do not appreciate all that can be done with the system. However, with time and experience they tend to extend their use of the system and then they need more resources and features. From Windows 98 through to XP, only five years and three operating systems have elapsed (ME, 2000, XP). An operating system can easily become out of date for the task required as any new developments that occur immediately after the release of the operating system have rendered it outmoded. A classic example is Windows 95; this was released at the start of Pentium Technology, and the first systems to run Windows 95 were 75 MHz. By the time Windows 95 had ceased to be current, the processor speed was 233 MHz (three times the speed), the Internet boom had arrived and USB technology was commonplace, resulting in seven versions of the operating system.

You can 'service-pack' more recent operating systems in that the vendor will produce hardware and software updates to attempt to keep the system as current as possible. You could also install a completely new operating system. This is fraught with problems as the hardware may not be able to support the new system (Windows XP, for example, needs a base system of 700 MHz with 256 Mb of RAM to operate effectively).

Go out and try!

Visit the Windows Update homepage shown in Figure 62 by following the links from www.heinemann.co.uk/hotlinks. Scan your computer and its version of Windows for updates. You may find that the website has discovered that your computer requires many or no critical updates.

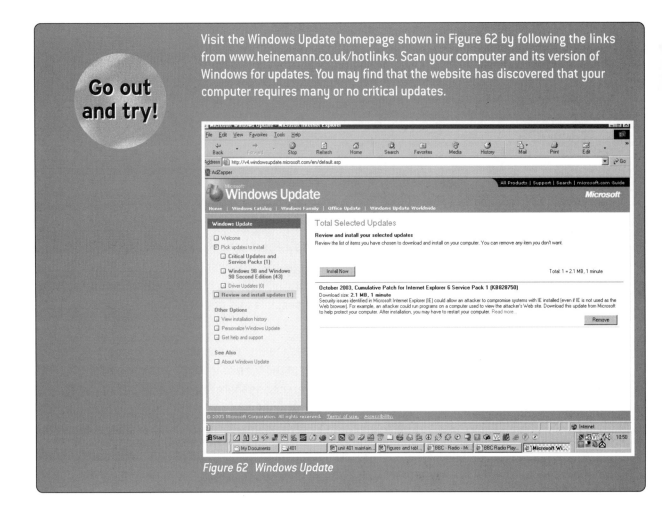

Figure 62 Windows Update

Some of you may believe that there is a conspiracy between a well-known operating system vendor, software creators and hardware manufacturers. As soon as you have bought an application and learnt how to use it, it's out of date and you have to invest your hard-earned cash in a new version of the application! Software outdates quickly as manufacturers and users strive to improve the features and functionality of the products that they are providing.

An easy to recognise example of this is Flash, a web-based multimedia application by Macromedia. Every year Macromedia have made considerable improvements to Flash to keep up with developments in website design and the increasing demands for interactive multimedia content on websites. Flash to date has survived seven versions (1, 2, 3, 4, 5, MX and MX 2004).

As you read this, think back to when you were aged 5–13. Your birthday or a festival was an excellent time to receive presents from your parents, grandparents and other relatives. You may have wanted the latest toy, whether it was a Barbie, Buzz Lightyear or Pokemon! Customers are often no different; they will come to you and say something like: 'This hardware is not the latest bright shiny toy; I want a new toy!'

Desire is fickle and customers, often through a lack of understanding, will want the latest technology. If it is inappropriate for the computer, you should advise them of potential pitfalls, but be prepared for the fact that they will still want it.

Problems are likely to occur when:

◆ the operating system is incapable of handling the new component
◆ there is not enough memory for the latest software
◆ the game requires a graphics facility that is not available on the current computer system
◆ the processor is too slow
◆ the computer is doing too much already.

Even if you don't agree with their choice, remain diplomatic and courteous at all times.

Systems replacement occurs when the computer is so far out of date or unsuitable for the task that it needs complete replacement. This will depend on the tasks that the computer carries out. Normally a computer is behind the times after 18 months and out of date by 3 years. Some organisations will then carry out the following processes:

◆ replace all computers in high specification roles after 3 years
◆ replace all computers in low specification roles after no more than 4 years, where out-of-date, high specification role systems can be used in this capacity
◆ dispose of computer systems either for destruction or recycling.

Normally after 3 years the computer system has no useful upgrade path.

Go out and try!

There are many good charity and voluntary organisations that recycle computers for developing countries or schools and charitable organisations in the United Kingdom.

Visit the Recycle-IT! website by following the links from www.heinemann.co.uk/hotlinks and read their site and newsletter. List all the worthwhile causes that they have supported.

4.3.2 Why must you coordinate with the user?

Working in the customer's environment means that you may be in their home, office or premises. You are an ambassador for your employer and anything you do (or don't do) will reflect on you and your organisation. If you are a freelance repair professional, a successful visit will ensure that you are called back again.

When you receive the call to go to a customer, you should obtain as much information as possible before you depart.

◆ You will need to know everything about what they perceive the problem to be so that you can have the correct tools, resources and spares (revisiting is often wasteful and can be seen as unprofessional).

◆ Find out where they are and the location of the computer.

◆ Confirm the time and make sure that you are early or have agreed a window of opportunity. 'I'm coming between 11 am and 12 noon' is better than 'I'll be there at 11 am' and you appear at 11.30.

While you are carrying out any maintenance on a customer's computer system, you must appreciate that you are preventing them from working on that system. You are effectively part of a hold up that could be costing them time or, more importantly, income.

You must ensure that you appear to be efficient and effective in the work you do. The customer may not understand computer technology, but that does not make them unintelligent or unable to spot that you may be wasting their time.

4.3.3 Who implements preventive maintenance?

Preventive maintenance is often implemented by three parties:

◆ the owner of the computer completes the preventive maintenance on the system as some customers have acquired enough knowledge to ensure the smooth operation of their own system

◆ you have been commissioned by a customer to carry out routine preventive maintenance tasks as they do not have the skills to complete this task by themselves

◆ the owner of the system is an employer that has scheduled periodic maintenance of all systems in their control, and you will visit each system on a pre-agreed timetable to carry out a series of routine maintenance tasks.

Preventive maintenance can also be:

◆ scheduled by customer agreement, i.e. the customer has paid for contracted periodic maintenance, over periods of once a month, three monthly, bi-annually or once a year

◆ generated through an automated system, e.g. a customer will get a maintenance visit when they have used so much paper or ink or toner, or the customer gets a preventive maintenance visit based on the number of help desk calls or system failures that may have occurred.

PRACTICAL TASK

Looking at the resources that your centre or employer uses, how often would you expect that the computers have been checked?

What evidence is there of a maintenance record card or log?

4.3.4 What resources are required to complete preventive maintenance?

There is an old adage, *'a workman is only as good as his tools'*. While this statement is old fashioned and male biased, it's true for everyone who is attempting to carry out a professional job. When you are in front of a computer completing preventive maintenance or carrying out a repair job, you must have the tools, skills and resources.

With computer systems you cannot cover for every eventuality. The skill is to prepare for the majority of problems. The common resources you are likely to require are:

◆ computer tools, which will include size 1 and 2 screwdrivers, an anti-static wristband, a compressed air canister, lint-free cloth and anti-static bags

◆ licensed copies of common operating system software, if you need to complete an update or install/reinstall system components

◆ licensed copies of common applications for installation or reinstallation

◆ driver and utilities disks for common cards and external devices (most companies will use one type or manufacturer for a specific device)

◆ replacement components (hard drives, floppy drives, CD-ROMS, CD-burners, DVD-ROMS, memory sticks, network cards, USB cards, graphics cards, etc)

◆ emergency boot disks

◆ anti-virus software, including a 'magic bullet' disk

◆ a firewall application

◆ diagnostic software

◆ your personal skills, knowledge and experience.

4.3.5 What do I do if I encounter problems?

Once you have stopped panicking, take time to think the problem through. Often a problem can be solved by systematic thought. Consider these questions:

◆ What is happening?

◆ What could the fault be caused by?

◆ What is the faulty component controlled by?

◆ What is the faulty component connected to?

A computer system is complex and each component has many likely interactions. When you sit at a faulty computer look at Figure 63 and ask yourself what might be the cause of the fault.

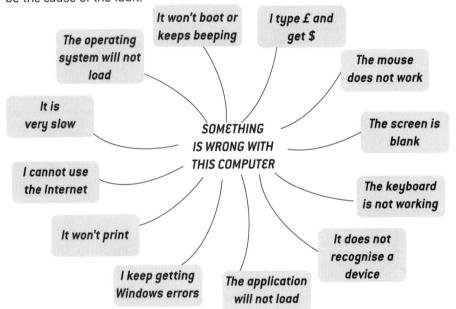

Figure 63 Fault-finding

The following are some of the reasons for the faults listed in Figure 63:

◆ **It won't print.** This could be caused by the printer's drivers not being installed, the wrong drivers for the printer being installed, the printer's not switched on, a faulty cable or a faulty printer (don't forget it may need ink or paper).

◆ **It won't boot or keeps beeping.** The keyboard may have a button stuck down, or you may have a fault with the processor, BIOS or motherboard.

◆ **I type £ and get $.** You have the wrong regional settings. The default for Windows is the United States keyboard. You need to go into Control Panel and set it to UK(English).

◆ **The mouse does not work.** Is it connected? Does it need replacing? Is there a fault with the PS2/serial port? Is Windows detecting it? If it is a wireless mouse, is it fully charged?

046493

- **The screen is blank.** Have you switched the monitor on? Is the monitor faulty? Is the graphics card faulty? Have you plugged the monitor into the graphics card?

- **The keyboard is not working.** Is it plugged in? Have you connected it to the right port (you can mistakenly insert it into the PS2 mouse port)? Does it need replacing?

- **It does not recognise a device.** Have you installed the appropriate drivers? Is the device working correctly on another system? Will your version of Windows work with the device? Is it plugged in correctly?

- **The application will not load.** Is the link working correctly? Has it been deleted or uninstalled incorrectly? Is there a licensing issue? Is there a conflict with another application? Is there enough memory for the application to run correctly?

- **I keep getting Windows errors.** Is there enough hard drive space? Do you have enough memory on your system? Is there a virus? Has something been removed?

- **I cannot use the Internet.** Is your network/Internet connection working correctly (you may need to get information from someone else to ascertain this)? Are your operating systems network settings correctly configured? Has anyone removed or changed the cable?

- **It is very slow.** You may have a hard drive memory or virus issue. Are you trying to get your computer to run too many applications?

- **The operating system will not load.** Start crying! You may have an issue with memory or the hard drive. If you can start the operating system in safe mode then you may be able to recover. Otherwise it is likely that you need to reinstall the system.

Once you have read Unit 403/404 and Section 401.5, you should be able to solve most of these issues.

PRACTICAL TASK

If your study centre has a PC repair facility, arrange suitable supervision so that you can work on an old computer and complete a series of fault-finding tasks.

Look for issues with:

- the PC hardware
- the operating system
- any applications.

Consider these questions:

◆ Does it take a long time to start?

◆ Are any parts of the system running too slowly?

◆ Are there any issues with the display?

◆ Are there any issues with the keyboard or mouse?

◆ Are there any error messages?

◆ Are there too many applications in start-up?

◆ Are all additional facilities working correctly?

4.4 Useful diagnostic routines in preventive maintenance and repair

Repair, fault-finding and preventive maintenance rely on technical experience and common sense. An experienced engineer can often pinpoint a problem because they have encountered it before.

Through time you will adopt common systematic techniques in diagnosing faults on any computer system. Figure 64 is a comprehensive flowchart for fault diagnosis on a standard computer system.

To maintain your skills and develop good diagnostic routines as a good engineer you must follow these rules:

◆ Maintain knowledge of new developments in the computer hardware and software sectors.

◆ Be prepared to try out new operating systems, components and applications as they appear on the market.

◆ Keep yourself current by taking the time to read manuals, text books, guides and websites on new products.

◆ Note that new developments include interesting variations on technology, especially where technologies merge. Keep an open mind and be prepared not to dismiss a manufacturer's attempt to revise technology. Often the variation becomes the innovation (optical mice, for example, have been available for over fifteen years but have only become commonplace in the last two years).

◆ Ensure that you are also aware of the limitations of the technology. Overloading processors, memory and hard drives have been the ruin of many a good computer and engineer's reputation.

◆ Remember that learning does not finish at school or college. Going on courses in technology and maintaining or attaining certification are the marks of a professional in the computer industry.

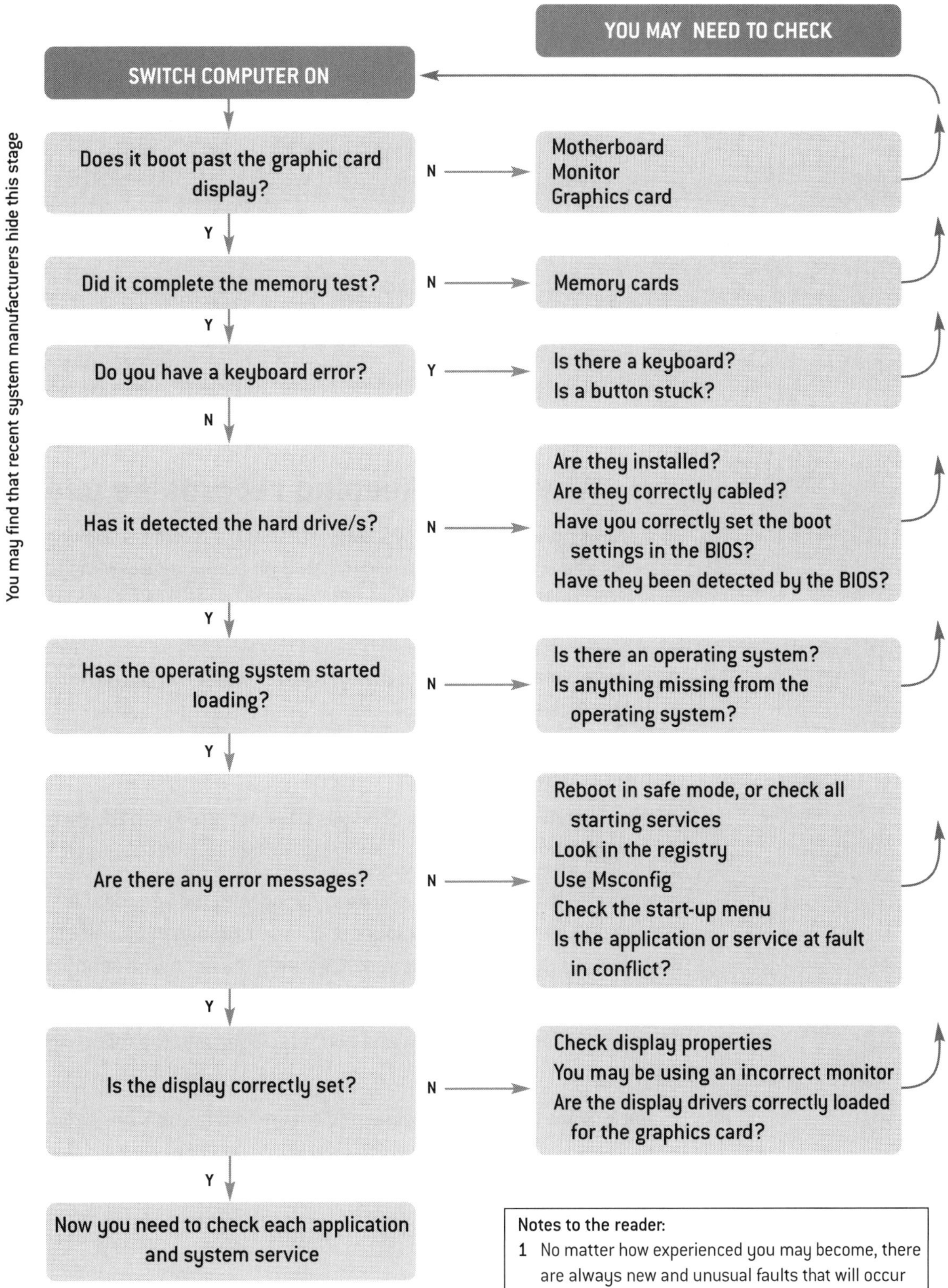

YOU MAY NEED TO CHECK

SWITCH COMPUTER ON

You may find that recent system manufacturers hide this stage

Does it boot past the graphic card display? — N → Motherboard / Monitor / Graphics card

Y

Did it complete the memory test? — N → Memory cards

Y

Do you have a keyboard error? — Y → Is there a keyboard? / Is a button stuck?

N

Has it detected the hard drive/s? — N → Are they installed? / Are they correctly cabled? / Have you correctly set the boot settings in the BIOS? / Have they been detected by the BIOS?

Y

Has the operating system started loading? — N → Is there an operating system? / Is anything missing from the operating system?

Y

Are there any error messages? — N → Reboot in safe mode, or check all starting services / Look in the registry / Use Msconfig / Check the start-up menu / Is the application or service at fault in conflict?

Y

Is the display correctly set? — N → Check display properties / You may be using an incorrect monitor / Are the display drivers correctly loaded for the graphics card?

Y

Now you need to check each application and system service

Figure 64 Systematic fault diagnosis

Notes to the reader:
1 No matter how experienced you may become, there are always new and unusual faults that will occur that you cannot prepare for.
2 You may wish to use this chart in Section 5 of this unit.

Go out and try!

Professional certification is the difference between a career in computing or it becoming 'just a job!' Leaders in the computer industry such as Microsoft, Cisco, Novell and CompTIA all provide a wide range of professional courses that are suitable for an engineer like you.

Visit their websites by following the links from www.heinemann.co.uk/hotlinks and list the certifications that can be completed and the industry sector that they can help you in.

The e-Quals, Information Technology Practitioner (ICT Systems Support) is similar to the CompTIA A+. Compare the two qualifications and consider the advantages of also having the A+.

Check if your school or college is offering any of the qualifications. You may find that they are an academy for Cisco, Microsoft or CompTIA.

4.5 Why would keeping records be useful?

As a professional you will be working with many customers, looking after their systems and ensuring that they can use their computer systems to run their business and hopefully make a profit (or more importantly not make a loss). You can easily encounter problems when:

◆ there are many computers that you have to maintain as part of the customer's system

◆ there are many members of the customer's organisation or department that you have to liaise with

◆ through time, many faults or issues have occurred with the same system or application.

To ensure that the customer is always happy with the service that you provide on behalf of your employer or yourself (you may be self-employed), it is necessary to keep accurate records during the life of the contract or the existence of the computer system.

Keeping records provides you and your employer with the following advantages:

◆ tracking the lifecycle of a request to ensure that the task has been completed

◆ being able to identify if a system has the same fault reoccurring

◆ being able to identify if the same people are involved

◆ tracking the fault history of any system.

4.5.1 Tracking the lifecycle of a request

Paperwork may be the bane of civilisation, but without it your organisation can be reduced to chaos. When managing any reported fault or issue from a customer your employer will ensure that there is an appropriate system in place (either computer- or paper-based) that tracks the task from the original call to the completed job.

The computer/paper system may have five stages:

◆ logging the original request

◆ assessment of resources required for task

◆ feedback or referral from engineer sent on task

◆ feedback or referral from customer

◆ follow up if required.

The original request may come in person, by email, phone, fax or post. You will need to record:

◆ the customer's details

◆ details of the system at fault

◆ date/time/circumstances when the fault occurred (or was noticed).

It is important that you, or a representative from your employer, agrees a date/time that you will go and spend time with the customer's system to resolve the fault. In most cases you will go to the system, though occasionally the customer may bring the computer (like a laptop) to you.

Before you go to solve the fault for the customer, an assessment of resources is required. This may be completed by yourself or a suitably skilled supervisor or an experienced colleague. You will need to identify:

◆ the required tools

◆ any software applications

◆ any software diagnostic tools

◆ any drivers

◆ spare/replacement hardware components

◆ any media (CDs, printer toner etc).

Systems, just like life, are not straightforward so you may find that you are unable to fix the system and need more resources than were expected. Alternatively, the customer report might not have been accurate. As long as you are polite, courteous and professional then you will get positive, but concerned, referral and feedback from the customer. It is important that your referral lists all the known issues in an accurate and technical manner so that the solution is provided correctly.

Customer satisfaction is paramount to good professional standing as well as to continued business with that customer. Many companies will employ representatives to follow up your work with a customer review. This allows your employer to:

◆ monitor your performance and review any training or discipline as required

◆ adapt their services to better handle the varied customer requirements.

PRACTICAL TASK

With your customer support, key skills communication or information technology tutor, create a customer request tracking system. Design a form that will capture the following details:

◆ customer's name
◆ department
◆ address
◆ other contact details
◆ date and time of request
◆ details of system involved (processor, memory etc.)
◆ details of fault (this may be in the customer's own terms)
◆ date/time the fault was noticed
◆ what was being done on the system before the fault occurred
◆ resources required for the task
◆ date/time of repair/maintenance
◆ feedback from task by engineer
◆ feedback from customer
◆ signatures of customer and engineers.

4.5.2 If a system has the same fault reoccurring

The advantage of keeping accurate records is that you can see if the same faults (or similar faults) are reoccurring on the same system. These are often caused by an undiagnosed hardware or software fault on the system. This can enable your employer to:

◆ satisfy the customer by sending in a specialist response to the problem
◆ create a new fault-free system for the customer and use it to replace the faulty system.

4.5.3 Identify if the same people are involved

By keeping accurate records of faults, your employer can clearly identify if the problem with the system is the person who is operating it. This is not necessarily a negative issue. From this you can recommend training and support for the individual, resulting in improved performance and a customer with skills to use your system effectively.

4.5.4 Tracking the fault history of any system

By keeping accurate records of problems with the system, your employer can look carefully at how they can improve the system in the future. Computer systems often only have a three-year life, so in that time they can be quickly improved for the next version. Many software systems are constantly under development; revisions are being provided on a continual basis, with new versions of the system being released almost yearly.

Go out and try!

Microsoft is the world's largest software manufacturer. Amongst many other products, they produce well-known operating systems and applications.

Visit www.heinemann.co.uk/hotlinks to go to the Microsoft website.

◆ Find out how you can update their operating systems.
◆ Discover how many versions of Windows and *Office* have been available since 1993.

4.6 The legal requirements involved in disposing of any waste

While this section may not seem to fit into a chapter on maintaining equipment and systems, with the intervention of the European Commission in many aspects of the working environment you have to conform to acceptable procedures in the disposal of:

◆ printer ink cartridges

◆ printer toner cartridges

◆ paper

◆ monitors

◆ processor base units.

Paper and printer toner/ink can all be recycled by a variety of organisations. The recycling of printer ink and toner can save your employer or customer money because most recycling companies will:

◆ pay you for your waste paper or donate a percentage of their profits to worthy charities

◆ sell you recycled ink or toner at a lower than 'new' price in exchange for your empty cartridges.

Go out and try!

Using a suitable search engine, search for toner/ink recycling companies and find out who will offer the best price in your area.

It is now illegal to dispose of computer monitors (and any cathode ray tube technology, like an old television) in conventional waste. Companies that wish to dispose of old computers, including their monitors, have to pay for a disposal bin to be delivered from a specialist disposal company.

There are now many organisations including Recycle-IT! Limited that specialise in the recycling and reuse of computer technology. Your employer can benefit by giving the computer to such an intermediary and so provide developing nations, as well as local schools and volunteer organisations, with much needed low-cost technology.

5 Successful fault-finding

Before reading this section, you may wish to reread Section 4.4 (page 82) and look at Figure 64 (page 83).

The skill of fault-finding is like flying. Flapping your wings won't get you into the air. You need to take that running leap off the cliff to see if you've got what it takes.

Initially fault-finding is a skill that seems like the dark magic of the grand wizard, full of mystery and understood by a few. Actually, for most of the time, it's very straightforward and you tend to improve your skill with practice. While you may not know how to fix every problem (as you may not have encountered them before) you should soon become proficient at successfully fixing the majority.

This section will help you:

◆ to identify that there is a problem with a computer system

◆ in the use of diagnostic tools

◆ to know what you need to find out

◆ to recognise common faults

◆ to know what to do when you have found the fault

◆ to solve common faults.

5.1 How do I know that there is a problem?

Computer problems can be very obvious (something is not working or the whole system is not working correctly) or they can be unnoticed (the system has a virus, or is beginning to run slower than normal).

Knowing that there is a problem is based on knowing how a computer operates and recognising that something is happening that is outside the norm. For example, your parents may know you very well (or you may think that they don't) and are very good at spotting when something is wrong (problems with girl/boyfriend or at school/college). Unfortunately, your teacher may not know you so well. They have to work with many people and may not spot when something is wrong unless you tell them or a disaster happens.

With computer systems, there are some obvious issues:

◆ it's not starting
◆ there is no display
◆ fire and smoke are billowing from the monitor or power supply (yes, this can happen!)
◆ the keyboard is not responding
◆ the mouse is not working
◆ the printer is not printing
◆ you cannot get on the Internet
◆ the software is not loading
◆ you cannot save
◆ it stops during the boot process
◆ the time is wrong
◆ there is no sound
◆ you get the wrong characters when you type
◆ you are unable to open an application or a file
◆ the CD/DVD-ROM drawer will not open.

The art of problem solving is being able to recognise that there are faults with the system even though everything appears to be functioning normally to the untrained user. Perhaps:

◆ the Internet connection is slower than normal
◆ the computer takes longer to boot than it should
◆ there is unexplained hard drive activity
◆ the computer crashes (blue screens or error messages) more often than is normal

◆ the mouse lags behind your use

◆ you can type faster than the computer can output

◆ applications that use graphics are painfully slow

◆ some applications take a long time to load.

5.2 Using diagnostic tools and techniques

In the practical task on page 69, you may have spent time using the diagnostic tool *FreshDiagnose*. Included as part of the application is a benchmarking tool, which is useful when you are not able to identify if there is an issue with the computer system.

FreshDiagnose will give you a picture of how the system is running now, so if you create a series of benchmarks over a period of time you can detect a drop in performance. Normally you may choose to benchmark a computer once a year for a customer. You may do this task more often if the performance of the computer system involved is critical to the operation of the customer's business. You need to spot any drop in system performance, and rectify it as soon as possible (this type of task is more likely to be carried out on a web, application or file server).

PRACTICAL TASK

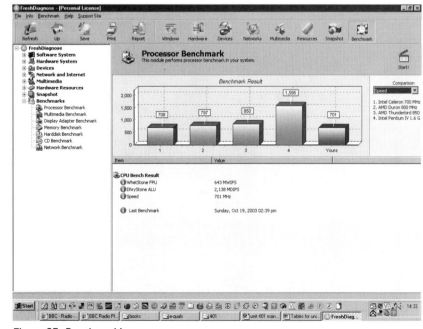

Using *FreshDiagnose*, benchmark your computer for a period of one hour and monitor its performance as you make changes to the system.

Using the tool shown in Figure 65, benchmark your computer's

◆ processor

◆ multimedia

◆ display adapter

◆ memory

◆ hard disk.

Figure 65 Benchmarking

With the permission of the person that owns/manages the computer you are using, obtain a licensed copy of a major application such as Microsoft *Office* and install it. Once the application has been successfully installed, run the previous range of benchmarks again and compare the results to the original benchmarks.

What are the differences in performance? Look carefully at the processor, memory and hard disk.

Many professionals have varied opinions on what is the best way to fault-find and diagnose problems with computer systems. However, there are commonplace techniques for diagnosing less than obvious faults and issues with performance on any computer system:

◆ check to see if there are too many applications in the Start menu/Startup

◆ find out what services may be running using Windows Registry, MSCONFIG, Task Manager or applications such as *FreshDiagnose*

◆ check if there are any other background applications being loaded by other means

◆ check the swap file size

◆ look at the system performance monitor

◆ find out if there are there any hardware conflicts.

5.2.1 Too many applications in the Start menu/Startup

The temptation is to buy or download for free many interesting applications (games, tools, etc.) and install them all on your computer, because your hard

Figure 66 Start menu/Startup

drive is big and it can handle it. Through time and lack of care you will find that your computer is slowing down, takes a long time to boot, that there are many icons in the system tray (the bottom right hand corner of your screen) or that it takes a long time to run any application.

Because of all of this you will probably find that Windows has a wide array of icons in the Start menu/Startup, running services that, while you will need them, you do not need them running all of the time.

PRACTICAL TASK

Look at the Startup submenu on your computer and list all the applications starting. Check with your computer hardware tutor if they are required. If any are not, drag and drop them into the Recycle Bin.

5.2.2 Services

Services are applications that run in the system tray, but also run in the background unnoticed. Windows use services to manage many applications:

- web servers
- printing
- firewalls
- LAN/WAN and MODEM communication (networking)
- task management
- graphical applications
- dynamic link libraries
- media players
- browsers
- anti-virus software.

What is it?

Service: An application that runs in the background of the system to enable Windows to operate or provide resources for applications that you may use.

Some services can be malicious applications (Trojans) or, more commonly, unwanted applications that generate adverts on your computer, or spyware that monitors the websites you visit for marketing purposes.

There are many ways to find out about the services being run by Windows:

◆ carefully work your way through the Windows Registry

◆ press Ctrl-Alt-Del to activate the Task Manager

◆ if using Windows 98, run MSCONFIG

◆ run applications such as *FreshDiagnose*.

The **Windows registry** is a database that holds comprehensive information on all features and configuration information for your computer's current system. This is done by a system called **registry keys**. Each key is an element of data that reports a setting for an individual component of Windows.

To access the registry, you need to activate Start menu/Run, type in **regedit** and click OK.

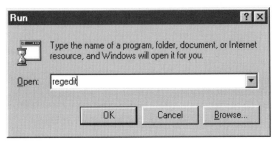

Figure 67 Accessing regedit

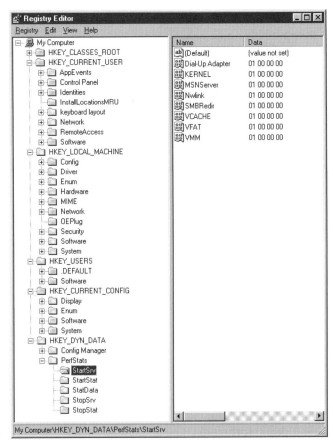

Figure 68 Regedit

As you can see there are five major (called root) keys:

◆ HKEY_LOCAL_MACHINE

◆ HKEY_CURRENT_USER

◆ HKEY_CURRENT_CONFIG

◆ HKEY_USERS

◆ HKEY_CLASSES_ROOT

The **HKEY_LOCAL_MACHINE** key holds information on the hardware environment for your computer. This will include all peripherals, input and output devices as well as core system components. The HKEY_LOCAL_MACHINE also contains information on **SAM (security access modules)** for the whole system in Windows 2000.

Through the use of the **HKEY_USERS** and **HKEY_CURRENT_USER** keys, your system can have multiple users and varied profiles on any workstation. If there are no users, the system will run a default user profile. When you log onto a Windows 2000 computer your **HKEY_USERS** profile is copied to the **HKEY_CURRENT_USER** key entry.

The **HKEY_CURRENT_CONFIG** key is used for machines that need different hardware profiles. If you are the owner of a laptop, you will be aware that you can add other cards using the PCMCIA slot, often on the fly. This is also true of technology that uses the USB connection, where you can use plug and play to add a digital camera, printer or scanner to a computer for a short period of time.

What is it?

PCMCIA: Personal Computer Memory Card International Association is an organisation that regulates the technology used for the credit card sized slots in laptops.

Windows uses the **HKEY_CLASSES_ROOT** key to manage all files associated with *Explorer*. So when you click on a .doc icon then *Word* will be opened and when you import a JPG image into *Publisher* then the correct object manager is used.

To find which services are running on your computer you can look at the following keys, through regedit:

◆ The load entry which is held at
   HKEY_CURRENT_USER\Software\Microsoft\Windows(98/NT/2000)\CurrentVersion\Windows\load.

◆ The Userinit entry, which is held at
   HKEY_LOCAL_MACHINE\SOFTWARE\Microsoft\WindowsNT\CurrentVersion\Winlogon\Userinit.
   This can initiate programs when the system boots. You'll usually see an entry for userinit.exe, but this key can accept multiple comma-separated values, so other programs can add themselves onto the end of the entry.

◆ Unlike the load and Userinit entries, the Explorer\Run entry works in both the
   HKEY_CURRENT_USER and **HKEY_LOCAL_MACHINE** keys. You can find the Explorer\Run key at
   HKEY_CURRENT_USER\Software\Microsoft\Windows\CurrentVersion\Policies\Explorer\Run and at
   HKEY_LOCAL_MACHINE\SOFTWARE\Microsoft\Windows\CurrentVersion\Policies\Explorer\Run.

◆ The RunServicesOnce key is designed to start service programs before the user logs on and before the other registry autostart keys start their programs. You'll find the RunServicesOnce key at **HKEY_CURRENT_USER\Software\Microsoft\Windows\CurrentVersion\RunServicesOnce** and at
   HKEY_LOCAL_MACHINE\SOFTWARE\Microsoft\Windows\CurrentVersion\RunServicesOnce.

◆ The RunServices key loads immediately after the RunServicesOnce key and runs before the user logs on. You'll find the RunServices key at
   HKEY_CURRENT_USER\Software\Microsoft\Windows\CurrentVersion\RunServices and at
   HKEY_LOCAL_MACHINE\SOFTWARE\Microsoft\Windows\CurrentVersion\RunServices.

◆ The RunOnce\Setup key's default value specifies programs to run after the user logs on. The RunOnce\Setup key is in the **HKEY_CURRENT_USER** and **HKEY_LOCAL_MACHINE** keys. You'll find it at **HKEY_CURRENT_USER\Software\Microsoft\Windows\CurrentVersion\RunOnce\Setup** and at **HKEY_LOCAL_MACHINE\SOFTWARE\Microsoft\Windows\CurrentVersion\RunOnce\Setup**.

◆ Setup programs typically use the RunOnce key to run programs automatically. You'll find this key at **HKEY_LOCAL_MACHINE\SOFTWARE\Microsoft\Windows\CurrentVersion\RunOnce** and at **HKEY_CURRENT_USER\Software\Microsoft\Windows\CurrentVersion\RunOnce**. The RunOnce entry in the **HKEY_LOCAL_MACHINE** runs associated programs immediately after logon and before the other registry Run entries start their programs.

◆ By far the most common registry location for autorun programs is the Run entry, which you'll find at **HKEY_CURRENT_USER\Software\Microsoft\Windows\CurrentVersion\Run** and **HKEY_LOCAL_MACHINE\SOFTWARE\Microsoft\Windows\CurrentVersion\Run**. The Run entry in the **HKEY_LOCAL_MACHINE** runs immediately before the Run entry in the **HKEY_CURRENT_USER**, and both keys precede the processing of the Startup folder.

PRACTICAL TASK

Open the Run prompt and start regedit. Look carefully through the registry and identify the keys previously listed. Check all the applications that are supposed to be running on your system against the keys listed by regedit.

List all the keys that are running services that your system does not need.

Changing keys is a task that takes great care as you can upset Windows and give it anther opportunity to crash. The easiest way to remove any entries from the registry is to find a key using regedit and to delete it. Power users, which you will become, will export the database and create their own edits of the database which they will then reload into the registry.

Searching the registry

First, open regedit and use Crtl-F to open the search menu, enter the HKEY_CURRENT_USER\Software\Microsoft\Windows\CurrentVersion\Run key and start the search.

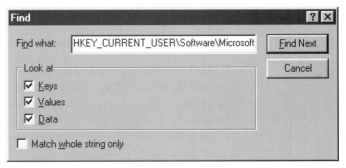

Figure 69 Searching for a key

Then, once you have found the appropriate key entries you can right-click on the individual keys to delete the entry. (Windows will check if you are sure!

Once you have done this, unless there has been a full backup taken of the registry, there will be no going back.)

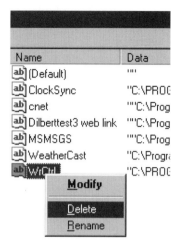

Figure 70 Deleting a key

Go out and try!

There are many websites that provide comprehensive information on managing and editing the registry. Visit www.heinemann.co.uk/hotlinks and go to the Registry Guide for Windows where you can review all the different ways you can amend the performance of Windows through regedit.

The **Task Manager** is a service in its own right. It controls all the applications and services that are currently using processor time and memory resources in your version of Windows. To access the Task Manager to see the services in operation, press Ctrl-Alt-Del simultaneously.

For Windows 98 the Task Manager acts as a separate program in conjunction with *Explorer*. When you press Ctrl-Alt-Del you see a window with a list of services currently running as in Figure 71.

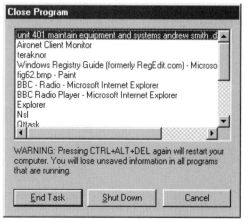

Figure 71 Task management in Windows 98

In Windows NT/2000/XP and 2003, the Task Manager is a more comprehensive resource. When you press Ctrl-Alt-Del you can access other resources to manage your computer as seen in Figure 72.

Figure 72   Ctrl-Alt-Del in Windows 2000

When you press on the Task Manager option you see three tabs: Applications, Processes (which includes all services) and Performance.

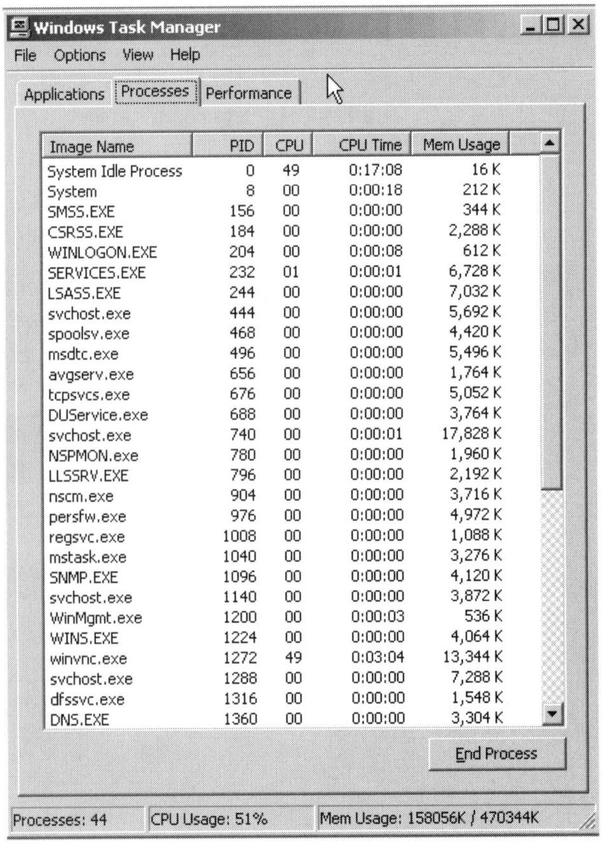

Figure 73   Processes in Windows 2000

Each process contains important information:

◆ process name: the name of the program, utility or service that Windows is running

◆ process identifier (PID): a unique ID that the system gives to an application or service (so multiple sessions of the same service can legitimately run)

◆ process resource: how many processor resources (as a percentage) the service is currently using (this is useful for finding services that are slowing the computer down)

◆ CPU time: how long the application has been running in hours, minutes and seconds

◆ memory usage: how much system memory the service is taking up.

If there is a process you feel is not required, you can select the process and press the End Process button. Be careful, though! You may stop an essential service and need to reboot Windows.

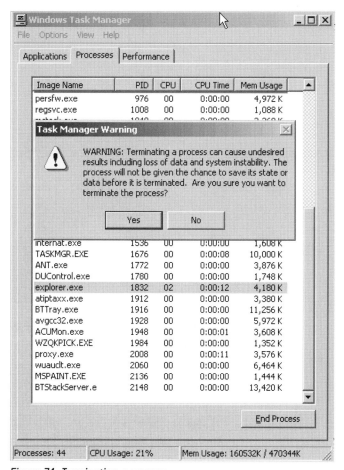

Figure 74 Terminating a process

PRACTICAL TASK

Before starting this task, make sure that you have saved all your work and closed all applications.

Using Windows 2000 or XP press Ctrl-Alt-Del and activate the Processes tab on the Task Manager. Look for the *Explorer* process and terminate it.

What happens? The desktop should disappear. To regain the desktop, you can start the process again by selecting the File menu and the New task option. When the Run window appears, type in *Explorer* and press Enter. You will find that the desktop has restarted.

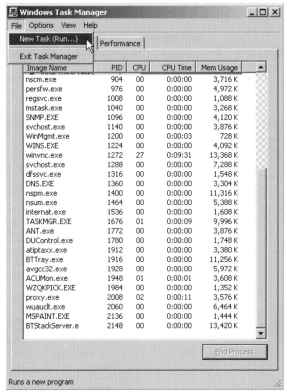

Figure 75 Starting a new process

Note: If this task fails, restarting your computer will resolve any problems.

While Windows 98 is now an old operating system, you are likely to encounter many customers over the next 3–5 years that have to run Windows 98 because of legacy systems or the prohibitive cost of upgrading. If you are looking for any services that may be installed you can use an application called MSCONFIG which can be found in Start menu/Run and type in MSCONFIG.

As part of MSCONFIG you will find the Startup tab; this lists all the applications and services Windows has been instructed to load at Startup. By clicking on the check box for any application, you can prevent that application from loading the next time Windows restarts.

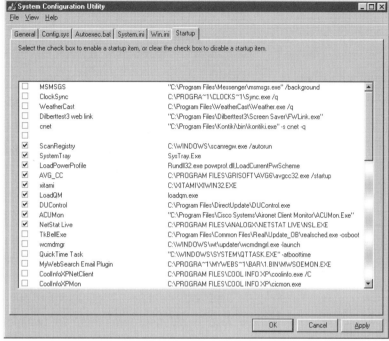

Figure 76 MSCONFIG/Startup

FreshDiagnose will provide you with comprehensive information on your system's current configuration. To find out what services are being run at start up, look in the software system StartUp screen.

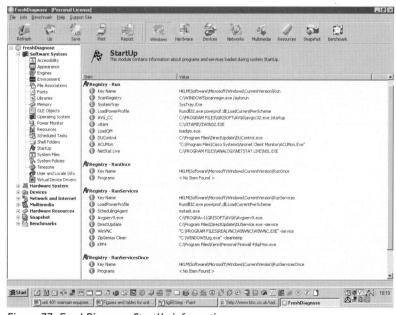

Figure 77 FreshDiagnose StartUp information

Looking for services applications that may be slowing down the performance of a computer system is a time-consuming process. You need to be careful and systematic, sometimes trying an application by removing it and then returning it if there is no noticeable change.

5.2.3 Background applications being loaded by other means

There are many other ways of loading applications onto your computer to drain the performance of the processor or memory.

Looking at a computer can be like being a detective, taking a detailed look at each component of the system and inspecting it to see if it is the cause of your problems.

To find out if such applications exist you need to look carefully at the following.

◆ For older systems such as Windows 98 you need to look in the C: drive. There may be three files called msdos.sys, autoexec.bat and config.sys. Each contains information that affects the boot process of Windows and loads other external applications to affect the system.

◆ Also for older systems there are two older versions of the registry called win.ini and system.ini. In each of these is a load option, and so the system will run a variety of applications on start up.

◆ Some web pages can contain *Active X* script that can run a variety of processes.

◆ Microsoft *Outlook* can run *Visual Basic* script.

◆ If your computer is connected to a network, the login process may activate a remote scripting or application delivery system that will add new processes to your computer system.

5.2.4 Swap file size

A **swap file** is a virtual memory system that utilises space on the hard drive to store various Windows applications information during the running operation of the computer system.

The swap file is used as a short-term memory solution when the computer's active memory is too full for a new process to join it. Any applications or processes that are not currently using processor time are moved (or swapped) into an area of hard drive storage called **virtual memory**.

There are issues when your system uses swap files to store computer memory:

◆ hard drive storage is slower and less reliable than chip-based memory

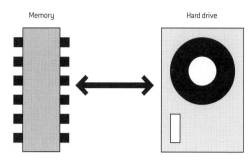

Swap space or virtual memory

Figure 78 Swap Space

◆ the time it takes to swap information from memory to the hard drive is slow and will reduce the performance of your operating system.

All versions of Windows support swap space, and this is normally referred to as its virtual memory. It can be found in Windows 2000 by entering Control Panel/System Properties and selecting the Advanced tab. In this section you will find the Performance options. Click on this and click on the Change Virtual Memory option.

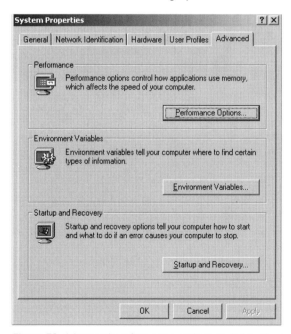
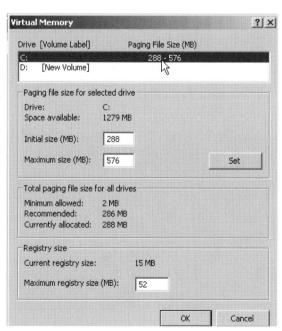

Figure 79 Advanced performance options and virtual memory settings

You can set the smallest size that virtual memory should be. This is slightly larger than the size of your system's memory. The largest should be approximately twice the size of the computer's systems memory.

It is worth noting that you can manage the size of the registry.

Go out and try! Look at a computer with Windows 2000 and ascertain the size of the virtual memory. Is it twice the size of the system memory?

5.2.5 The system performance monitor

Working on the Task Manager in Section 5.2.2 (page 97), you will have already seen the system performance monitor. To recall the system performance monitor, press Ctrl-Alt-Del and select Task Manager, and select the Performance tab.

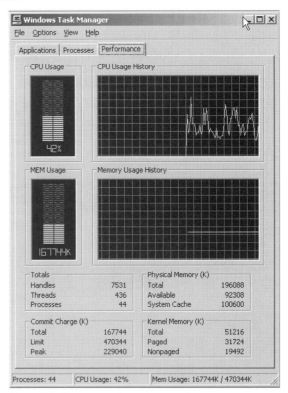

Figure 80 System performance monitor

The system performance monitor is passive; you cannot change anything that it is doing. However, it is a useful tool.

◆ You can check on the process performance when the computer is running an application.

◆ You can look at the process performance when the system is apparently dormant, as this is a strong indicator of the hold that services have on the performance of the computer. The computer used for Figure 80 is a Windows 2000 server configured as an Internet proxy server, and while the image was being taken, the server was managing a large quantity of traffic across the system.

◆ You can identify memory usage. Each process and service has to occupy a portion of system memory. Is the value close to the system memory limit? This may indicate too many processes or services, or that your computer system needs more memory.

Go out and try!

Using your computer, enter Ctrl-Alt-Del and look at the system performance monitor:

◆ What is it currently doing?

◆ How much memory is in use?

◆ How much memory does your system have?

5.2.6 Hardware conflicts

A hardware conflict is where two components on the same system are attempting to share the same resources being offered by your computer's operating system. While this is an obscure reason for a system to slow down (as normally it will only affect the devices involved), it has the potential of adding extra processing time to the system because an operating system like Windows will try to resolve the conflicts when the two devices send information to the system.

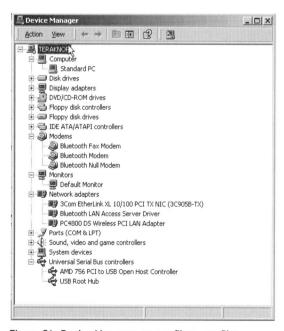 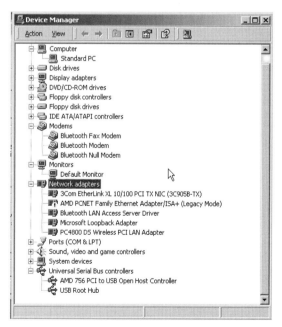

Figure 81   Device Manager: no conflicts; conflicts

Figure 81 shows the Device Manager which can be found via Control Panel, System Properties and the Hardware tab. The left-hand screen in Figure 81 shows a system that, as yet, has no conflicts; the right-hand screen shows that a conflict has occurred with a network card competing for the same resources as another system component.

Go out and try!

Using your computer enter System Properties and find the Device Manager. Check to see if there are any conflicts (removing them will be covered in Unit 403/404).

5.3 What information do I need to gather?

You may not be the professional that eventually solves a user's problem, but over the phone, via email or in person, you may have to gather an accurate picture of the problem with the computer system. It is important that you have a clear and comprehensive picture of all the issues so that the repair is accurate and time is not wasted on multiple attempts.

◆ Can the computer boot up? If not, what point does it reach?
◆ Are all the peripheral devices (mouse, keyboard, printer, scanner, digital camera) working?
◆ Are you able to connect to the network?
◆ Are you able to connect to the Internet?
◆ Is there any sound through the speakers?
◆ Can you open *Explorer* to browse the computer?
◆ Is the display on? If so, what is the quality of the display?
◆ Is there a burning smell coming from the back of the computer?
◆ Does the computer beep continuously at start up?
◆ What sounds does the computer make? Listen carefully to the base unit, not the speakers.

Each of the aforementioned queries forms the basis for recognising common faults, to be explored in the next section.

5.4 Recognising common faults

Developing your skills as a computer maintenance professional means that you have to be able to recognise common faults at a glance. This will speed up your work and save time in needless searches for other problems that may not be there. While faults can be varied and technical, you need to be able to identify issues with these components:

◆ plug fuse for base unit or monitor
◆ CMOS battery
◆ video board
◆ motherboard
◆ monitor
◆ ball in mouse
◆ optical mouse
◆ keyboard

- CD/DVD-ROM drive or CD/DVD writer
- floppy disk drive
- hard drive
- printers
- printer driver
- NIC or MODEM
- data cables.

Finding faults requires a systematic approach to working with technology; this technique is often referred to as **troubleshooting**. To successfully troubleshoot a problem, you will need to take these steps:

1 Check for power.

2 Check if the system works with a replacement component.

3 Check if the system works with a replacement power or data cable.

4 Check if the fault is not with the component but with an application that is using it.

5 Check if the fault is not with the components but with a device that is connected to it.

Section 5.6 (page 118) explores how you may be able to solve these common faults.

5.4.1 Plug fuse for base unit or monitor

One day you or someone else switches a computer on and it does not start or you can hear the computer booting up and there is no display or power-on light on the monitor.

The power cable that runs from the wall socket to the computer or monitor is the primary source of power. If there is a fault with the cable, then the whole system will not start. Often people will spend hours attempting to repair a computer or monitor, when they have neglected to identify that the power cable was at fault.

Monitors and computer base units should be protected by a 13-amp fuse.

Power cable (called a kettle lead)

5.4.2 CMOS battery

What is it?

CMOS: Complementary metal oxide semi-conductor, is the material used to store information in the BIOS (basic input output system) chip. It requires relatively low quantities of power to retain the information.

Go out and try!

CMOS is a material that is used as part of the BIOS. Using the Internet, carry out some personal research to discover where it is in common use in computer technology.

The CMOS battery provides a continuous supply of power to the BIOS and the system clock, allowing the computer system to retain information about:

◆ the current date and time

◆ system start-up requirements, so that the BIOS can load the correct services when the computer is switched on.

Like all batteries, in time the CMOS battery's performance will decay. The battery is a unit that is recharged by the motherboard when the computer is operational but, with each 'recharge and use' cycle, there is a slight degradation in performance.

This problem is more likely to occur on older computers, though you may occasionally find the problem occurring on newer computers.

This fault will make itself apparent when the computer is switched on and you have one of the following problems:

◆ the BIOS has reported that the CMOS checksum is incorrect, and this has been caused by a loss of power to the CMOS

◆ the date/time has reverted to the system default time, which may be midnight on 1 January 1990.

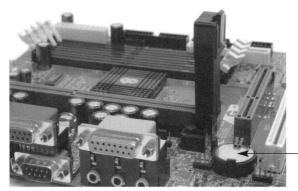

CMOS battery

CMOS battery

5.4.3 Video board

The video board (or display adapter) is the source of much pleasure and pain for computer users and computer maintenance professionals alike. If a fault occurs on the video board, you will initially suspect that you have a fault with the monitor or the motherboard.

The only symptom of a fault with a display adapter is that you see nothing. This is a result of:

◆ the video board not starting, so the computer system is not active

◆ the video output being faulty and the monitor not receiving a signal.

5.4.4 Motherboard

Motherboards are complex systems that can fail completely or you may find that various sub-systems have failed. The symptoms of a motherboard failing include:

◆ the computer will not start

◆ the computer will start but the system sends a series of beeps via the onboard speaker

◆ devices such as your MODEM, network card or soundcard do not work because the PCI bus has failed (see Unit 403)

◆ your hard drive, CD-ROM or floppy drives do not work because the IDE data bus is not operational (see Unit 403)

◆ your video board or monitor is not operational

◆ you can't use the USB port

◆ you cannot print

◆ your mouse is not working

◆ the keyboard is not working.

Motherboard

5.4.5 Monitor

The video board may be the cause of the apparent fault with your monitor (see Section 5.4.3).

Now that there are two types of monitor in common use, for the average computer user the faults can be very different. This section looks at common faults found with the CRT monitor and the TFT monitor.

> **What does it mean?**
>
> **CRT:** *Cathode ray tube is a vacuum sealed electron gun that sends charged particles to a screen coated with phosphorus. This is the same technology as your family television.*
>
> **TFT:** *Thin film transistor is the flat screen LCD (liquid crystal display)-based technology used in laptops and the newer popular flat-screen monitors.*

CRT and TRT monitors will both suffer commonly from these two issues:

◆ all monitors are vulnerable to the whims of the motherboard and the video board so there may be no apparent display

◆ if there is a fault with the connector, the monitor may display a tinted colour scheme (in purple, green or blue).

CRT monitors are more complex and faults with the components inside can produce a wide range of visual effects as demonstrated in Figure 82.

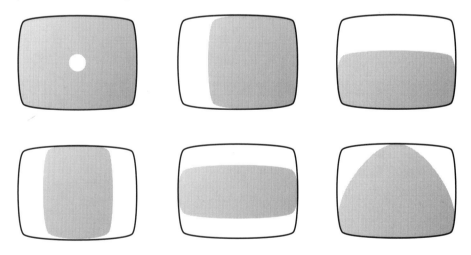

Figure 82 CRT faults

Each fault is caused by problems with the equipment that directs the electrons to the front of the monitor.

TFT monitors' main fault is damage to the screen itself. The liquid crystal system is a delicate structure that is easily ruptured, producing a rainbow affect in the damaged area of the monitor.

5.4.6 Ball in mouse

The mouse ball is the mechanism which allows Windows to work out the position of the pointer on the screen and the speed that you are moving the mouse. You will notice if you have problems with the mouse if:

◆ the pointer on the screen is jumping around when you move the mouse

◆ you are moving the mouse faster than the pointer is moving across the screen

◆ the pointer on the screen is moving faster than your movement of the mouse.

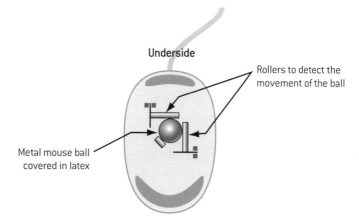

Figure 83 The mouse ball

5.4.7 Optical mouse

An optical mouse is mechanically simpler than the ball-based mouse. It measures the reflection of a light source to calculate the position of the Windows pointer.

You may notice similar problems with the optical mouse as those described in Section 5.4.6, except that computer users that are using an optical mouse may find that the Windows pointer can have a life of its own.

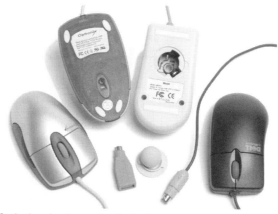

Optical and opto-mechanical mice

5.4.8 Keyboard

The keyboard is a complex array of switches, and there are many opportunities for failure to take place. Problems with the keyboard are likely to be local, involving the operating system and related to the motherboard.

These are the faults you are likely to encounter:

◆ when you type you get the wrong output for the symbol keys you pressed

◆ characters appear without you typing

◆ you press a key and multiple characters appear

◆ nothing happens

◆ some characters work; others do not

◆ the computer keeps beeping every time you press a key.

5.4.9 CD/DVD-ROM drive or CD/DVD writer

For the purposes of fault-finding CD-ROMS, DVD-ROMS, CD writers and DVD writers all behave the same, despite their being all different technologies. The reason for this is simple; the technology contained in the sealed box will send the same information as far as the motherboard and the operating system are concerned.

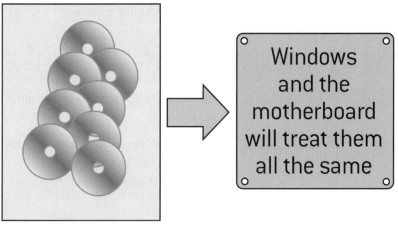

The computer could contain a CD-ROM, DVD-ROM, CD writer, DVD writer

Figure 84 CD/DVD technology

These are the faults that you are likely to encounter through using CD/DVD technology:

◆ the drawer does not eject

◆ the drive makes an unholy sound!

◆ you are unable to play music CDs

- you have problems writing CDs and DVDs
- you cannot read a CD or DVD
- the CD or DVD is not being auto detected
- the CD or DVD is ejecting at an unexpected moment.

CD-ROM drive

5.4.10 Floppy disk drive

Although it is the oldest storage technology found inside a PC, with the smallest storage capacity, floppy disk drives are still popular:

- the cost of a floppy drive is less than £4
- it is an excellent backup system to use to boot the computer if all else fails
- many users have large quantities of legacy data held on floppy drives that they may wish to access
- it is still a quick and effective mechanism to move small quantities of data.

Floppy disk drive faults can lie with both the mechanism and the media, and so changing the floppy disk may be the solution. In everyday use, you will encounter the following common faults:

- you are unable to insert a floppy disk
- you are unable to remove a floppy disk
- the floppy disk is damaged or unreadable
- your computer is unable to write to the floppy disk
- the floppy disk drive makes an inappropriate crunching sound.

Floppy disk drive

5.4.11 Hard drive

Being the main storage medium for the operating system and all personal files and applications, the failure of a hard drive tends to cause the greatest consternation amongst users and computer technologists alike. The failure of a hard drive may lead to the loss of work; the loss of work will often cause an anxious customer to become upset.

Hard drives are complicated and delicate systems, and can fail through age and wear. You will not be able to solve all hard drive faults, no computer professional can, but there are specialist companies that provide hard drive recovery services.

Go out and try!

There are many companies that provide others with a hard drive recovery service.

Using a popular search engine, search the web to find three companies that offer hard drive/data recovery services. Compare the fees they charge and the products they offer.

You may encounter these hard drive faults:

- a head crashes when the hard drive has completely failed and the read/write head has locked or hit the magnetic platter
- the driver motor can fail
- the boot sector can become corrupted

◆ the computer may not boot if there is a fault with the IDE or SCSI bus

◆ the BIOS will not detect the hard drive

◆ the operating system is not correctly installed

◆ the hard drive has corrupt sectors or tracks.

What does it mean?

IDE (integrated drive electronics) and *SCSI (small computer system interface)* are commonly used to transfer data from storage devices to the main computer system.

5.4.12 Printers

There are three types of printer technology in commercial use, and you will encounter different issues according to the type.

If you are called out to a laser printer you may encounter the following problems:

◆ no image or output

◆ paper jam

◆ loss of power

◆ printer overheating

◆ lines in output

◆ faint image or output

◆ corrupt image/output being created.

If you were called out to an inkjet printer you may encounter the following problems:

◆ no output

◆ paper jam

◆ ink being spilt or sprayed

◆ loss of colour or certain colours

◆ misaligned output

◆ stripes in output

◆ grinding sound!

Line printers are often used for continuous stationery such as invoices, despatch notes and wage slips. They are used commercially but rarely in the home environment. If called to a line printer, you may encounter these problems:

◆ the tractor feed is not holding the paper

◆ the head has jammed

◆ the head has lost contact with the ink ribbon.

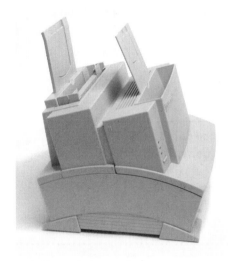

An inkjet and a laser printer

5.4.13 Printer driver

A printer is a mechanical device that needs software installed in the host operating system to control it. Each printer has a unique driver written specifically for the version of operating system installed on your computer.

If the wrong driver is installed or the driver has become damaged or deleted, then the printer is likely to:

◆ do nothing!

◆ display absolute garbage!

5.4.14 NIC or MODEM

The NIC (network interface card) and MODEM are used to connect the computer to external systems. Achieving this is inherently complex and often prone to failure (often due to the IT professional not doing his or her job properly). Common faults tend to be based on the loss of communication between your computer and the remote host.

5.4.15 Data cables

Your computer has a myriad of data cables connected to it internally and externally. You may find that on the standard computer system there are cables that connect:

◆ the hard drive to the motherboard

◆ the CD/DVD/ROM or writer to the motherboard

◆ the floppy drive to the motherboard

NIC and MODEM

◆ various USB devices to the motherboard

◆ CD-audio to the sound card

◆ external systems such as USB/Serial and parallel devices to the ports.

Finding faults with cables can be problematic and requires a systematic approach to discover what may be wrong (check power, check cable, check device). Most cable faults occur when there is:

◆ damage to the cable

◆ damage to the connector.

Cables

5.5 Now I have found the fault, what do I do next?

Congratulations! You are a technical expert. You have found the problem. The team are celebrating. So what happens next? The customer wants the problem solved.

The next step is critical as the solution will make more work for you (or your employer) as well as dictating when the customer can have their faulty system back in use. You have to consider how critical the problem is and how urgently the customer wants to reuse the system before you consider how you may choose to solve the problem. Unfortunately for you there is no right answer, only different ways for the customer to become displeased if you get it wrong. Here are some likely solutions:

Replace the component. Unless it is the hard drive, where you have to consider data recovery issues, this is often the quickest and easiest solution. The faulty component may be disposed of or sent to a specialist for repair.

Use the skills of another. Admitting that you are unable to solve the problem often requires courage as no one wishes to appear incompetent. Asking for advice is not always possible when you are working on the problem alone. (Consider mobile computer repair professionals who have to rely on their skills to complete the job.)

Sending the device away for repair is costly and time-consuming and is only done when the problem is genuinely beyond your remit or the component is too technical. (For example, there are some specialist printers available that you would not attempt to repair.)

Offer a complete replacement system. This can be time-consuming and costly, as well as cause problems, as the replacement is unlikely to be the same as the original and will lack the data on the computer that it needs for transferring. This solution is only to be considered as a last resort.

5.6 Solving common faults

This section provides you with likely solutions. Unfortunately there will always be the fault that you have never encountered before and this book cannot cater for everything.

5.6.1 Plug fuse for base unit or monitor

Replacing the cable will solve the problem. The cable offering the power can be obtained for less than £1 and is effectively disposable. If the fuse has failed it can be replaced by one with the same rating.

If the power cable has failed you may have a greater problem with the monitor or base unit; there may be an electrical fault with a component or the power supply that will cause a spike and this has caused the failure of the power cable.

To rectify this you have to be a qualified PAT tester to discover the problem and pass the issue onto a skilled electronics engineer. Often power problems are caused by the power supply which can be replaced independently or as part of a new computer case. An ATX computer case can be purchased for £15.

PRACTICAL TASK

With the consent of your supervisor or tutor, open up an old computer base unit (this will need to be an AT case which will be a 200 MHz computer or slower) and also open up a new computer base unit (this must be an ATX case, which will be found on all processors post 350 MHz).

Ensure that it is not connected to the mains and that you have appropriate anti-static protection.

Compare each power supply and motherboard. What is the difference in power cables, plugs and sockets?

Follow the links from www.heinemann.co.uk/hotlinks and compare standards for different motherboard, power supply and case formats.

5.6.2 CMOS battery

If the CMOS battery is the removable watch type then you can go to a high street retailer and purchase a suitable replacement. On some older motherboards the CMOS battery was a sealed soldered unit that could only be repaired by:

◆ replacing the motherboard
◆ removing the battery and soldering an equivalent replacement (which may not exist anymore).

PRACTICAL TASK

With the permission of your supervisor or tutor, open the base unit of a computer that it is good working order and has a removable CMOS battery. Ensure that the computer is not connected to the mains and that you have appropriate anti-static protection.

Remove the battery and attempt to reconnect the computer (to monitor, power, keyboard and mouse). What error message do you get? Will the computer start? Did the BIOS reset? Will the system detect all the components?

5.6.3 Video board

Video cards can be very problematic so there are many likely solutions to the problem.

◆ Replace the monitor if you had installed the wrong type and the monitor is not compatible with the resolution of the video board.

◆ If the SVGA socket is damaged on the video board then the video board needs replacing.

◆ If the SVGA plug on the monitor is damaged in that the pins are bent, this requires the replacement of the monitor (on a sealed unit) or the monitor cable.

◆ The operating system may not be using the correct drivers for the video board, thus requiring the installation of manufacturer specific drivers. You may need to go into safe mode and download the drivers from the manufacturer's website. (Note that most video boards will work on 660 × 480 with 256 colours.)

◆ The AGP or PCI bus may not recognise the video board (or vice versa, the video board does not recognise the AGP or PCI slot). In this case, you may need to update the drivers on your operating system to manage the AGP or PCI system.

◆ If there is no output at all, replace the monitor first. If there is no success, then replace the video board. If there is still no success, it is the motherboard that needs replacing.

5.6.4 Motherboard

There are no serviceable components on a motherboard, so if you have clearly identified that it is the motherboard that is faulty then it must be replaced (Figure 85). Some companies, such as ADT, do complete board level repairs but they are uncommon and are often serving regions as large as Europe due to demand.

5.6.5 Monitor

If you have managed to identify that the monitor is at fault, don't try to repair it. It is unlikely that you will be able to. Monitors are computer resources that may last for years or briefly run and then fail. If a monitor is faulty, you can send it to a specialist to repair. If it is under warranty send it to the manufacturer or original retailer.

The only fault that you can solve is if the pins on the plug have been bent (often caused by ham-fisted users who put the plug in the wrong way). This fault can be easily resolved by:

◆ using a pair of tweezers to straighten the pins, or

◆ replacing the cable.

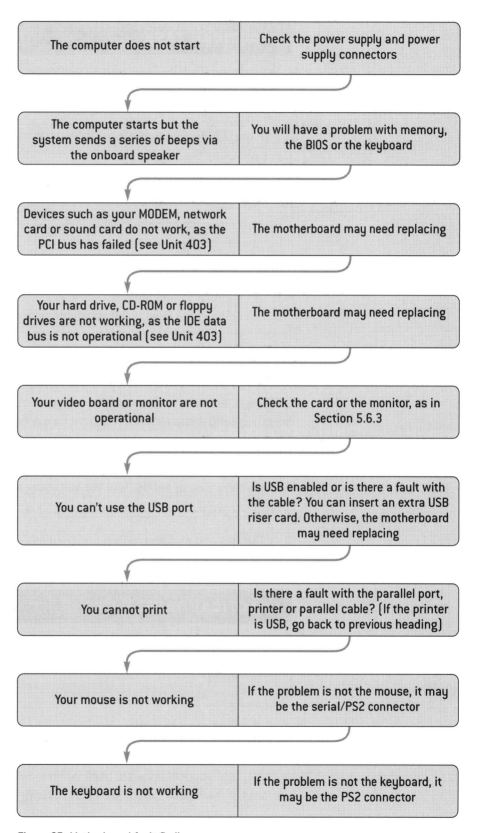

The computer does not start	Check the power supply and power supply connectors
The computer starts but the system sends a series of beeps via the onboard speaker	You will have a problem with memory, the BIOS or the keyboard
Devices such as your MODEM, network card or sound card do not work, as the PCI bus has failed (see Unit 403)	The motherboard may need replacing
Your hard drive, CD-ROM or floppy drives are not working, as the IDE data bus is not operational (see Unit 403)	The motherboard may need replacing
Your video board or monitor are not operational	Check the card or the monitor, as in Section 5.6.3
You can't use the USB port	Is USB enabled or is there a fault with the cable? You can insert an extra USB riser card. Otherwise, the motherboard may need replacing
You cannot print	Is there a fault with the parallel port, printer or parallel cable? (If the printer is USB, go back to previous heading)
Your mouse is not working	If the problem is not the mouse, it may be the serial/PS2 connector
The keyboard is not working	If the problem is not the keyboard, it may be the PS2 connector

Figure 85 Motherboard fault-finding

PRACTICAL TASK

This task can only be done with an old unused monitor and you must get implicit permission from a tutor or supervisor. You will need to obtain a small screwdriver and a small pair of tweezers before you start this task.

Take the D-type plug that connects the monitor to the PC and bend back one pin using the small screwdriver.

◆ How will this affect the image being displayed on the monitor when it is plugged into the PC?

◆ How many pins do you have to bend and which pins do you have to bend to change the image colour?

◆ What colours change on the monitor?

Once you have completed this task make sure that you repair the damage by using the small tweezers to straighten the monitor cable pins.

5.6.6 Ball in mouse

Cleaning a mouse will often solve the problems of the ball causing the cursor on screen to jump erratically. When you turn a mouse upside down you can undo a small cover and remove the ball. Completing the following steps will ensure that the ball will run freely and the cursor will not jump across the screen.

1 Clean any dust or debris from the ball using a dry tissue.

2 Use a cotton bud to clean any debris away from the internal rollers.

3 If there is any stubborn debris attached to the rollers use a small craft knife to scrape it away.

PRACTICAL TASK

Open an opto-mechanical mouse and identify the internal components. Look where dust and debris gather and clean away any that have accumulated.

5.6.7 Optical mouse

Optical mice are famously fault free, and if one fails you have to replace it outright. Often optical mice are used without a mouse mat on a multitude of surfaces. If the mouse cursor starts 'shuddering' you will have to:

◆ check if any dirt/fluff has collected in the light sensor, and remove it with a cotton bud, and/or

◆ provide a mouse mat because the surface is changing the angle of reflection of the light emitted by the sensor.

What does it mean?

Angle of reflection: When you look in a mirror, the angle of reflection is the same as the light source. When the angle changes, you will not see the reflection come back to you.

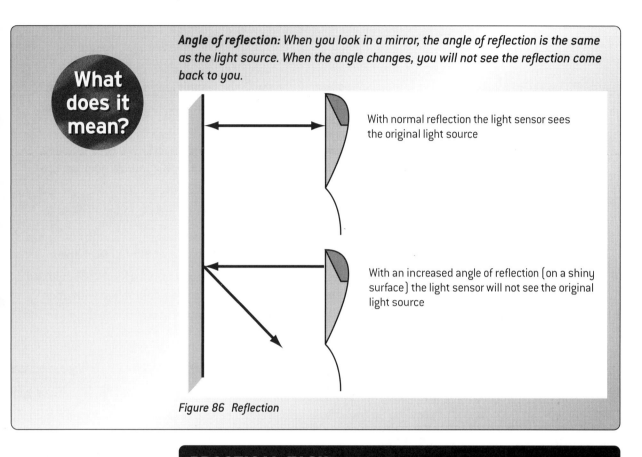

With normal reflection the light sensor sees the original light source

With an increased angle of reflection (on a shiny surface) the light sensor will not see the original light source

Figure 86 Reflection

PRACTICAL TASK

The way Windows controls mice is the same, regardless of the technology used to control the mouse. Start Settings/Control Panel and open the mouse icon.

Many users have problems with using the mouse as the controls are too sensitive or restrictive, preventing them from using the mouse effectively. Using the Buttons and Motion tabs, calibrate the motion and click speed of the mouse that you are using.

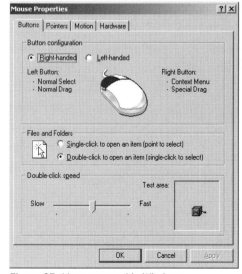

Figure 87 Mouse control in Windows

5.6.8 Keyboard

With a keyboard you are equally dependent on the operating system and the hardware that is being used. When trying to resolve any faults, consider the following issues:

◆ Is the keyboard connected?

◆ Are you using the right keyboard? The United Kingdom keyboard has a different standard from countries like Germany, France and the United States.

◆ Is the correct keyboard driver loaded? Windows will use United States settings by default. This makes life difficult with symbols such as £, $" and @.

◆ Is the keyboard dirty? The keys may be stuck down. You may need to clean the keyboard.

◆ Look at the type-matic rate. The keyboard may be set too sensitive.

◆ If the keyboard keeps beeping every time you press a key, the keyboard buffer is full and this means that there is a greater problem with your operating system. You may need to restart the computer to diagnose the problem.

PRACTICAL TASK

Following on from the practical task on page 123, you will also find in Settings/Control Panel the keyboard icon; double-click on it to open the option.

On this screen, calibrate the speed of the keyboard response time in Windows, change the keyboard type (as some users have specialist keyboards) and configure the locale (country used).

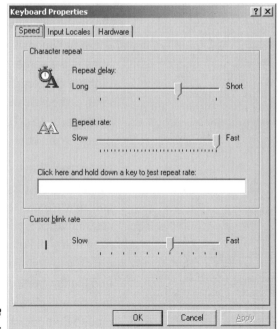

Figure 88
Keyboard settings in Windows

You may find that you will also need to configure the regional settings of the computer, which can be found in Settings/Control Panel/Regional Settings.

Here you may need to set the system to your local region as this will have an effect on how the keyboard behaves.

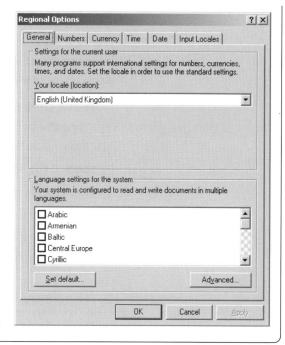

Figure 89 Regional Options

5.6.9 CD/DVD-ROM drive or CD/DVD writer

CD/DVD technology now costs so little that, if you have a problem with various CD/DVD components, it is often more cost-effective to replace the system outright. At the time of going to press you could purchase the following items for the following prices:

PC CD-ROM	£10
PC DVD-ROM	£22
PC CD writer/rewriter	£35
PC DVD writer/rewriter	£100

Naturally prices will drop!

However, if you have a fault with any of the above systems, it is worth checking if:

◆ the CD/DVD media is damaged

◆ the IDE or SCSI cable is connected correctly from the motherboard to the CD/DVD unit

◆ there is power going from the power supply to the CD/DVD device

◆ the software you are using correctly detects the CD/DVD device

◆ you are not trying to write data at a speed too fast for the quality of the media.

A little known issue with CD/DVD devices is that if there is a fault with the earth from the device to the motherboard, it will stop the whole system from working.

5.6.10 Floppy disk drive

Like CD/DVD technology, floppy disk drive technology is now so low cost that it is more effective to dispose of the faulty item rather than repair it. However, if you encounter problems with a floppy disk drive, make these checks:

◆ eject a stuck floppy disk by gently sliding a knife from left to right to left inside the bottom and top sides of the disk. This will release it from the catch inside the drive

◆ check if the 34-pin cable is the correct way around in the case

◆ check to see if the 'write protect' lug is closed on the disk

◆ confirm if the disk is full by using Windows *Explorer*

◆ confirm if the disk is damaged or corrupt by using Scandisk as well as Windows *Explorer*.

5.6.11 Hard drive

Under no circumstances must you ever attempt to open a hard drive. Doing so will damage the hard drive by letting dust into the delicate system, as well as invalidating the warranty.

What does it mean?

*A **warranty** is an agreement that guarantees that the manufacturer will repair faulty products for a period of time after the item is sold. Companies like PC WORLD will offer to sell you an extended warranty to increase the repair cover of your computer system.*

Problems that you *are* able to resolve include:

◆ replacing the IDE or SCSI cable, if the hard drive is not communicating with the rest of the system

◆ ensuring that the hard drive is switched to master or slave, according the hardware configuration (see Unit 403)

◆ running Scandisk or Defrag to complete operating system repairs on the structure of the hard drive

◆ checking whether there is no boot sector and the operating system needs to be installed (or reinstalled)

◆ checking whether the BIOS needs to be flash upgraded (you will need to go to the manufacturer's website) so that it can manage the hard drive. (This often happens if you install a new hard drive on an old system and the system does not recognise the size of the hard drive.)

PRACTICAL TASK

Using the version of Windows available on your own computer, complete a comprehensive analysis of the integrity of your hard drive. To accomplish this you will need to run Scandisk and Defrag:

To access Defrag, click on Start/Programs/Accessories/System tools/ Disk defragmenter.

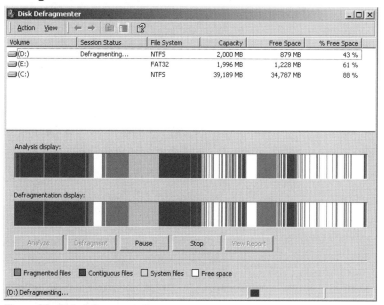

Figure 90   Disk defragmentation

Note that Windows 95/98 has a different version of Defrag but the operation is similar.

Defrag is a tool that rearranges (tidies) all the files on the hard drive to create more space for larger files. You could have 2 Gb free on a hard drive, but because the free blocks are all less than 100 Mb in size it is difficult to save large files.

Once you have started Defrag, click on the Defragment button.

Scandisk is a tool that has been available since DOS version 5 and was a feature in Windows 95/8; it checks your hard drive if you do not shut down your computer correctly.

In Windows 95/98, you can find Scandisk by entering Run/Scandisk.

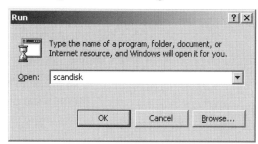

Figure 91   Obtaining Scandisk in Windows 95/98

Otherwise in Windows 2000 etc. you have to run an older command called CHKDSK, which you can access by entering Run/cmd then typing chkdsk.

```
C:\WINNT\system32\cmd.exe                                          _□×
Microsoft Windows 2000 [Version 5.00.2195]
(C) Copyright 1985-2000 Microsoft Corp.

C:\>chkdsk
The type of the file system is NTFS.

WARNING!  F parameter not specified.
Running CHKDSK in read-only mode.

CHKDSK is verifying files (stage 1 of 3)...
File verification completed.
CHKDSK is verifying indexes (stage 2 of 3)...
Index verification completed.
CHKDSK is verifying security descriptors (stage 3 of 3)...
Security descriptor verification completed.

  40130338 KB total disk space.
   4395260 KB in 31496 files.
     10340 KB in 2018 indexes.
         0 KB in bad sectors.
    101450 KB in use by the system.
     65536 KB occupied by the log file.
  35623280 KB available on disk.

      4096 bytes in each allocation unit.
  10032584 total allocation units on disk.
   8905820 allocation units available on disk.

C:\>chkdsk /?
Checks a disk and displays a status report.

CHKDSK [volume[[path]filename]]] [/F] [/V] [/R] [/X] [/I] [/C] [/L[:size]]

  volume        Specifies the drive letter (followed by a colon),
                mount point, or volume name.
  filename      FAT only: Specifies the files to check for fragmentation.
  /F            Fixes errors on the disk.
  /V            On FAT/FAT32: Displays the full path and name of every file
                on the disk.
                On NTFS: Displays cleanup messages if any.
  /R            Locates bad sectors and recovers readable information
                (implies /F).
  /L:size       NTFS only:  Changes the log file size to the specified number
                of kilobytes.  If size is not specified, displays current
                size.
  /X            Forces the volume to dismount first if necessary.
                All opened handles to the volume would then be invalid
                (implies /F).
  /I            NTFS only: Performs a less vigorous check of index entries.
  /C            NTFS only: Skips checking of cycles within the folder
                structure.

The /I or /C switch reduces the amount of time required to run Chkdsk by
skipping certain checks of the volume.

C:\>_
```

Figure 92 CHKDSK

PRACTICAL TASK

With the permission of your tutor or the person that owns the computer, restart the computer, press DEL or F2 and enter the BIOS. While each BIOS is slightly different, you can always find the same information.

You should be able to find a section that detects hard drives. Run this utility and identify:

◆ the storage capacity of the hard drives on your system

◆ the number of cylinders on the hard drive (this represents the number of drive platters)

◆ the number of sectors that are on the hard drive (each is used by the operating system to store data)

◆ whether this utility detects the number of CD-ROMs or other media.

5.6.12 Printers

While faults differ according to the printer technology, solutions can be summarised as follows:

◆ When you have a paper jam, carefully and systematically remove the paper and any debris from the printer. You must open all doors and lift all flaps/covers. With all printers you must take care not to make contact with the printing mechanism as this can be hot (laser printer) or create a mess (inkjet). You will need to reload the paper ensuring that it is in good condition when placed in the paper tray.

◆ If there is a problem with ink or toner you may need to run the printer through a cleaning cycle. If it is an inkjet printer, using a piece of paper towel on the head helps. With a laser printer, shaking the toner cartridge can help. For a line printer, you simply change the ribbon which comes in a cartridge.

◆ If any printer is making an inappropriate sound, once you have eliminated a paper jam, you need to send it to a suitably qualified professional, whom the manufacturer recommends. Most printers are not user serviceable. You will find that if you attempt to dismantle a printer, you will have difficulty in reassembling the system.

◆ If there is no output or the output is 'garbled' the likely issues are: no driver, wrong driver, fault with the connector on the PC or printer, or a faulty printer cable. Driver reinstallation is simple, and can be done with the resources provided from the manufacturer's CD or website (see Section 5.6.13). Printer cables are low cost and easy to replace, as most systems now use USB. Faults with connectors are more problematic as they are directly soldered onto the board of the PC.

PRACTICAL TASK

Using the version of Windows on the computer you are using, enter the Printer menu. You will find this in Start/Settings/Printers.

Figure 93 Printers

Right-click on one of the printers that is installed on your system and select the Properties option.

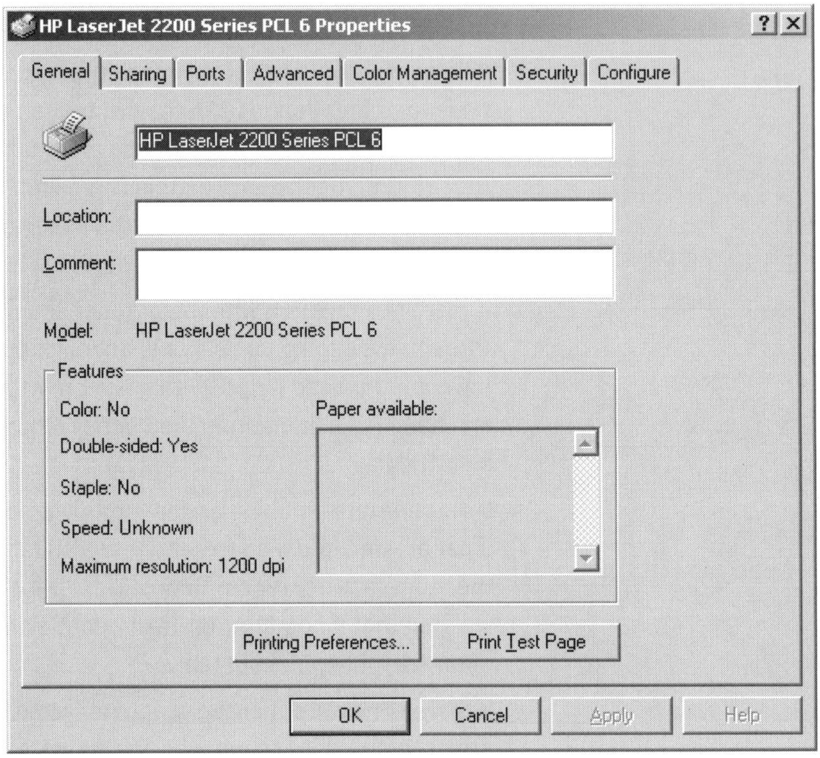

Figure 94 Printer options

Task one
Click on Print test page and check the quality of the printout.

Task two
If your printer offers you the opportunity to use the Change printer preferences, click on this option and look at what you may be able to achieve.

5.6.13 Printer driver

All printers are different, and you cannot use Epson drivers for Hewlett-Packard printers and vice versa. When you install a printer, Windows may detect the printer and offer the correct driver if the printer is older than the operating system. With continuous development and improvements in printer technology, you are more likely to need to install the printer driver when you install the new printer.

When you right-click on the Printer/Properties options you have the opportunity to change the printer driver.

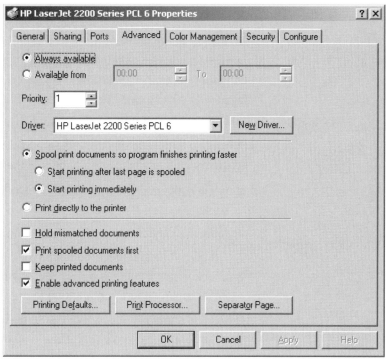

Figure 95 Printer driver options

PRACTICAL TASK

Using the printer installed on your system, find and click on the Printer driver option. Using the 'hardware/driver' wizard change the printer driver to one that is unrelated to the printer that you are running.

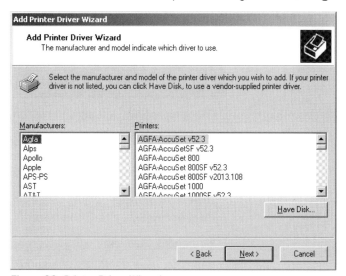

Figure 96 Printer Driver Wizard

Once complete, attempt to print. Does it work? What is the result?

5.6.14 NIC or MODEM

Troubleshooting faults with a NIC or MODEM can be very complex as this requires a good knowledge of networking. (If you do well on this course you can progress to the Level 3 networking course.) Nevertheless you are always faced with a multitude of causes for a MODEM or a NIC not working and the resulting loss of communication.

In working with both devices, you may be able to solve communication problems by applying one (or more) or the following solutions:

◆ Is the cable plugged into the NIC or MODEM and connected to the wall socket?

◆ Does the cable that is connected to the NIC/MODEM work on another system, or in another wall socket?

◆ Check to see if there is a fault with the network/phone system with your ISP or organisation's networking team.

◆ Does another NIC/MODEM of the same type work instead?

◆ In network properties, is TCP/IP or another suitable protocol installed?

◆ In system properties, is the NIC or MODEM recognised?

◆ If TCP/IP is correctly installed, is the network addressing correctly configured (automatically detect settings may be appropriate)?

What does it mean?

TCP/IP (Transmission control protocol/Internet protocol) is a method used to send data from computer to computer across networks and the Internet.

PRACTICAL TASK

Checking the networking settings on Windows is not difficult, but it is essential that you do not change the settings on a pre-configured computer. Otherwise you may prevent it from communicating with a network or, even worse, prevent another computer from being able to communicate.

To access network setting for a computer, right-click on My Network Places or Network Neighborhood if you are using Windows 98.

You need to find the local area connection and select Network Properties; once you have done this you should be able to find the TCP/IP settings.

Using Figure 97, identify the settings.

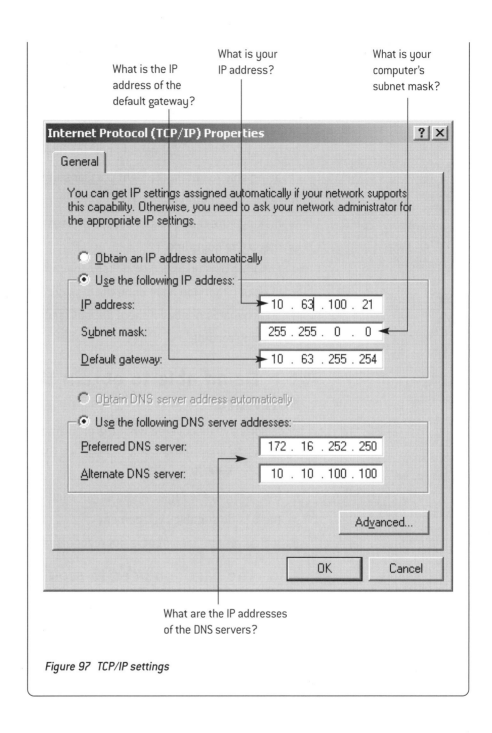

What is the IP address of the default gateway?

What is your IP address?

What is your computer's subnet mask?

Internet Protocol (TCP/IP) Properties

General

You can get IP settings assigned automatically if your network supports this capability. Otherwise, you need to ask your network administrator for the appropriate IP settings.

○ Obtain an IP address automatically
⦿ Use the following IP address:

IP address: 10 . 63 . 100 . 21

Subnet mask: 255 . 255 . 0 . 0

Default gateway: 10 . 63 . 255 . 254

○ Obtain DNS server address automatically
⦿ Use the following DNS server addresses:

Preferred DNS server: 172 . 16 . 252 . 250

Alternate DNS server: 10 . 10 . 100 . 100

Advanced...

OK   Cancel

What are the IP addresses of the DNS servers?

Figure 97 TCP/IP settings

5.6.15 Data cables

Cables connecting various internal and external devices to the computer are often prone to faults. Once you have found the problem and eliminated the fact that it may have been the device or port that it is connected to, the problem is easy to solve by replacing the cable.

6 Fixing the system

With the skills that you have developed in reading and putting into practice this module and the understanding that you can obtain from reading Units 403 and 404 you can be trusted to 'get the job right'. But doing the job is not technical skill alone. You have to develop skills in:

- being able to obtain the right part, or software
- reading the manual
- making sure that you can access the system to fix it
- managing your time
- ensuring that you successfully fix the problem
- checking that you have done the task correctly
- doing what is needed if there are still issues with the system
- keeping records.

6.1 Being able to obtain the right part, or software

Once you have discovered what the problem may be with the computer system, you are often expected to replace the faulty component. This can very problematic if:

- the part you are replacing no longer exists
- there is no suitable replacement
- the current replacement is not recognised by the system.

6.1.1 The part you need to replace no longer exists

Older computer systems rapidly become victim to the constant march of development in the computer industry, where what was once commonplace technology is rapidly outmoded, superseded or ignored with the development of new technology. While it may be possible to purchase replacements, they become more expensive due to their rarity value. A classic example occurred in the late 1990s when computer memory changed from 72-pin SIMMs to 168-pin DIMMs. Older systems that needed SIMMs for any upgrade or replacement suffered because the price of DIMMs dropped and SIMMs crept up (even though they were of a lower standard than their DIMM counterpart).

What does it mean?

SIMM: single in-line memory module. Older standards in memory meant that these 72- and 30-pin sticks could hold from 1 Mb to 32 Mb of data.

DIMM: dual in-line memory module. The basis for the current memory standard started at 32 Mb and is currently available in sizes beyond 1 Gb.

You or your employer can overcome this by ensuring that there is a small surplus stock of all required spares. You may find that this is not done unless the system is critical, due to the prohibitive cost. Or you could go to computer repair shops or computer fairs to scavenge for replacements (although not a guaranteed option and the replacement may be faulty or incompatible).

Go out and try!

Follow the links to the online shops from www.heinemann.co.uk/hotlinks to see if you can find SIMMs, AT motherboards or cases on either site.

6.1.2 There is no suitable replacement

With many different form factors (computer cases) and motherboards available as well as those created in the past, if major systems fail it is difficult to replace them.

Processors can fail and it is easy to replace them if the slot type is in common use. As technology ensures that the speed of processors doubles every 18 months, the slot that processors use changes as well. Since 1996, processor slots such as socket 5, 7, slot A and socket 370 are totally incompatible.

This means that, with a computer that is over 18 months old, unless you buy a new motherboard, processor and suitable system components (memory etc.), there is no suitable replacement option available.

6.1.3 The current replacement is not recognised by the system

As time marches forwards the currency of your operating system and speed of your motherboard wander backwards. You may replace your graphics card with a new superior system but find that it is no longer compatible.

Manufacturers will only create drivers for your operating system while it is current. Organisations such as Microsoft update their products at least every two years. You will find that Windows 98 will not work with many newer technologies.

Motherboards operate at a speed called a **clock rate**. Very soon new hardware will operate at greater speeds and become incompatible with your system. Older motherboards operated at speeds of 66 MHz whereas you can now obtain systems that operate at 200 MHz.

What does it mean?

Clock rate is the number of electronic cycles per second; a processor instruction clock rate is always faster than the data clock rate of a motherboard.

6.2 Reading the manual

One of life's greatest mysteries is why manufacturers create manuals and professionals don't read them. As you become more experienced you will be able to remember tasks and how to install, fix and configure a variety of complex systems. As a matter of pride, many of you will not consider looking for written help.

Many problems with computer systems and the devices that you may attach to them are known and documented by the manufacturers.

Instead of creating a situation where you are constantly stuck with a recurring problem that you are unable to solve you could:

◆ read the manual provided

◆ consult online help

◆ look at the read.me file.

Motherboards, printers, scanners, digital cameras etc. all come with a printed manual. In some cases, this may be a CD that contains a large PDF or *Word* document. They all have guides to installation, configuration and troubleshooting and potential problems.

What does it mean?

PDF (portable data format) is a standard created by Adobe for web- or CD-based documents that cannot be edited.

Windows has a useful facility, cunningly called **Help**. If you press F1 you will activate Windows context-sensitive help system. This means that, if you are in any application or Windows feature, you can activate the related Help files.

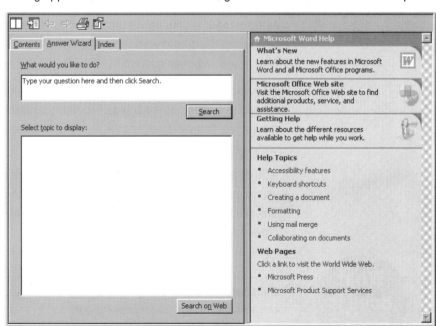

Figure 98 Windows context-sensitive help

As you can see from Figure 98, you can search through Help by typing in the required keyboard to identify your problem.

Some help systems are web based and you will be lead though a system on your CD or hard drive that will link to the latest help on the manufacturer's website. Most manufacturers will duplicate this help on their website so that you are able to resolve any issues with their products.

PRACTICAL TASK

Task 1
Using the Windows help, search for assistance on printer problems. You should obtain a link to the printer and network trouble-shooters.

Task 2
Go to the Hewlett-Packard website from www.heinemann.co.uk/hotlinks and type in the search field: Laserjet 2200 problems. You will find a series of links to support and driver pages. Find the one that lists all known issues.

On some older, smaller or less commercial applications you will encounter read.me or readme.txt files. These simple documents act as a guide to the application. These are equally as useful as professional manuals/help guides and tend to contain the same quality of information.

PRACTICAL TASK

Look at all the applications installed on your computer. Look in the Start menu as well as searching through C:\program files. Identify how many have read.me or other text files that contain information about the application.

6.3 Making sure that you can access the system to fix it

Often you will not know where the 'errant' computer system is located, especially if this is your first call to the customer. Before you embark on what may become a fruitless journey:

◆ find out where the computer is located

◆ ensure that there is someone there to meet you

◆ check if you need keys, ID or other means to gain access.

In most situations, arranging an appointment and confirming location and directions with the customer are satisfactory. However, many organisations have internal security so you may need to obtain keys/swipe cards or appropriate supervision to access the equipment. Checking in advance is of paramount importance; the customer will not perceive your inability to access the computer as a good reason for your not being able to fix it.

6.4 Managing your time

Going to a faulty computer system and sitting with it until it is fixed is not good time management. As is often the case you will have many other tasks awaiting your attention. Before you go to complete the work, you need to obtain an accurate idea of what the problem is. This will enable you to estimate the time you will take in completing the task and what resources you may need to take with you.

When working with computer systems, you should follow these common good practices:

◆ Overestimate the time you are going to take by 50%. This will cover travel and unforeseen faults (as the customer does not always give you accurate information). If you take less time, this is a positive and you can progress onto the next task.

◆ Ensure that you are well equipped for the job. This may include tools, replacement hardware or software. Leaving the job to fetch something that you forgot (or did not realise that you required) adds time to fixing the problem.

◆ Multi-task, so if you are visiting one customer, check to see if there are others in the same area that need work done. This will dramatically reduce your travelling time and improve your effectiveness. If you are working for a company, and you are visiting one department for one task, check to see if you might visit other computers in the same section.

◆ Some tasks require patience while you are waiting for an application or an operating system image to load. (Instead of sitting there like the proverbial lemon, do something useful with that time.)

◆ Keep the customer informed. If they know that a task may take a certain amount of time or that it will take you at least two visits, then they tend to be more accommodating and make less calls to the help desk.

6.5 Ensuring that you successfully fix the problem

An incomplete job leaves a dissatisfied customer. Dissatisfied customers complain and tell others about your poor service. This in turn generates a poor reputation which reduces the amount of work that you will get.

If you are unable to fix a problem, don't leave it and don't give the customer a tall story. (They may not be technical, but that does not mean that they are unintelligent.) Get help, ask a more experienced professional, contact the manufacturer's helpline and read the manual. But make sure that by the time you leave the customer for the last time, their system is restored to its former glory.

6.6 Checking that you have done the task correctly

While there may be similarities between this section and Section 6.5, there have been many professionals who believe that they have successfully fixed the problem only to be called back to the job as this was not the case.

Communicating with the customer also includes getting them to demonstrate the problem and checking once the task is done that you have returned the system to a state that is acceptable to them.

Many people have often misunderstood instructions. For example, a common mistake with printers is that the technical support will come along and test the page using a monotone *Word* document. Whereas, if they used the Windows printer test tool, the output will demonstrate if there are any faults or simply that the colour ink cartridge needs replacing.

6.7 What to do if there are still issues with the system

There are some problems that are not fixable without completely replacing the hardware. This is the last resort and can only be done with the customer's consent, and considering any financial and warranty constraints.

6.8 Keeping records

Day after day you work on many computer systems and start to notice that a certain brand of mouse keeps losing its ball or that a popular type of soundcard fails after three months of use. Or you have one customer that always manages to damage the printer under their control. What can you do about this? You inform your supervisor and he or she says: 'So what. Prove it.'

Most organisations have a major systems support function to keep track of all work that is done by you and your colleagues. This powerful tool allows them to track:

◆ common faults with software and hardware

◆ problematic customers, companies or departments.

Successfully identifying a common fault with software or hardware can enable managers to answer two important questions:

- Is this a product that we no longer wish to support or purchase?
- Are we doing something wrong? Do we need to look at our procedures or provide suitable staff training?

By tracking records, you can also identify:

- whether a customer needs to be charged more, or offered a different service contract
- whether they may have received a substandard system
- whether they need some basic training to reduce the number of calls.

Go out and try!

Visit www.helpdesk.com and look at the help desk software that is available. Compare the products listed on site and identify if they offer call management, asset management and knowledge management solutions.

7 Tips for passing the module

As this is a core module, you will be assessed in two ways by your tutor and City and Guilds:

1 You will complete an assignment, and you will be given no more than three hours to complete the task set.
2 You will complete a computer-based examination, in which you will be limited to one hour to attempt no more than 40 questions. (Note, however, that City and Guilds may change this to improve standards.)

7.1 The assignment

Your assignment will be scenario-based and will involve you carrying out a series of preventive maintenance tasks on a personal computer system. It is essential that you clearly follow health and safety procedures and show that you are aware of ESD precautions. You may be supplied with a Fault Reporting Log Sheet and preventive maintenance log; on these you will need to record faults and any remedial actions taken. The assignment may contain set tasks like these:

1 Unplug the computer system and inspect all components.
2 Check for any external damage or deterioration.
3 Clean the base unit, monitor, mouse, keyboard and printer.
4 Remove accessible covers (not the monitor).

5 Remove dust and debris from the base unit, mouse, keyboard and printer.

6 Inspect the interior of the base unit and other devices for damage or deterioration.

7 Replace covers, reconnect the system and restart.

8 Carry out troubleshooting on any problems or defects encountered.

9 Suggest possible causes of any problems encountered.

10 Carry out a system or data backup.

11 Carry out a system or data restoration using the backup created.

12 Complete a routine operating system maintenance procedure, e.g. disk cleanup and/or defragmentation of disk.

7.2 The examination

Use the accompanying questions to practice (the answers are listed at the end). Don't cheat; the practice is a worthwhile exercise:

1 What is the safest way of lifting a heavy object that is on the floor?

    A With your ankles, taking the strain on your feet.

    B With your back straight and knees bent.

    C With your arms out.

    D Bent over.

2 PAT is an acronym for.

    A Preventative Appliance Testing.

    B Portable Application Testing.

    C Private Address Translation.

    D Portable Appliance Testing.

3 Which of the following is *not* a hazard?

    A The power supply on a computer base unit.

    B The toner used in a laser printer.

    C The fire alarm system.

    D Cleaning chemicals.

4 ESD precautions are in place to protect

    A You.

    B The computer.

    C Your employer.

    D Your colleagues.

5 Anti-virus software has to be updated regularly

    A To regularly scan the memory.

    B To regularly scan the computer.

    C As new viruses are created on a daily basis.

    D As new faults are found with your operating system.

6 A firewall is used to

    A Protect the network from you.

    B Keep the anti-virus software up to date.

    C Enable the computers access to the Internet.

    D Protect the computer from unauthorised access.

7 Files can be hidden using

    A The hide option in *Explorer*.

    B The UNATTRIB command.

    C The file manager option in *Explorer*.

    D The folder options dialogue window.

8 Which of these is not a fault caused by a keyboard?

    A The computer emits a long beep.

    B The computer fails to boot.

    C The computer fails to start.

    D The £ is replaced by a $.

9 A senior manager calls in desperation to report that the printer will not print. What should the technician ask to troubleshoot the problem?

    A Is it our printer?

    B Is the printer still under warranty?

    C Has anything changed with the printer or computer recently?

    D Is there another printer that can be connected to the computer?

10 Which part of fault-finding is important to help avoid repeating repairs that were performed previously?

    A Gathering of information.

    B Identifying of the problem.

    C Following the correct implementation of the solution.

    D Reading previous documentation of the problem and its solution.

11 Which computer component starts POST?

    A BIOS.

    B CMOS.

    C CPU.

    D Hard drive.

12 Reading the manual is considered to be

    A Bad luck.

    B Uncommon.

    C The professional solution to a problem.

    D A demonstration of your inability to do the job.

Good luck!

Answers to questions: 1B, 2D, 3C, 4B, 5C, 6D, 7D, 8D, 9C, 10D, 11A, 12C

Customer support

Introduction

Knowing how to deliver high standards of customer service is a continuous challenge that all organisations face. Customers' expectations are higher than ever before and the world of technology is one of the key influences in raising customer demands and expectations.

A little over ten years ago, things were very different:

◆ a postal strike had an enormous impact on the daily operations of a business

◆ buying the weekly shopping involved travelling to the local shop or supermarket

◆ researching a subject meant a journey to the local library for most individuals.

The evolution of improved technology has brought us the power of email and online shopping services. It has helped those that are housebound become more independent, and it has provided variety in learning and teaching methods. The impact on society of developments in IT is enormous. It has created more choice, improved the speed and methods in the way we operate and, in doing so, it has empowered all our lives.

With improvement comes pace. Technology is moving so fast that many users need guidance and support in getting their technology to work well for them. Knowing what the customer needs to work well within their own environment is the key to success.

IT professionals have to provide a high standard of professionalism to meet customer demand. This demand stretches a technician in many directions dependent on his or her role:

◆ working as part of an internal helpdesk structure – responding to questions and queries for its company employees

◆ working as a field technician visiting customers and fixing or resolving problems in a face-to-face situation

◆ working as part of an external helpdesk structure – supporting customers that buy the products and services including customers that do not work for the company.

This unit relates to the City and Guilds Equal Information Technology Practitioner (ICT Systems Support) Qualification. By reading this unit, you will explore the main issues that will be encountered in the world of technology, communication and customer service, typically known as **end user support** in IT terminology.

This unit aims to provide you with the information you need, both *theory* and *practical,* to deliver the right balance of your technical professionalism with interpersonal skills. These have to be displayed so that the support delivered to the customer is timely, effective and meets the customer's needs and expectations.

1 Providing technical information and support

To be effective in a support role, the right balance of technical information is required alongside the interpersonal skills to relate knowledge to the user effectively.

Customer support is about identifying a customer's needs and providing a solution. It is not only concerned with what a technician knows; it is focused on how that knowledge is used to meet the customer's need. When it is done well, technical knowledge converts itself to 'support' as viewed by the user. This instils customer loyalty and creates greater job satisfaction.

Support is judged by the speed at which queries are resolved and the way this is communicated by a technician.

This first section looks at six important topics:

◆ responding professionally to customers – the skills mix

◆ methods of providing technical support

◆ sources of technical support information

◆ the support team

◆ keeping a log

◆ health and safety

◆ software applications.

1.1 The skills mix

First impressions count.

◆ Over the telephone, the first impression starts from the first ring tone and is judged by how long the customer is kept waiting in a queue. Once the telephone is answered, the support desk will be judged on how the customer is greeted and the flow of the conversation. Each stage is assessed by the customers, although they will not verbalise it in most cases unless it is not meeting their expectations.

◆ With face-to-face situations, it will depend on the first visual contact the users have with the technician and the organisation (if they are a user visiting the business premises). Impressions are powerful and set the 'image' of support long before a query is explained, let alone solved.

However communication happens, it is important to respond to customers in a prompt and professional manner. Knowing what prompt and professional

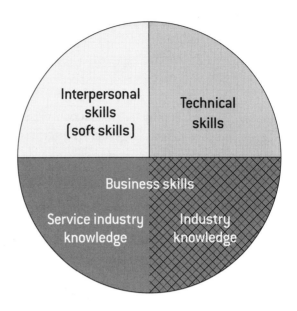

Figure 1 The professional skills mix

mean and how one achieves this is the challenge for anyone working in IT, let alone any other industry.

Professionalism

When baking bread, you need to have the right ingredients, appreciate the reasons why you need to have enough 'air' in the dough and how to 'knead' it to get the right result so that the bread will rise. So it is with professionalism. The term is used to explain the coming together of a number of areas. This takes time but makes the difference to the polished outcome. There are a number of skills required (Figure 1). Some are essential and some desirable. Professionalism can be seen, heard and most importantly felt and it is what all organisations want of their staff. When service is provided to a high standard, it creates enthusiasm, job satisfaction and the willingness to build on what is being done. This has a knock-on effect through all the work that is done within the support structure.

Business skills

These are the general skills that a practitioner in their chosen field needs to have to function effectively. These are skills specific to the customer service and support industry, such as understanding the importance of meeting customer's needs and knowing how to manage their expectations. They are broken down into industry knowledge and service industry knowledge.

Industry knowledge: Some support functions hire people who understand the specific industry in which the company is engaged, such as manufacturing, education, retail or financial. This knowledge makes it easier for an employee to understand the company's goals and therefore to contribute accordingly. Many help desks recruit from within the company and value candidates that have the skills and knowledge that pertain to the product or service being sold. For example, a company that sells accounting software may seek help desk personnel who have an accounting background. The benefit of employees with this knowledge is that the analyst will understand the customer's needs and appreciate the impact on the customer's business when a product fails. This empathy goes a long way towards securing customer loyalty.

Service industry knowledge: When hiring support technicians or analysts, many organisations will look to see if candidates have a practical knowledge of 'service' and helping others. If they find this when scanning through CVs and resumés, this indicates that the candidate has already grasped an understanding that delivering a professional service is vital and that customers look to them for help.

Technical skills

The level of technical skills that are required within the IT field will vary depending on the customer's needs. Technical skills are required to support a specific product of technology that a help desk needs. As a minimum, companies will expect people applying for entry level positions to be computer literate. They must have experience of using computers and know how to use Microsoft Windows as well as popular software packages such as Microsoft *Word*, *Excel*, *Access*, etc. Depending on the job role, analysts at different levels will be expected to have skills and experience in a 'specific' area. For example, a technician who has a role within an internal help desk supporting a complex computing environment may require a broader base of skills, including experience with network environments, operating systems, applications and hardware systems.

Interpersonal skills

These are otherwise known as **soft skills** and are the qualities people need to deliver not just a satisfactory service but an outstanding service in a professional manner. These skills have an impact within the scope of team work, as well as an incredible impact on the customer. The term 'behaviour breeds behaviour' is common. People normally adapt to environments based on the messages they encounter. Most of the ways we experience positive experiences will depend on individuals possessing these skills:

◆ listening skills
◆ verbal skills
◆ customer service skills
◆ problem-solving skills
◆ writing skills
◆ team skills.

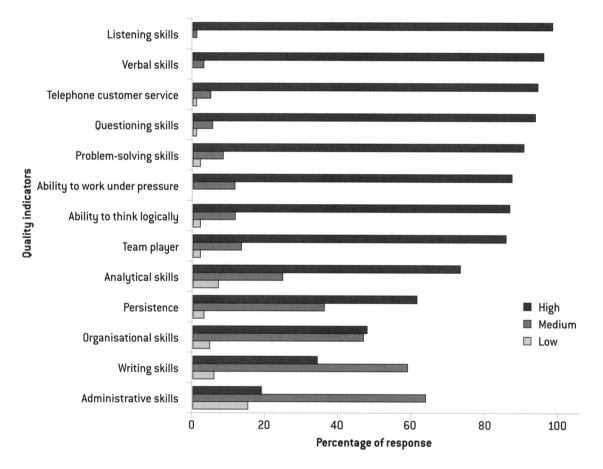

Figure 2 *Help Desk Institute Customer Support Practices Report*

PRACTICAL TASK

Investigate support team roles at your college:

1 List what you feel are the essential qualities for the support role.

2 List what are the desirable qualities for the role.

   Discuss your findings as a group.

Go out and try!

Put your assessment skills to the test.

Spend some time observing a customer service environment (preferably IT related in your college or an experience you have had of a help or support desk, but it could be any environment).

Draw up an observation sheet that will help you to gather the information.

Think about the skills that create professionalism. Now answer the following questions:

◆ How long did it take to be served?

◆ Was the assistant/technician/colleague polite and prompt?

◆ How did they display their listening skills?

◆ Did you feel as though you were taken seriously? What made you 'feel' that?

◆ Were any issues explained using an appropriate level of language – could you understand what was being said?

◆ Were you assured that 'the situation' has been/will be resolved?

◆ Did you learn anything to help you should the situation occur again?

◆ Were you given adequate time to explain and to ask further questions?

Where to start – knowing your customer

Everyone experiences being a customer at some point or other. Many people find themselves providing a service to others, their customers, whatever their job or task may be:

◆ a student undertaking a period of study

◆ a lecturer setting out to help learners achieve a goal

◆ working part-time in McDonald's

◆ a newly appointed technician working as part of a team for IBM.

Everyone is serving and working with a purpose for someone else, and everyone is relying on others to provide a service to them – as customers. It is important to find out as much as you can about your customer's use of ICT so that you can relate to the importance of the software/hardware etc., and the impact that this has on the working environment.

What does the customer need?

Ask any user what he or she wants from a PC and the list will probably be quite short: 'One that works every time I switch it on and does not crash.' Users take for granted all the other things they expect – they only ever remember those things that go wrong.

Depending on the job role that a user has, his or her needs of IT will vary. All of them will have some fundamental requirements from an IT support function. Given that a user will be looking for a combination of ways to use ICT, it is important to look at two main points:

◆ What equipment are they likely to be functioning with on a daily basis?

◆ How are they using it?

A technician's role is to build up an accurate picture of these points quickly .

Hardware

A user may be someone on the go all day long with a laptop and other equipment, such as a fax/printer or a mobile phone with Bluetooth technology, to allow access to emails and the Internet. Extra hardware may be needed, such as a better resolution printer, for someone in the design team. Users need the minimum configuration to allow them to operate their PC: keyboard, mouse and screen.

Having been assigned the required hardware configuration, the user then needs this to work every time the computer is switched on. This is where the problems really start. All equipment fails at some time and it is then that the support team need to step into action.

Software

Apart from the operating system (such as Windows, which will allow the user to log on), each PC should have the standard applications:

- word-processing
- spreadsheet software
- database software
- communications software.

Depending on what type of work the user does, there may be other essential software needed, such as DTP software, a graphics package, project management software, financial systems, etc. There may also be software that has been specifically written for the organisation. For example, a publishing house may have a special system to calculate royalty payments due to their authors. All this software needs to be kept up to date, and the files produced need to be kept safe. This will mean that software updates will need to be done on a regular basis (with minimal disruption to the user) and that a backup procedure must be in place (with minimal effort on the part of the user).

Consumables

Consumables are the things that users really do take for granted!

- floppy disks
- CDs
- cleaning products for the mouse and the screen
- paper
- printer cartridges.

There needs to be a ready supply of these for every user. This will be dependent on the precise job requirements of each individual in an organisation. The equipment will then need to be maintained (kept clean), the software has to be kept up to date and each workstation supplied with consumables so that everything runs as smoothly as possible.

Maintenance in support is rather like house keeping duties at home. Often it goes unnoticed until someone stops doing it and things start looking more messy. That's when we know whether support is in place or not!

Goal and target setting in organisations

To be effective in business, every organisation sets out with a plan and an objective 'goal'. It often starts off with a mission statement that identifies the main purpose of the organisation. It answers the question: 'What are we here for?'

The obvious goal for any organisation is to make a profit and or gain the highest market share. They need to look at the competitive market they are in and to adapt to the continuous changes and improvements that are expected from their customers.

The main factors affecting the survival of a company are:

◆ competition

◆ increased customer expectation

◆ marketing – communicating the range of products and services in the most effective way

◆ selling methods for those products and services

◆ profits (these must be used wisely – for example, investing in research and development, better premises, staff training, etc.).

All these factors create the essential mix to ensure an organisation can survive. They are considered and reviewed continually.

Establishing knowledge about the organisation you work for is important. Most organisations will provide new entrants with a member of staff to act as a 'buddy' or 'mentor' to induct them through certain areas of information such as:

◆ products and services

◆ the range of the customer base, internal/external, private individuals or companies, etc.

◆ what performance measures employees are expected to work to, e.g. service level agreements (SLA)

◆ whom to refer problems to

◆ what equipment is needed, and how it is maintained and used

◆ details of the organisation's mission statement/customer service policy.

The information above is gathered over time and helps employees to become more effective for the organisation and to meet the demands of their customers. The quicker these are mastered, the more time that can be devoted to the main focus of your role: maintaining and improving the service delivery.

Mission statements

A mission statement is normally no longer than a paragraph and is written in a language that everyone can understand, customers and employees alike.

Here are two examples:

- *A water company:* To offer a quality of service that is acceptable, having regard for costs and effects on the environment and to remedy recognised deficiencies over a reasonable period.
- *A credit card company:* To supply products and services to our customers.

All organisations have goals. Some have an agreement which is set up between the IT support department and other departments within the same organisation, i.e. the end users.

Service level agreements

Service level agreements (SLA) and operational level agreements (OLA) are the terms and conditions that the organisation agrees with a customer. These terms are the level of service that the customer agrees to pay for. It is the very least that the customer can expect from the support function. In most cases, all support staff dealing on a day-to-day level with that customer will be aware of what standards they are working to.

An agreement will be a formal written document, legally binding contract by both parties, and will specify:

- the services the IT support function will provide
- the level of services, e.g. Bronze, Silver, Gold levels, or 2, 3, 4 star depending on the customer's needs
- how much it will cost.

To achieve the level of support, the manager of the IT support team must ensure a team of technicians is available as appropriate. He or she will be responsible for setting targets for the team and scheduling the work. Here are some targets that the support manager may set:

- to answer all incoming calls promptly, i.e. before the fourth ring
- to provide information and advice to end users within 10 minutes
- to identify a course of action within 20 minutes
- to solve the problem or provide replacement facilities within one hour
- to resolve a problem within 24 hours
- to keep the end user informed of progress.

Some of these targets may be unachievable in every case, so some targets may be made more achievable by qualifying them:

◆ to identify a course of action for 90 per cent of faults within 20 minutes
◆ to solve the problem or provide replacement facilities for 75 per cent of faults within one hour
◆ to resolve 60 per cent of problems within 24 hours, the remainder within 48 hours.

1.2 Methods of providing technical support

Customer support is about identifying a customer's needs and providing a solution. It is not just concerned with what a technician knows. It is focused on how that knowledge is put across to meet what the customers need. To communicate a message effectively, there are choices as to which method holds best for you and your user at the time the support is needed. Essentially, there are three main **methods of communication**.

◆ **Verbal communication:** The spoken word involves hearing the message. It could be a one-to-one conversation, either face-to-face or using the telephone, or one-to-many, as in a presentation or demonstration to an audience. Many interactions between a help desk analyst and the customer occur over the telephone. The technician's ability to communicate verbally is critical. They have to be able to solve problems but being remote from the customer means that their choice of language must be clear, confident and at the right pace. Patience and focusing are vital because some customers may need a lot more guidance than others. For example, a technician speaking to a first-time computer user will need to use more simplistic language when guiding them through a set of instructions.

◆ **Written communication:** This will involve reading the message. It could be on paper, for example, a report, handout or leaflet, or displayed on a whiteboard, OHP or blackboard. Supporting customers in this way is increasing. Help desk analysts have to write well to log calls, and they may need to develop procedures and to correspond with customers and colleagues via email.

Many companies now allow customers to directly access the help desk's tracking system to check on the status of their call if it is outstanding.

Some companies use their internal company Intranet or the Internet to publish answers to frequently asked questions (FAQs), hints and tips documentation, etc. Clarity and simplicity are vital to display the right image and greatly aid supporting the customer.

◆ **Practical communication:** With a demonstration you can show the audience, whether it be one-to-one or one-to-many, what you are doing and they can then practise this for themselves. This assists them in developing confidence and memorising what has been done. Showing a user how to do something and then watching them consolidate their knowledge is effective **training** and gets the message across quickly. Depending on the technician's role, this may be possible and will require all of his or her interpersonal skills.

◆ **Body language** can also be a powerful method of communicating feeling. The nod of a head communicates understanding; a person shaking his or her head depicts a different meaning. Body language can be used to support verbal and practical communication to good effect.

Did you know!

Professor Albert Mehrabian, the scientist most often quoted when thinking about body language, stated that the percentages of importance of the three major factors in communicating are:

◆ what we say	7%
◆ how we say what we say	38%
◆ body language	55%

This means that 93% of all communications relies on aspects other than the words we speak.

Check your understanding

Using the headings Verbal, Written and Practical, imagine you work for a busy internal helpdesk and that you provide technical support via telephone calls as well as helping users at their desk.

List for each method:

1 The advantages of providing technical support.

2 The disadvantages of providing technical support.

Consider what you need to be able to do to effectively deliver technical support information using these methods.

PRACTICAL TASK

◆ As a user of ICT within your college, list how many times you have needed help within a week.

◆ What categories did it fall into? Hardware, software, consumables?

◆ How was this provided? Demonstration? Over the telephone?

◆ What were the main methods that were used? Verbal, practical or written?

◆ What was the outcome?

◆ As a user, how did you feel? What was your impression of the IT support technician?

◆ What could have been done better and what was done really well?

◆ Compare notes with others in your group. What improvements would you like to see in how support is provided to users? Draw up some recommendations.

CASE STUDY

Maggie and the mobile

Maggie is a first-year student at Brentfields college. She has been there for ten weeks now and is enjoying her course. Having settled in well, she notices that all her friends have mobile phones and feels a little out of place without one. This weekend she has made the decision that she will purchase one. Having saved up and waited for a long time, she wants the latest edition. The Motokia C350 has caught her eye. It has lots of features.

◆ Colour screen.

◆ Remix polyphonic ringtones.

◆ Downloadable games.

◆ Changeable covers.

She has used a mobile before though she has never owned one. She will need some good advice from a customer service assistant who will need to lead her through the essential and useful information that she needs to be aware of.

You are the customer assistant!

◆ What needs do you feel Maggie has?

◆ Why does she really want this phone? How will you use that information to serve her properly?

◆ What questions will you ask her? Put the information in a logical order.

◆ What essential things do you need to tell her?

Make notes and then discuss your thoughts with your group.

The shop assistant serving Maggie has to establish some basic information before going on to explain features or benefits, etc.

◆ He or she will also have to be familiar with the product and technical specification that is for sale. This knowledge must already be in place before the customer is served.

◆ Then he or she has the challenge of relating the main features, e.g. downloadable ring tones, polyphonic sounds, to Maggie's reasons for wanting the phone.

◆ There are other considerations, such as level of usage and billing. Will she be a 'pay as you go' customer or would Maggie be better off with a 'contract'?

◆ Then there's the way the assistant puts the information across. Too technical and Maggie will feel jaded and confused. Too basic and Maggie may feel embarrassed and patronised.

It's a fine balancing act. The success of the sale will depend on all these factors and more. The success of IT support has similar challenges.

It may seem as though the process of supporting a customer's wants and needs is fairly simple but customers vary and 'one solution does not fit all'! The customer's expectations may make him or her appear fussy and fickle; this reaction could arise because of the choices they have made but also because of past experiences in requesting support. A customer knows how they want to *feel* when someone is serving or supporting them. As we are all customers this is common to everyone. You will no doubt have heard the phrase: 'It's not what you say – it's how you say it.'

The role of an IT support technician is to combine the right balance of technical knowledge with the right level of interpersonal skills for the customer/user to grasp what they are being told. Users need to have a positive image of support and some will complain that support technicians speak another language. There can be a culture of 'us' and 'them' – and often the support team are seen to be unapproachable, and/or unsympathetic to the needs of users.

Other users will see the support team as a group of reliable, helpful individuals who are in the background ready to solve IT problems and educate the customer in the process.

Having decided what the best methods of communicating a message to the user are, Figure 3 outlines the process which enables a technician to deliver support in an effective manner.

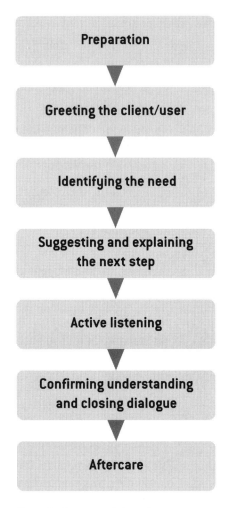

Figure 3 The essential service process

Preparation – 'If you fail to prepare, be prepared to fail'

- Equipment used must be in working order.
- Check all the logging software is operating.
- Complete all start of the day/end of the day checks.
- Workstations need to be neat and tidy.
- Be physically prepared! Is your appearance appropriate? Remember that first impressions count!
- Be mentally prepared! Workloads may be heavy, which can make the day seem long and support has to be consistent.
- Prioritisation of work – know what needs to be done first, what can wait, etc.

- Whom can you refer to?
- Find out what the most frequently asked questions are.
- Where can you find help?

Greeting the client/user

Thinking about the methods of communication that will be applicable, the initial contact with the user is crucial for setting the tone of the conversation. Whether it be telephone or face-to-face, you need to create a positive, approachable first impression. Always use the customer's name.

Check your understanding

- From the practical task you did on page 155, how would you assess the way the ICT technician greeted you when you had a problem?
- Consider their body language (if applicable), their tone of voice, and facial expression. Was it what you expected?
- Compare your answers with others in your group.
- List what you think are the essential qualities of greeting and establishing rapport with a user. Bear in mind that they may be irritated because something is wrong.

Identifying the need

Establishing what the problem is and what the user needs is vital so that an effective speedy solution is provided.

Questioning must be relevant and succinct; this will avoid further irritation. Remember that when asking questions you should always listen carefully to the answer.

- **Open questions** start with what, where, when, why, how, which. These are used to gather information. The user can then describe the situation. 'You say you haven't been able to access your email this morning, Mr Singh. What messages are displayed on your screen?'
- **Closed questions** are used to check understanding and clarify or seek agreement or contradiction. 'Can you see the icon for Internet Explorer, Mr Singh?'

  A closed question may then lead to an open question to elicit more information. 'Tell me exactly what you see on the screen.' Inviting the user to describe what they see will also help a technician if they are working remotely.

Suggesting and explaining the next step

When the problem has been accurately identified, it is then possible to go to the next step of suggesting what needs to be done to resolve it. The technician will either provide instructions for the customer to carry out or solve the problem directly in a face-to-face role.

Think about the customer's needs and provide support to users in the following scenarios.

◆ Bernie is frustrated because he keeps losing his files (he can't find them).

◆ Leroy needs to scan some material and fax it to a client. He has not used a scanner before but he does know how to send a fax.

◆ Jordan has returned from holiday to discover he has 367 emails. He is frustrated because he doesn't know how to separate important emails from lower priority ones.

In each case:

◆ identify the person's need

◆ state the idea that will solve the problem

◆ decide how you will explain this to your customer – verbally, by demonstration, or by written hints and tips

◆ as a role-play, act out the part of the IT technician.

Active listening

You have no doubt heard the phrase: 'You have two ears, one mouth. Use them in proportion.' Depending on the mode of communication available – i.e. face-to-face or telephone – the demonstration of good listening skills will vary.

When dealing with customers of any description, especially when you are in a support role, give the customer time to explain their situation before you go on to speak. Display the active signs of listening:

◆ **Maintain eye contact:** This tells the speaker that you are definitely listening. It gives them the confidence and motivation to tell you the situation they are facing. A close friend, parent or relative must have said to you at some time 'LOOK at me when I am speaking to you'.

◆ **Make notes/log the call:** If you are communicating by telephone, you will have to log the customer information. You may have an appropriate software package that will prompt you to ask questions. Otherwise, take notes. Consider advising the customer of what you are doing so that they realise you are trying to understand the situation in the most efficient manner possible.

◆ **Respond:** Having been told, or been shown, what the customer perceives as the problem, you now have to respond appropriately. This does not mean jumping in! It may mean that you need the customer to answer a few more questions. Use the customer's name and ask whatever else you need to know.

Confirming understanding and closing dialogue

Support is always about understanding. Get your message across so that the user feels they have learned something or at least have some idea of where to begin should the situation occur again.

The user may never fully like using the product but the support can bring them closer to feeling better about using it. So, remember that, wherever possible, it is about building awareness and confidence so that the user enjoys using the technology as much as possible.

Recap on any action that has taken place. Use closed questions to check they have followed what has been said. Close the conversation by asking them: 'Is there anything else I can help you with, Mrs Smyth?' This will allow the opportunity for any ambiguity to be dealt with and will confirm to you that the user is satisfied.

Aftercare

Aftercare is an essential part of support. It is done after a conversation has taken place between the user and the support technician:

◆ call queries are logged and closed
◆ orders for parts are carried out
◆ paperwork is fully completed
◆ problems are escalated to the right person etc.

By keeping this information accurate, statistics on performance levels and details of the most effective ways to deal with frequently asked questions can be maintained.

Check your understanding

Using the essential service process, map out at what stage each of the above happens, e.g. answering calls promptly relates to greeting the customer.

Discuss this with your group.

PRACTICAL TASK

- Observe your college helpdesk. What are the main methods used to support the users?
- Establish the most common queries the support team experience.
- Consider how the staff deal with the students and staff.
- What training is given?
- What documentation of hints and tips exists for users?
- Where is technical information located?

ASSESSMENT ACTIVITY

Consider what methods of communication are used in different settings and how they can deliver an effective support to users using the methods you describe.

- Explain the advantages and disadvantages of these methods.
- Explain how the helpdesk technician keeps his or her knowledge up to date.
- What technical skills do they need?
- What interpersonal skills do they need?

An IT technician supporting IBM customers may know what the solution is to their customer's 'blue screen' problem, but they can only provide the solution if the customer is able to understand what is being asked of or said to them. In many cases, the customer may already be infuriated at the loss of time in their workflow. The technician has then to overcome the challenge of calming the user down and leading them through a sequence of instructions and questions to put the solution in place. This requires great skill.

Depending on the technician's style of communication – tone, pitch, facial expression, practical instructions – the customer may or may not feel secure in what is being asked of them. If support is handled badly, the customer will not view the support provider as a professional. This will create a communication barrier for the technician, the customer and the technology they are using. This is the complete opposite of what support is about.

Customer support is the 'cement' in any service. It is one thing to achieve sales with a product that at first appears reliable, but it is the support and aftercare that overcome price objections, develop and increase customer loyalty, thereby increasing repeat business. Delivering quality IT support is the key to increased profitability and growth for any IT company.

PRACTICAL TASK

Put the above information to the test. Find out what IT customer support your peers, friends and family have.

◆ Look at price – is it the cheapest?

◆ What are they paying for?

◆ What is their experience of support?

1.3 Sources of technical support information

The technical skills required will vary according to the customer's needs. Technical skills are the skills that the help desk or field technician need to support a specific product and technology.

All organisations would like their staff to maintain a good level of technical knowledge, so that all the important and vital information is available to them to perform their duties to a professional standard. This will form part of an organisation's vision/mission.

Technicians need to maintain up-to-date knowledge within the sphere of their work. For example, within the mobile phone market, there are constant changes and new specifications. It is the same with computers and the peripherals that go with them.

Given that there may be a query on a piece of hardware or software, technicians need a solid reference base. They need to know where to look in case a fault occurs. The technical support knowledge exists in a number of formats and these can be categorised according to the source.

Paper

◆ **Manuals:** Will have details of the specification being used. Although these can seem very labour intensive, they play a vital role in providing the detail required on any one command or activity.

◆ **Procedures guides and notes:** Could be information drawn up internally from training activities that technicians have attended and, just as with manuals, may contain information that can assist the technician or the user instantly.

◆ **Manufacturer's documentation:** All software and hardware, unless created in-house, will have supporting manufacturing details which can be referred to in case the components fail and require replacement.

◆ **Libraries:** There should be a library of magazines, newsletters and articles. This can be a valuable source of knowledge providing information on technological trends. 'How to' and 'How things work' articles contain lots of useful illustrations and diagrams.

◆ **Logbook:** Many technicians keep a personal logbook and refer to this in the event of specific incidents that they have seen before. This can save time and provide an instant source of 'history' to a particular piece of hardware/software that has been installed.

Electronic media

◆ **CD-ROM:** This is easy to access and saves storage space. It may contain all the information in a flexible format that could be transferred to hard copy if required. Some software houses provide the bulk of their technical information in this format. Updated CDs may be sent regularly. Text retrieval will be based on a word or a phrase. Some of the paper-based sources above such as manuals and technical notes may be stored in this way.

◆ **Knowledge base:** This is a collection of information sources such as customer information, internal documents, policies and procedures with suggestions for possible resolutions. It does require management so that new resolutions and policies are added to the system. But it could be a very strong reference source for newly appointed technicians who need to gain relevant knowledge as fast as possible.

◆ **Websites:** There are many news groups where queries can be placed and speedy answers received. Some of these are provided by software houses. This can be a very valuable source, given that a problem experienced in one workplace has probably occurred elsewhere. Most subject areas will be covered and there are groups for Microsoft application users, Windows users, Novell users etc.

◆ **Help files:** Contained within a number of software packages, the search facility has a base of information that can assist the user in solving some of the most common errors or delays. This can be a good tool to highlight to users and has the added benefit of being instantly available.

Human support

◆ **Colleagues:** In-house support can be the most effective way to gain technical support in the early days of a technician's work life. Knowing the structure and whom to refer to is key to this success.

◆ **Specialists:** Technicians cannot be expected to know everything so, in cases where a query is outside the parameters of their experience, it is useful to refer to someone who is technically competent to a higher level. Such specialists may reside within the organisation or may be contactable via telephone helplines.

◆ **Practitioners and manufacturers:** As with manuals, details of online contacts or telephone contacts should be kept on all software and hardware.

PRACTICAL TASK

Interview your help desk staff at the college.

◆ Devise a questionnaire to find out the main methods they use to update their knowledge.
◆ Compile your findings.
◆ Gather a list of the websites that are frequently used.
◆ List the manuals that are kept.

1.4 Keeping a log

Here are a few reasons for recording/logging customer requirements for technical support and the outcomes:

◆ monitoring system trends
◆ identifying potential failures
◆ identifying user training needs
◆ identifying weak/unrealiable areas in the system
◆ Identifying potential improvements.

Fault report methods

It is important to establish a method for logging all information. If this method is not apparent, it will lead to misreporting of problems, failure to deal with reports in a timely fashion and therefore a multitude of complaints could occur. Professionalism requires a system that is used by all. Reports can be made in a variety of ways.

◆ **Verbal:** The support staff will speak to the user over the telephone. In this case, records kept will be either in paper format or will be entered on an on-screen system. Both will be completed by the technician as the conversation progresses and the customer will be asked for specific details about the problem.

◆ **Paper:** Many organisations still implement a paper-based reporting procedure. This requires the end user to fill out appropriate details on a support request form before submitting it to the support department. This acts as proof that the fault was reported through the proper methods, and they also act as a 'material reminder' to technicians of jobs that are outstanding.

◆ **Online:** This is the most modern method of reporting faults. A web-based form may be used or notification of a fault may be conducted via email. This does have the advantages of instant reporting and reduced effort on the user's part. There may be drawbacks. Given that the system is online, this method is of little use if the user cannot access the network.

Customer data

◆ **Customer information**

This will include specific information about each customer:

- ◆ name
- ◆ telephone number
- ◆ department or company name
- ◆ address or location
- ◆ customer number/employee number or user ID.

◆ **Incident information**

These are details of a problem or request:

- ◆ the incident category (hardware or software problem)
- ◆ affected component, such as printer or monitor, symptom date and time incident occurred
- ◆ date and time the incident was logged, analyst who logged the incident, description and severity.

◆ **Status information**

Given that there are various levels of problem escalation (see support team structure, page 168) data is recorded about the incident and its progress if it has not been resolved at level 1. This will include information such as awaiting parts or who has been assigned to the problem, the date and time this has been assigned, the current status and the priority. Once an incident record has been created, that record is continually updated as new information, such as resolution, becomes available.

◆ **Resolution information**

This describes how an incident has been resolved. It includes information to track service level compliance, details of the person or group who resolved the incident, the description of how it was resolved, the time and date this was resolved and what was found to be the cause.

Companies use the customer, incident, status and resolution data fields to create detailed tracking and summary reports and to perform **trend analysis**. This can also be used to track and monitor technician performance levels.

Analysing the results

If a support function is to be effective, there needs to be a system for reporting faults. Whatever the type of setting, procedures for collecting and recording support information are vital and benefits are then available:

- **Monitoring system trends**

  Careful examination of support data can reveal some recurring themes. It could be that individual users or even entire departments may have a tendency to report certain types of problems. For example, a system usage could show a heavy demand for printing during the same 1-hour period every afternoon with at least three jobs in the print queue at any one time. Recurring problems on a single machine could indicate that the machine requires complete reinstallation or replacement, while widespread problems might be solved by installing updated versions of software on a network.

- **Identifying any potential failures**

  Logging faults enables the support section to identify common problems with a particular model of hardware or software. This will then enable them to return goods to the manufacturer under warranty and will influence further purchases of this component, machine or software.

- **Identifying user training requirements**

  Keeping an accurate log may identify that training is required in the use of particular software or hardware, or for particular users or groups of user. Such trainining should reduce problems, user frustration and therefore reduce the need for user support.

- **Identifying weak/unreliable areas in the system**

  Any gliches in the system (or network) can be identified.

- **Identifying potential improvements**

  Having collected the data this knowledge base can be used to suggest ways of overcoming problems, time wasting and budget spending. This is valuable in determining the ongoing improvements that are vital to customer support.

What kind of information might be recorded?

As with any management information system, it is important to retain all information that will help to keep track of progress in solving any particular fault that has been reported and which may help to prevent similar problems happening in the future. Here are some questions that the computerised call logging system should be able to answer:

◆ Who reported the fault?

◆ When was it reported (the exact time as well as date)?

◆ Who was assigned to deal with this problem? At what time did this happen?

◆ What action did the engineer decide upon? When did this take place?

◆ What was the actual problem? End user error? Faulty hardware?

◆ Has the problem been fixed? If so, how was it fixed?

◆ What was the cost of repair (in terms of replacement equipment, engineers' time)?

Additional information can be gathered by analysing the data as follows:

◆ Are there any individuals who call in more regularly than others, and who could benefit from some extra training in the use of IT equipment and/or software?

◆ Are any items of hardware failing too often? Should an alternative hardware provider be found?

◆ Are the engineers coping with the flow of faults fast enough? Are additional support engineers needed?

PRACTICAL TASK

◆ Decide what information should be kept about faults reported to an IT support team.

◆ Design a paper-based or online fault report support form.

◆ Devise a database structure to record these faults and to track the action taken to solve problems

◆ What reports might this database provide?

◆ Design a customer information, incident status, and resolution form.

1.5 The support team structure

In large organisations, it is unlikely that all the team are experts in all aspects of the support role. It is more likely that each support worker will specialise in a particular area of support.

There are six main categories, or roles, within a support team.

◆ Front-line service providers.

◆ Dispatcher/help desk assistant.

◆ Level 1 specialists/technical support engineers.

- Field service engineers.
- Bench engineers.
- Purchaser.

In general **front-line service providers** are the staff who directly interact with the customers.

The **dispatcher** or **help desk assistant** then move the problem one stage further:

- Logs calls from customers detailing their problems onto a computerised call management system.
- Assigns jobs to field and technical support engineers.
- Processing engineers' reports and updating the call management system.
- Providing assistance to the support team manager, i.e. progressing repairs and liaising with sub-contract suppliers.

The **level 1 specialists/technical support engineers** fix the problems:

- Required for software related faults, taking responsibility for the job and liaising with the end user to determine the nature of the problem.
- Providing telephone support for the end user so as to resolve any issues, without having to visit the user.

◆ Where a visit is necessary, arranging a date and time and organising any resources required, i.e. software patches/manuals/drivers etc.

◆ Liaising with end user and external system suppliers/vendors to provide a permanent solution.

◆ Documenting the outcomes and sending reports to the help desk assistant.

Field service engineers may be necessary to fix problems on a customer's site:

◆ Required for hardware faults, taking responsibility for the job and liaising with the end user to determine the nature of the fault where possible and appraising which spare parts/loan equipment is needed.

◆ Collecting spares/loan equipment from stores.

◆ Diagnosing hardware faults.

◆ Providing a fix; permanently by use of new replacement parts/cleaning and servicing/reconfiguration, or temporarily by use of loan equipment.

◆ Documenting the outcomes and sending reports to the help desk assistant.

◆ On completion of repairs in the workshop by a bench engineer, returning repaired equipment to the end user.

Bench engineers work in the background:

◆ Processing incoming repair work, testing faulty items to diagnose fault or to confirm the field engineer's diagnosis and to determine if the fault is hardware or software related.

◆ Raising purchase orders for the sourcing of spares or, where appropriate, liaising with the purchaser to have the repair assigned to either the manufacturer for warranty repair or to a repair company.

◆ Carrying out repairs to equipment where practical.

◆ Carrying out functional tests to repaired items, processing associated paperwork and liaising with the helpdesk assistant to advise repair status.

◆ Providing telephone support to field and technical support engineers.

The **purchaser** has the authority to buy equipment and software:

◆ Reporting to the support team manager, sourcing equipment and services as required.

◆ Liaising with manufacturers and suppliers to obtain the most cost-effective solution/repair, and processing repairs.

◆ Processing of goods-in paperwork and booking stock items into the stock system.

◆ Controlling stock distribution to field service engineers.

◆ Organising the safe packing of new/repaired equipment that is to be sent to end users or for repair; and processing of despatch/repair paperwork.

Each person within the team will have specific skills and qualifications:

◆ The support manager's main skills will be in managing the support team and liaising with other parts of the organisation.

◆ The engineers will be supporting, installing and testing systems and will need a high level of technical knowledge and skills.

◆ The helpdesk assistants may not be as highly qualified as others in the support team, but their communication skills will be used in every contact with end users.

Within each job role, depending on the size of the team, there may also be trainees working alongside those with more expertise. Everyone in the team has a role to play, and is as important to the success of the team as every other person.

PRACTICAL TASK

◆ As a group exercise, arrange to interview people in the IT support team at your college to find out the job roles of each person in the support team.

◆ Between you, draw up a job specification for each member of the team.

◆ Find out what qualifications each person has and what additional qualifications they are working towards.

◆ Compare this with the job role of a technician working in a computer superstore.

The escalation process

A new technician joining the team will need to have an understanding of this structure so that problems that cannot be resolved at this first level of support can be referred (escalated to another point of contact). This is known as second level, then third level.

These are the stages of reporting, although the primary responsibilities lie with the front-line service provider.

◆ Receives customer problems, requests and inquiries that may be reported over the telephone, email, fax, the web, etc.

◆ Logs the incident having gathered relevant information about the customer and the incident (the electronic ticket is then updated continuously until the incident is resolved).

- Determines the nature of the customer's incident.
- Delivers a solution using various options (remote access, knowledge-based information).
- Documents the resolution thoroughly so that the help desk can reuse it. If it cannot be resolved, the front-line service provider determines how quickly the incident needs to be solved so that the problem is escalated to the right person.
- Records the incident's severity in the ticket, all steps taken by both the help desk and the customer to try to resolve the incident, with any additional information the customer provides (such as directions to their site).
- Escalates the incident to the correct level 1 specialist or level 2 specialist or external vendor, or subject matter expert (SME).
- Retains ownership of incident's status to the customer (such as when the customer can expect a field service engineer to arrive or when the ordered parts should arrive).
- Reviews the incident's resolution once it is identified to learn how the incident was solved or to determine what caused the incident to occur.
- Follows up with the customer to ensure he or she is satisfied with the resolution.
- Closes the ticket.

Tip: The term ticket goes back to the days when the fault was logged manually and a 'ticket' was issued. These days faults are often reported electronically but the term is still widely used.

Finding individuals for front-line positions with the right mix of technical and interpersonal skills is a challenge that all line managers face in today's marketplace. Getting the right balance is what is preferable; strong technicians may lack the right level of empathy or patience to do the job. On the other hand, customer-focused people may lack the right technical skills required to work in a complex computing environment. Some people prefer a 'hands-on' approach and may become dissatisfied when they realise their position demands that they spend a lot of time on the telephone. The employee and the company benefit when the right skills and position are matched with the right person.

The key elements that recruitment staff look for when accepting people for front-line support are those who genuinely like helping people and who work well with others. There are many companies that believe technical skills can be developed more easily than interpersonal skills and are willing to hire people with strong evidence of interpersonal skills, and a customer orientation. The company then bolts on the technical training so that they can do their work effectively.

Companies that are supporting highly sophisticated technology will, at times, hire people with strong technical skills and provide extensive customer service training.

The role of the support technician

Depending on the organisation's function and structure and where you fit within it, your customer base and their needs will vary.

CASE STUDY

Fast food outlet

Haruki works in a fast food outlet on a Saturday serving behind the counter. He takes customer orders. His primary customer is 'Joe Public'.

Tomoko works in the same store but she provides the fillings that go on the fishburger. Her primary customers are the staff who are taking the orders placed by the public. Haruki's customers are **external customers** because they are not connected to the business in any other way than as someone wishing to buy a particular item (food in this case). People come in and ask him for a double cheeseburger with fries. He carries out the request.

To deal with his primary customers, Haruki will each day prepare himself by:

◆ ensuring the tills are operating

◆ checking that the right amount of cash (float) is in the till

◆ making sure the stock is ready to serve the customers

◆ checking with other colleagues to make sure everything is expected to run smoothly ... there haven't been any incidents (staff sick, till shortages from the day before, etc.)

◆ preparing himself visually; neat tidy appearance

◆ preparing himself to meet and greet the customers in the style that the outlet wishes him to.

Haruki listens, identifies what his customers need and then responds to them in a timely, efficient way.

Tomoko's primary customers are **internal**. To provide service to them, she will ensure the fillings are placed on the buns and that they are then placed in the appropriate serving sections.

In preparation for her day and onwards, Tomoko:

◆ will understand the importance of keeping an eye on the volume of food that is needed at any one time

◆ will ensure enough fries are cooked and ready

◆ will inform her section manager if stock is low, etc.

Her priorities are different from those of Haruki but are every bit as essential to the operation of the fast food outlet.

CASE STUDY

Northpark College

Jill is the Manager of the IT support team at Northpark College. There are 800 students and 65 staff, and computers of various types dotted all around the campus. The library has a suite of 40 networked computers. These are used for individual study and research, much of this being on the Internet. Students are not encouraged to bring laptops into college, but most teachers have their own portable laptop PCs, or use one of six PCs networked to the college system. There are other networked PCs in each department of the college.

Jill has a team of five technicians and, between them, they are expected to keep all the systems running.

◆ Are Jill's customers internal or external?

◆ What preparation will need to be done to ensure customers are supported well?

◆ Draw up an organisation chart.

◆ How will problems that cannot be solved by her staff be escalated to the next level?

◆ How does serving internal customers differ from that of external customers?

◆ List the methods of communication that Jill's team will use when communicating with an IT student who understands how computers are configured and compare these with that for a tutor who only uses software applications.

◆ Discuss your findings as a group.

The role of a typical support technician then depends on how the support is organised. It could be that the support is in-house, otherwise known as **internal support**. Or it could be that this is outsourced to a specialist company which would be **external support**.

A typical day for a support technician will be very varied. Some of the time the support technician will be at the desk of the user who needs help. At other times, he or she will be answering email queries and keeping a record of faults that have been reported, and how these have been dealt with. There will also be times when the support team are testing equipment that does not seem to work. If a reported fault cannot be identified and fixed straightaway, the faulty equipment may be removed from a user's configuration and a replacement installed so that the user has continuous usage of a PC. However, the faulty part still needs to be fixed and put back into use.

The support technician might have to do any of these tasks:

◈ set up a PC ready for a new employee who will be arriving to start work that morning

◆ assign user IDs and passwords for all employees, and change passwords for those who forget them, or whose passwords become compromised

◆ maintain equipment, e.g. clean a keyboard

◆ change the hardware configuration, e.g. add more memory, upgrade a peripheral

◆ change the software configuration, e.g. install new software

◆ supply consumables, e.g. take a delivery of paper and distribute it to each stationery cupboard within the building.

The support technician is not just there for when things go wrong. Prevention is more effective than cure so if he/she knows how to prepare and anticipate the demands of his customers, e.g. in providing an adequate paper supply, the easier the job can be. The support technician may also be involved in training end users or preparing training material.

Check your understanding

In small groups, compile a team skills grid like the example in Table 1.

◆ In the first column, agree on a list of 10 tasks that you think an IT support technician should be able to do. Tick the other columns to show which of you can already do particular tasks.

◆ Decide on a training plan to upgrade the skills of your team. Make sure everyone can demonstrate at least one task to the others in the group. Even if everyone thinks they are proficient at a particular task, it can help to see how others do it.

◆ If there are tasks that none of your group can do, think about how you could resolve this problem. Who, or where, can you turn to for help?

Table 1 **Skills grid**

Task	Person A	Person B	Person C	Person D	Training plan
Task 1	✔		✔	✔	C demonstrates to B
Task 2		✔	✔		B demonstrates to A and D
Task 3				✔	D demonstrates to A, B and C
...					
Task 10	✔	✔			A demonstrates to C and D

Write a job specification for a help desk assistant. Compare this with that of a trainee field service engineer (concentrating on software problems of users) or a trainee technical support engineer (concentrating on hardware problems). Decide what training needs that a help desk assistant would require if promoted to one of these support engineer roles within a large IT support team.

PRACTICAL TASK

◆ What type of structure is employed by your college?

◆ How are incidents escalated?

Draw up the structure and discuss with your colleagues.

1.6 Health and safety

Wherever you work, health and safety will be a compulsory duty. *Everyone* is responsible for health and safety within a working environment.

Organisations have a duty of care to their employees to ensure their workplace is both safe and reasonably comfortable. This impacts on the standard of the office environment which should have the following:

◆ adequate ventilation

◆ sufficient good light

◆ a comfortable temperature.

It also affects computer users and the equipment that is provided in the following ways:

◆ monitors should be adjustable and fitted with filter screens if glare is a problem

◆ chairs should be adjustable so that employees can sit comfortably at the keyboard and monitor

◆ regular breaks from using the computer should be encouraged

◆ desks and floors should be free from trailing cables

◆ the computer users themselves must not tamper with any electrical equipment or consume food or drink while working at the computer, in case of spillages.

Detailed information on health and safety is covered in Unit 401 (page 3).

IT technicians may be located within an organisation that deals with in-house customers who bring problems to the support section; or the technician may visit users at their own desks. Field support engineers may also visit customers' premises to collect faulty equipment or to fix problems. Health and safety issues will vary according to the location and the role being played by the IT technician and such issues have to be considered in these different situations all the time.

When speaking on the telephone, it is important to be clear with instructions, ensuring that customers are not encouraged to 'fiddle' with cables or unscrew parts of a computer that must be repaired by experts. Knowing how to retain 'safe' work practices for the customer, the organisation and the employee (i.e. you the technician) requires thought.

Check your understanding

Consider all aspects of health and safety for a technician working in these environments and list the main hazards:

◆ Working on site, visiting users at their desks (just like your college technicians).

◆ A peripatetic worker, visiting customers at their premises.

◆ A helpdesk technician supporting clients on the telephone.

Health and Safety at Work Act 1974

This Act sets out what is expected of employers to safeguard their staff. However, it also stresses that employees are responsible for their own safety and the safety of their co-workers around them. So, as an employee within the IT support section, it will be important to be aware of the safety precautions that you need to take and ensure you follow all guidelines laid down by your employer.

PRACTICAL TASK

ICT legislation affects the scope and role of all IT support staff.

Listed below are the most important Acts:

◆ Health and Safety at Work Act etc 1974

◆ Copyright, Designs and Patents Act 1988

◆ Electricity at Work Regulations 1989

◆ Computer Misuse Act 1990

◆ Obscene Publications Act 1992

◆ Data Protection Act 1998

Pick two of these and draw up a summary.

1.7 Software applications

You need to be aware of and be able to describe software applications that allow provision of technical support:

◆ email
◆ call logging
◆ CRM (customer relationship management) database.

Customers may choose to report faults/problems in various ways, dependent on whether the support function is in-house or external. The methods for documenting faults will vary. The most important point is that there needs to be a definite procedure for reporting faults. This should be established by the IT support function as far as possible.

Email

This is a common method of reporting faults. A web-based form can be used or emails can be sent to the support department. From the customer's point of view, it is instant and easy to complete. However, it will be of little use if the fault to be reported means that the customer cannot access the network!

Call logging

Whenever a fault is reported, it should be logged using appropriate organisation software. The information will help to identify trends and to track progress on a call. It can also be printed and referred to when considering improvements.

The log should include all the salient points that need to be recorded. At its simplest level, it may be sufficient to record the nature of the fault, the date of the report and the staff member making the report.

The appearance of the logged information will vary from organisation to organisation. In general, though, the following information will be held:

A reference number: This can be selected by a call logging package and will allow quick viewing of faults reported, and their current status.

Date and time the fault was reported: This should also identify the support member who received the fault report, if it was taken by phone.

Contact details of the person reporting the fault: In-house support technicians could simply record the person's name, department, room number and extension number. Third party support technicians may need full contact details, e.g. the contact's address, if the technicians need to go out to the site. (This will probably already be stored on the support function's database.)

Fault description: This should include a description of the system that has developed a fault such as its location, machine number or serial number in the case of users with access to multiple machines as well as details of the fault's symptoms.

Steps taken towards fault resolution: The form should record actions taken by technical support, as well as identifying the members of staff who took these actions, and the date and time such actions were taken. This is vital in ensuring quality of service, especially when supplying third-party support, where technicians must adhere to service level agreements (SLAs). If the fault is resolved over the phone during the initial call, this should be recorded and the duration of the call logged.

Third-party involvement: If it is under warranty, faulty equipment can be returned to the supplier or manufacturer for replacement. Also some specialised repairs may need an item to be sent off to another third party. The fault report form should note these details. Sending off faulty components for replacement does not resolve the problem. Fitting the replacement when it arrives is considered the actual date of resolution.

CRM – customer relationship management

This term is used by the support function rather than being another type of support given to a customer. The key to understanding this term is in the 'relationship management' of CRM. The support function is constantly aiming at maintaining and building a healthy relationship with users. To do this successfully, it requires a means of recording as much history and information on a client as possible. This is usually logged by way of a database that helps to build a picture of the user and their interaction with the organisation. CRM is a marketing database that has the facility to record all customer activity. This will include:

◆ help desk queries/enquiries made
◆ ordering patterns
◆ credit ratings
◆ a history of the customer's involvement in marketing promotions.

Check your understanding

Search on the Internet for customer relationship software.

How could a technician use information to assist them in dialogue with the customer?

2 Identifying potential improvements in the customer's use of resources

To make improvements for a customer, it is important to have as much information available about the customer's use of the computer system, noting what software/hardware they are currently using. Examining a history of faults that have been reported will help to build a picture of the customer, their user needs and experiences at any given time.

2.1 Methods of gathering and recording information

There are various methods for collecting information on customers. These take a number of forms, depending on the organisation's policies and how determined they are to remain customer-focused. Are they reactive or proactive?

Building relationships is about using the information available, so the method(s) chosen need to match the information needs.

◆ Questionnaires and surveys.

◆ User logs. These records may be paper-based or photocopies of paper-based data. It is also possible to produce a printout of logged data.

◆ Printouts of logs.

Questionnaires and surveys

Verbally questioning the user to determine their uses, needs, experiences, etc. is usually done over the phone but could be face-to-face dependent on the 'setting'. Designing **questionnaires** can help a support desk to analyse their effectiveness and the customer's frequently performed tasks, obtaining written customer feedback.

Customer surveys are a series of questions that ask customers to provide their perception of the support services being offered. Whether conducted annually or on an ongoing basis, these surveys are an excellent way to measure the strengths and weaknesses of existing support services.

Surveys provide an insight as to whether customers perceive their needs are being met, unlike more quantifiable metrics.

◆ Number of calls.

◆ Average time taken to solve an incident.

◆ Number of calls escalated to next level.

These can be conducted during telephone calls, in paper form or by email by asking the customer to complete and return these over the Internet.

Event-driven surveys are a series of questions that ask customers for feedback on a single recent service event. The results of these give management the ability to measure the performance because they give feedback on the analyst who handled the event. This would be generated within 48–72 hours of the service event.

Overall satisfaction surveys are a series of questions that ask customers for feedback about all calls they made to the help desk during a certain period of time. Help desks use these responses to identify areas for improvement. Some help desks also send surveys to customers who did not contact the help desk in the previous 6–12 months to determine if they lack faith in the help desk's ability to satisfy their needs. Usually, the help desk conducts overall satisfaction surveys annually or semi-annually.

These are an excellent way to measure the quality of help desk services because customers are providing feedback. Management uses the feedback obtained from these surveys when defining the help desk's goals.

User logs

There are many forms of user log:

◆ support logs
◆ event and audit logs
◆ access logs.

A **call logging system** can examine the most frequently asked questions, faults that have been noted and resolved and possibly any events that may have occurred.

CASE STUDY

CityGem PLC take pride in providing a good level of service to their customers. They want to ensure they stay at the forefront of service, remaining ahead of their competitors. Once every year, they hold an extensive survey using feedback from their largest customers. They do this to find out what their customers needs are and to see if the service they are providing is coming up to scratch. After analysing the results, they invite their customers to a breakfast meeting. The event is seen as a 'thank you' to the customers who have given them the feedback. After

---

breakfast, the company Director for CityGem presents the results: good and bad.

- What are the benefits of the exercise to CityGem PLC?
- What are the benefits to the customers?

Benchmarking

Benchmarking is the process of comparing the help desk's standard performance metrics to another help desk in an effort to identify improvement opportunities.

2.2 Preparing accurate records

Every support group has a responsibility to maintain a current database of the organisation's hardware and software:

- complete systems
- peripherals
- connection hardware network
- hardware or consumables (e.g. printing paper, toner, cartridges, disks and CD-ROMS).

This will be logged down to each individual machine, and is a bit like a stock take of goods held. The data recorded by a support group or help desk should be kept as part of a hardware and software audit. This is important to track recurring or developing problems and will help in the support section's role to recommend, implement and identify ways of preventing future delays.

The types of information needed can be categorised as hardware or software.

Then, a database of information may be developed to record important characteristics of each computer.

- The manufacturer, model, and serial number of each computer in use.
- Details of the hard disk types and capacity.
- Details of floppy drive quantity, type and capacity.
- Details of motherboard adapter slots – number and type.
- The manufacturer, model and serial number.
- Location of each item of equipment.
- Purchase date of equipment and details of guarantee.

◆ Maintenance agreements.

◆ There should also be copies of the CMOS settings for each machine. Ideally, these should be disk copies for easy restoration (using a CMOS saving/restoration utility). As a minimum, there should be manually recorded details, particularly of the hard drive parameters.

◆ For each computer, there should be copies of each machine's configuration files including the Windows Registry, .ini files and, sometimes, autoexec.bat and config.sys files.

◆ Details of cards fitted to each machine including their purpose (e.g. scanner or fax card), manufacturer, model and serial numbers.

◆ Details of hardware setting such as DIP switches or jumper settings on the motherboards and cards.

◆ Copies of all installation guides, hardware manuals and technical notes.

◆ Master copies of all the installation disks.

◆ Details of the service history for each item of equipment.

There are various methods of collecting this information. It may be kept as a combination of paper-based and/or computerised data … so long as it is suitably backed up!

Software

In the same way that hardware is recorded, a record of all software installed is vital.

◆ Details of the operating system being used (e.g. Windows XP, Linux).

◆ Copies of all the software master disks or CDs.

◆ Details of the service history of each item of equipment.

This will include updates to versions sometimes known as service packs, automated updates, or hotfixes, e.g. Windows 95 had seven updates! Windows 98 had a second edition.

Check your understanding

To keep an accurate audit as far as possible, design a hardware and software form for recording all the information of the equipment used in your college.

◆ Who do you think should control this information?

◆ How long do you think it would take to document all the specifications for each individual computer?

PRACTICAL TASK

Using the forms you have created, prepare accurate records of existing resources being used in your classroom.

Hardware data collected must show:

◆ complete systems

◆ peripherals (scanners and printers)

◆ connection hardware

◆ network hardware

◆ consumables (e.g. printing paper, toner cartridges, disks)

◆ and CD-ROMS.

Software data collected must show:

◆ operating system in use

◆ versions

◆ installed applications or components

◆ utilities.

As an additional point, what other considerations need to be taken into account with regards to software?

Other methods used for keeping records

As a way of recording additional detail, it's a good idea for all technicians to keep a **personal logbook** – or lab-book record – in addition to any existing paperwork that is necessary.

The logbook should be hardbacked and lined on one side with alternate pages left blank to enable the technician to sketch, draw diagrams, flow charts, etc. As work is done, detailed notes are made of the equipment, configurations, observations, procedures and so on. This not only adds to the 'history' of events but can often serve as a welcome 'training reminder' on similar or common faults that have been resolved in different ways.

◆ A lab-book can save a busy technician time by letting him or her quickly revisit an earlier chain of events, without having to go through the case history again.

◆ Records like these enable someone else to take over a task if the original technician is away sick, on holiday, etc.

◆ It can serve as a good reference in identifying trends over a period of time or contribute to effective team meetings, where other issues may crop up but escape the memory of the team.

◆ If the records are kept accurately enough, they can also help to identify problematic equipment that keeps coming through the section.

2.3 Providing recommendations to customers

Recommendations form an important part of customer support. If a technician has established a customer's needs and collected data on them, it follows that the information should be put to good use to improve the use of IT for the user. This may be done:

◆ face-to-face

◆ by telephone

◆ in writing.

CASE STUDY

A company has a number of ICT workstations in their administration and sales department. The company keeps a record of problems they encounter with the equipment and software. A case history has revealed four issues:

◆ A heavy demand for printing during the same 1 hour period every afternoon with the print queues displaying at least three jobs outstanding at any one time.

◆ A steady use of the printer during the rest of the day, with the majority of the demand from one workstation.

◆ System fault records show a continuing problem with a printer indicating heavy use and little or no preventive maintenance (i.e. frequent paper jams).

◆ Call logs show two users having difficulties using their applications with complaints from a number of users about slow printer response at certain times of the day.

From the information:

◆ Provide two recommendations for improvements of the customer's use of the system.

◆ Provide at least two recommendations for improvements to the customer's use of the system.

◆ Decide what method you could use to put the information across.

3 Improving a customer's use of resources

3.1 Frequently performed tasks

Technology, by definition, is about identifying areas where a process can be made more effective and efficient. To some users, effective might mean that it saves time; to others it might mean that it saves money. To others again, it might mean both of these points and also offer improved security.

If the time is taken to understand the frequently performed tasks by a customer, the IT section can then assist the user in setting up and configuring the system to be automated.

The type of procedures that are automated will vary dependent on the user but there are some that are vital to the maintenance of the computer system. Let's look at some of these.

Backups

Backups are used as a technique to store important data so that it can be recovered at a later date.

Ever since the advent of computers, industry, commerce, government organisations and society have become increasingly dependent on their use and the data/information that is stored on them.

- If a company like Amazon were to lose access to their data for a short period of time, the organisation could lose hundreds of thousands of pounds in potential income. In real terms that means jobs.
- If a bank lost information on stock exchange transactions or details of customer withdrawals the cost and legal implications would be phenomenal.

So, in all cases, data that is created, maintained and stored on computers requires a backup to be stored separately. It will be a technician's role to assist a user in recommending and setting up the procedures so that the user doesn't have to make a mental note. If it can be automatically undertaken, all the better.

Go out and try!

In Unit 401 you had the opportunity to implement a backup system as part of your role in supporting a customer. Now, carry out a backup of your computer and devise a system with a friend where you can store a copy of your data at their home and you can return the compliment by backing up their computer and keeping a copy of the data at your home.

Data transfers

Imagine a popular high street retail outlet selling clothes. They have a head office at a central point that handles stock turnover, and data on transactions that are handled by all its high street branches. In order to do this the sales, goods returned, etc. are all processed at the tills in the branches. This information is collated throughout the operational day. At the end of each day, the branch activity is reported electronically by all the branches to head office advising of their takings, stock purchased, returns by the customer, etc. That transfer of information is referred to as a **data transfer**. This will enable the central function to keep an eye on the purchasing trends of the general public, identify areas where sales are low (or equally important where sales are high), identify lines of stock that are selling well or not, etc.

Data transfer can be done by two means:

◆ by foot
◆ using networking technology.

By foot may seem antiquated but, in systems or organisations that rely on security and off site backups taking place, this is an effective and safe method.

Networking technology is reliant on a stable infrastructure, and you may choose to manage the equipment that enables this process to take place. Many organisations have to move a large quantity of data on a daily basis. It is therefore commonplace for companies to have multiple lines between sites for data transfer as well as having a backup line in case the main communications line is cut.

An excellent example of a company that uses a main communications line for daily data transfer as well as a backup connection is a national newspaper. Consider News International who are based at Wapping in London for the journalism, editorial, marketing and advertising management of *The Times* and *The Sun*. They will have printing presses that have to run each evening for distribution overnight so that you (or your family) get the newspaper in the morning. This means that they will have printing presses in more than one city so that they can quickly distribute the final copy. If one version of the paper is not printed, due to a loss in communications, the result will be that the newspapers will not be distributed for a major part of the country. This will result in a loss of income, good faith with the customer that buys the newspaper as well as the advertisers who have paid considerable sums of money for you to see information about their product.

As with backups, if there is a way of automating this to assist the branch and head office staff it will save time and reduce opportunities for human error.

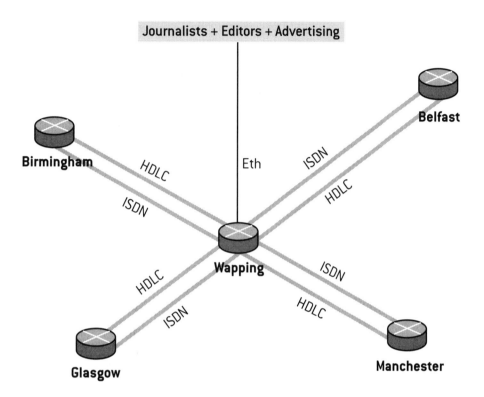

Figure 4 *A possible network for a new national corporation*

Virus scan

Every computer must have suitable anti-virus software and every organisation must have a procedure to deal with viruses and the protection of the computer system. In Unit 401 you had the opportunity to install an anti-virus application as a problem solving and preventive maintenance technique for your user.

PRACTICAL TASK

◆ Write a short report (no more than 400 words) on the differences between a virus, worm and Trojan.

◆ Using websites such as the McAfee Security site (follow the links from www.heinemann.co.uk/hotlinks), identify what the latest virus threat is and what impact it will have on a computer if infected.

When a computer system is infected with a virus, an organisation will have the following issues:

◆ The company may experience loss of business time and income while the computer system or individual computers are out of action.

◆ The company is exposed to outside attack and possible commercial damage as someone gains access to their system.

To prevent virus attacks or at least ensure the damage is minimal, a company will install anti-virus software. A strong corporate anti-virus solution will:

◆ update all workstations on a daily basis with the latest anti-virus database

◆ monitor all server access

◆ configure all workstations to alert the network administrator as soon as a virus is detected.

Firewalls and **network traffic monitoring tools** will detect any potential attacks or virus infected traffic (especially worms and Trojans), and **mail servers** can be configured to quarantine any infected mail.

Email

Many organisations now use email as an effective tool to automate communication of information and resources to employees, suppliers and customers. Note: this is not to be confused with SPAM.

What does it mean?

SPAM, named after a song by Monty Python, is a technique used to:

- *Send mailings to thousands (and often millions) of email addresses to sell a variety of products that often relate to the sexual services industry.*

- *Attack a mail server or email address with millions of emails per hour in an attempt to cause damage.*

Commonplace acceptable uses of email as a method for automated communication include:

◆ sending corporate updates including newsletters, company policy, monthly financial statements, etc.

◆ informing customers or suppliers of a change in corporate details, e.g. services that you are providing (or require)

◆ distributing additions to software (**critical updates** and patches)

◆ warning customers of problems with a product.

CASE STUDY

The *UK Herald* is a new national newspaper, based in the Edgbaston area of Birmingham. As part of the distribution structure they have a local printer as well as others in London, Edinburgh, Cardiff, Manchester and Belfast.

In a short report answer these questions:

◆ How could the newspaper set up a system that will enable reliable data transfer?

◆ What 'defences' would an organisation of this size require against viruses and where would you choose to configure them?

◆ What would be the best system of backups?

◆ How would the managing editor use email as an effective method of communicating with the journalists?

◆ How would the network manager use email as an effective method of communicating with technical and non-technical staff?

3.2 Benefits of automated procedures

The aim is to provide a user with a simple and positive image of the technology they use. There will be situations that technicians and support staff can identify that would make the user's daily life easier, such as using automated procedures. This is what computers are for. Make them do the work for you.

In the everyday use of computer systems you can instigate the following automated procedures.

◆ Set up new styles in a word processing application to save time and effort.

◆ Create a simple macro in *Excel* or *Word* to carry out a routine task.

◆ Add a button to an application to save time and effort.

◆ Ensure that some spelling corrections are automated.

◆ If required, automate scheduled data transfers.

◆ Configure your email application to automate email send and receive at regular intervals.

◆ Where appropriate, automate regular backups.

Depending on your use and experience of a word processing application like Microsoft *Word* you may find that sometimes creating a document can be time-consuming; you have to keep changing **font style**, text colour and point size. Life can become easier when you know how to set up a style.

Using Microsoft *Word*, in the top left hand corner of the tool bar, there is a double-A symbol. Click on this to activate the style pane.

double-A

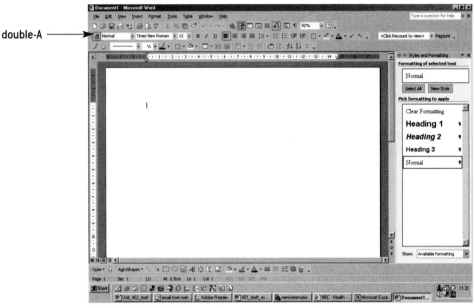

Figure 5 The Style pane

If you click on the New Style button, you will be able to choose the font details you require.

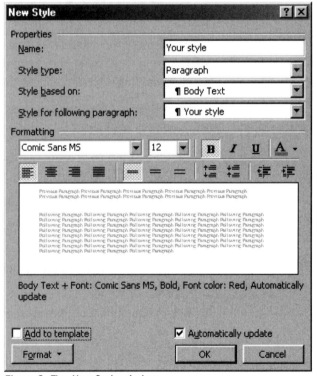

Figure 6 The New Style window

You will have to name the style and decide what style of font, text colour and point size you require. You can decide whether this style is going to apply to a paragraph or a table, or whether it will apply to a bulleted list.

Once the new style is installed, you can click on it at any time to convert your text.

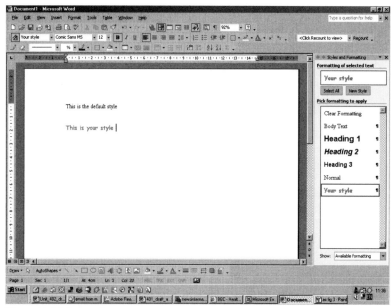

Figure 7 Adding style

A **macro** is a small program or pre-recorded routine that depends on the task that is required, and is designed to save time for the user. For example, you can create very complex macros that edit or compile documents.

Macros is in the Tools drop-down menu section of *Word*.

When you start recording the macro, you must give it a name and choose whether you wish to assign it to the tool bar or set it up as a keyboard shortcut.

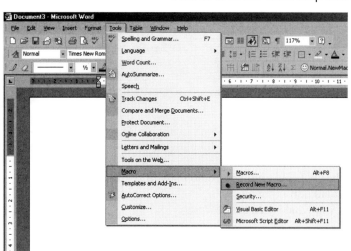

Figure 8 Record New Macro option

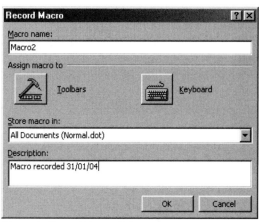

Figure 9 Record Macro dialogue box

You can drag the macro onto the tool bars and edit the appearance of the button.

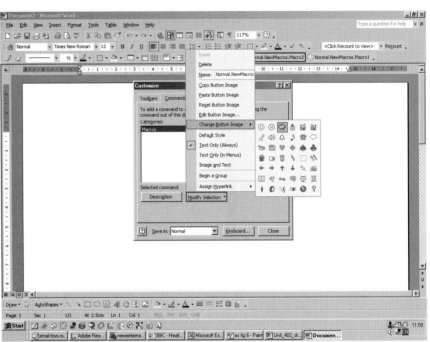

Figure 10 Creating the macro button

Once you have pressed Close, you can start the recording process. In this example, you could type a common verse of a song or a well-known poem.

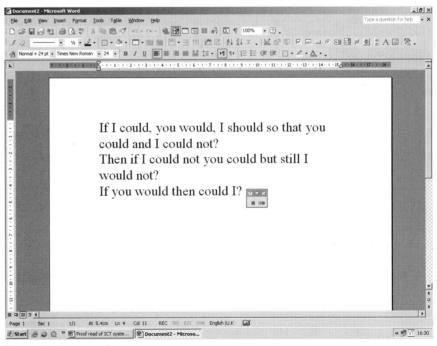

Figure 11 The recording process

When you next press the button that you have created, you will find that the macro will do the keying for you.

Macros can be used to automate menu tasks such as Find and Replace as well as options in the Format, Tools and Table dropdown menus.

Go out and try!

◆ Create a macro that will change all text to uppercase (Tip: You will need to select that which needs to be done with Ctrl-A).

◆ Create a macro that uses a keystroke as a shortcut.

Adding a button to an application is the creation of a simple **shortcut**. Sometimes, the keystroke or the menu route is time-consuming or inappropriate. (Remember you may be working with someone who has a physical disability and will need you to make the application accessible.)

If you have ever completed some Maths formulae in *Word* for your homework you will appreciate how time consuming it is to change the text to superscript for mathematical powers (like $2^2 = 4$).

To do this 'normally', you need to highlight the text, open the Format/Font window and check the Superscript box.

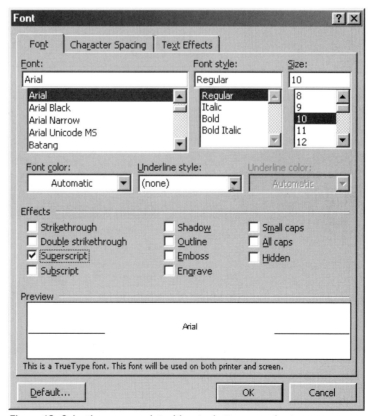

Figure 12 Selecting superscript without a button as a shortcut

Instead, you could add a button so that this repeated task can be done quicker. In the Tools/Customise option, you can add the superscript option to the toolbar by using drag and drop.

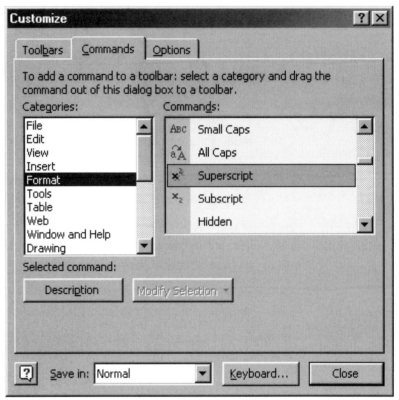

Figure 13 The superscript button

While typing a long document you may have wished that the computer could do some of the typing for you, or correct some of your more common mistakes while you are typing. *Word* is capable of detecting mistakes; it shows them by using a red underline and if you right-click *Word* can also provide hints. You can automate the process according to the work that you are typing. This is available in the Tools menu, as the **Autocorrect option**.

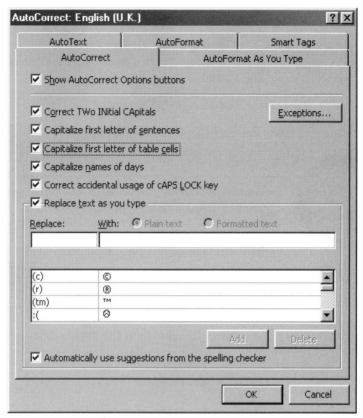

Figure 14 The AutoCorrect feature

You can add anything you wish and decide on what the AutoCorrect needs to be. Try out the following examples:

◆ use csm for computer systems maintenance

◆ use cpu for central processing unit

◆ use tcp for transmission control protocol/Internet protocol.

Type them in and you will find that *Word* will automatically offer the full forms to you. This feature can be very useful when you have lots of jargon to type.

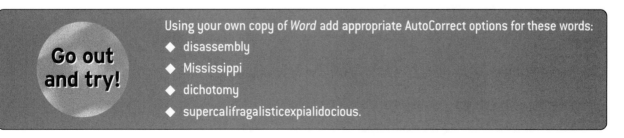

Go out and try!

Using your own copy of *Word* add appropriate AutoCorrect options for these words:

◆ disassembly

◆ Mississippi

◆ dichotomy

◆ supercalifragalisticexpialidocious.

The scheduling of **automated data transfers** and **backups** is often done by using a system utility like the Microsoft Task Scheduler (see Unit 401, page 63). Some network systems use versions of the file transfer protocol. In the underlying operating system (or the command prompt), you can use a command called Copy to move files from your computer to a remote system such as a file server.

The format of the command is:

COPY source-file(s) destination-file(s)

You have to include the command as part of a batch file that will be run by the Task Scheduler.

*A **batch file** is a file that contains automated system commands. For any Microsoft product, this will have a .bat file extension.*

Your email software may be automating the sending and receiving of mail without your realising that this is happening. This is a throwback to a time when the speed and availability of communications were considerably limited. Normally you can automate the transfer of email:

◆ when you connect to the Internet with a modem

◆ periodically, every 30 minutes

◆ when you close the mail application.

If you have a permanent connection to the Internet, you may wish to configure this service to update every 5 minutes.

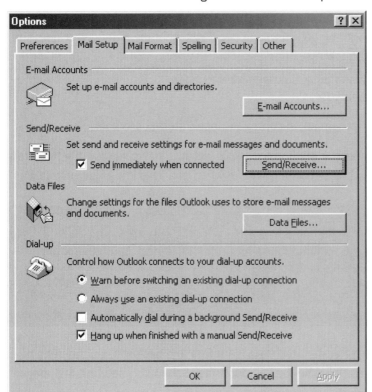

If your computer has Microsoft *Outlook* installed, use the Tools/Options window and select the Mail Setup tab. From here, you can access the Send/Receive options.

Figure 15 Email options

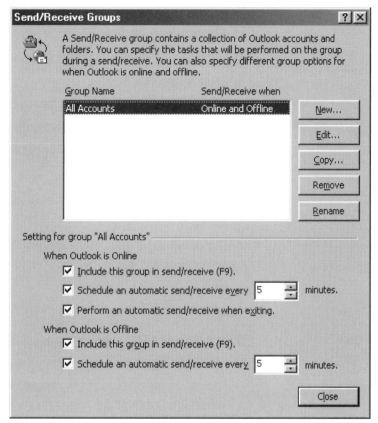

Figure 16 Setting how your email application sends and receives mail

You may choose how often your mail application will manage mail, online and offline.

What does it mean?

Offline means that you have closed Outlook *but as it is running in the background it will notify you of any mail that comes into your Inbox.*

Here are some suggestions for automated procedures:

◆ setting up new styles
◆ creating a simple macro
◆ adding a button
◆ scheduling data transfers
◆ automating backups.

3.3 What to automate

Automation depends on the user and the work that they carry out. It is important that you interview them and comprehensively assess their needs. When you are working with the user, remember that they are your customer.

Their satisfaction should be important to you. They may not keep coming back to you, even with minor problems, if you incorrectly assist them.

When assessing the user's needs find the answers to these questions:

◆ What is their role?

◆ What software do they commonly use?

◆ What do they do with the software that they commonly use?

◆ What data is critical? What data will need a regular backup or data transfer?

You also need to assess the user.

◆ Ask them to 'demonstrate' their use and watch them for no more than five minutes.

◆ Look carefully at their individual needs. If they have any disabilities consider how they can be appropriately assisted.

◆ Look at their technical experience and how automation could help them.

◆ Assess where further training may be required.

From this you can identify what you could do to help the user:

◆ You might set up new styles for someone who is an extensive user of *Word*.

◆ Adding simple macros might reduce repeated tasks or make a process accessible for someone with a disability.

◆ You could add a button (or buttons) to an application for ease of use.

◆ You might automate spelling corrections for someone who has to type many technical terms. This can also be used for someone with an autistic spectrum disorder such as dyslexia.

◆ You could schedule data transfers to ensure that essential data is sent to a remote location.

◆ You might automate email send and receive to ensure that a user's mail system is up to date.

◆ You could complete an automated backup to ensure that critical data is safe.

CASE STUDY

Victoria Smith has worked for the Ridgeway local government offices as a legal advisor for the last 5 years. She has a brittle bone disorder which means that she often uses a wheelchair and can suffer discomfort when typing for long periods of time.

Using Microsoft *Word* is an important part of her job. Being a determined and independent personality, she wishes to continue using this application, but has agreed that she needs it to be configured to help her in the completion of her legal reports that have to be submitted to the local government councillors.

Write a report (approximately 1000 words) on what assistance you could give Victoria, using the skills you have learnt in automating applications and procedures for users. You may wish to include screen grabs as part of this report.

4 Creating routine and complex automated procedures

4.1 Creating automated procedures

Automated procedures are a benefit to a user. They can offer:

◆ a source of reliability, e.g. in the use of backup and data transfer to ensure that their data has a fail-safe in the event of system failure

◆ consistency in making sure that they carry out the same process as everyone else, e.g. in choosing to employ a corporate style sheet

◆ through backups and data transfer, the assurance that there is a contingency if the system fails

◆ efficiency and effectiveness for the user in the work they do.

In this section you will be expected to automate:

◆ a backup

◆ a timed data transfer

◆ a scheduled virus scan

◆ scheduled maintenance

◆ the creation of shortcuts and hyperlinks

◆ applications.

4.1.1 Backup

Completing a backup should be part of normal maintenance.

◆ The *ZipGenius*, application (page 37) uses a compression format that can be used on most systems and is related to the inbuilt compression tool in Windows XP.

◆ Windows XP uses a comprehensive facility called **System Restore**. This allows you to take a 'snapshot' of the current system (files and system settings), so that you can return the system to a previous state. System Restore, by its very nature, is automatic and will make backups when there is a change to the system.

◆ On computers with Windows 98, there is a backup utility in Programs/Accessories/System Tools. When started, you are given the choice of starting a new backup job, restoring data from a previous backup or opening a backup that has been completed.

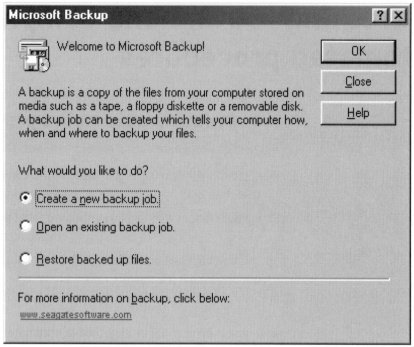

Figure 17 Starting a backup

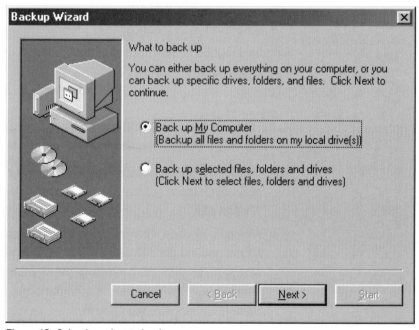

Figure 18 Selecting what to backup

You are then provided with the opportunity to back up the whole system or to back up selected files. The choice will depend on how much space you have available to store the backup. (CD/DVD burners are now considered excellent backup media.)

You may elect to back up every file or, for the sake of storage, complete an **incremental backup** and back up new or modified files.

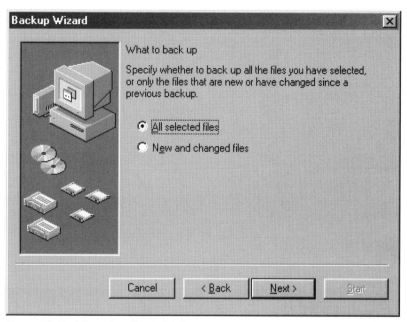

Figure 19 Deciding what files to back up

You will need to specify the folder in which to create the backup and whether the file is to be compressed and verified.

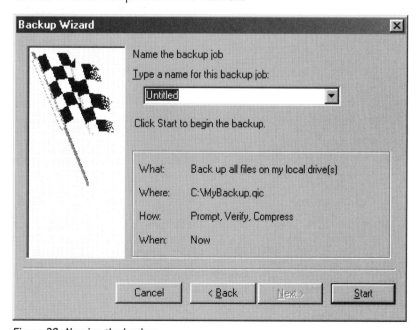

Figure 20 Naming the backup

You need to name the backup (try the day and date) and press Start.

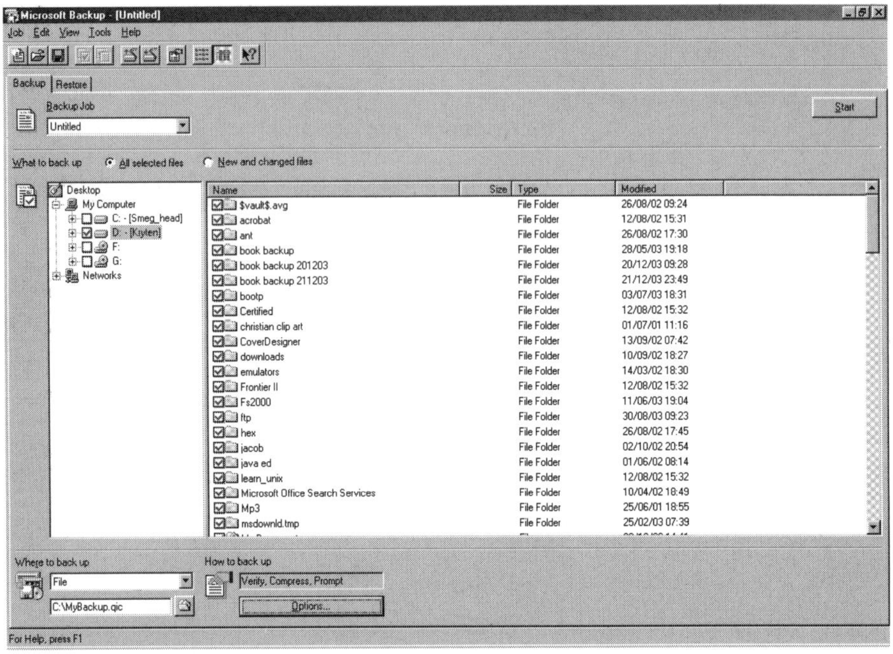

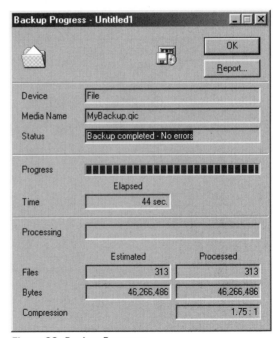

Figure 21 Selecting the files to back up

Go out and try!

Microsoft *Backup* is a comprehensive tool. Look at some of the features it offers:

◆ backing up the registry

◆ selecting specific files or directories for backing up.

Figure 22 Backup Progress

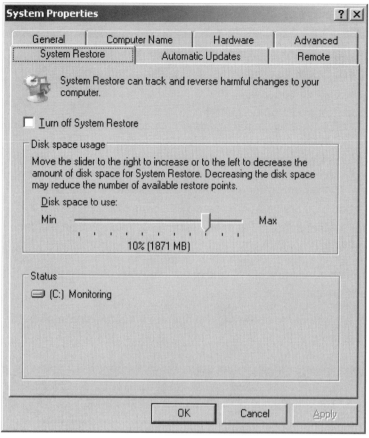

Figure 23 Windows XP restore

The Windows XP System Restore facility is activated by default. It can be found by right-clicking on the My Computer icon and selecting Properties; or you can access it via Control Panel/System Properties.

You can decide the quantity of hard drive space that is to be used for the images. It is recommended that you use no more than 10% of your hard drive for images.

You can create a task in the Task Scheduler to routinely prompt you to create a restore point. Depending on how paranoid you are, daily or weekly will suffice. This can be done by using the System Restore wizard which can be found in Start/Programs/Accessories/System Tools.

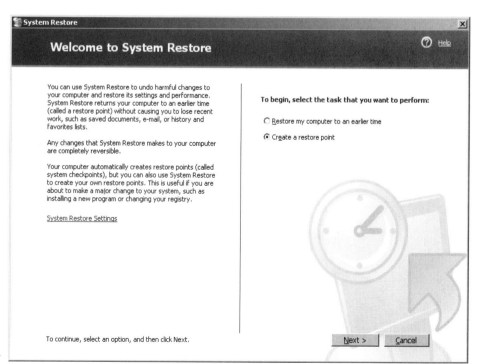

Figure 24 Setting the Windows XP restore point

PRACTICAL TASK

Using an appropriate version of Windows, complete a backup of the My Documents folder. Create a schedule using the Task Scheduler that will complete a daily backup and ensure that the backup is incremental (that is, it will back up new and modified files).

4.1.2 Timed data transfer

Many commercial applications offer automated data transfer as part of their remit. In this section, you are going to create a batch file and then create a schedule that will be that data set (your My Documents folder will be the data that you will transfer).

This will work in all versions of Windows, and minor variations between the operating systems are catered for.

Step one: Create a batch file to automate the operating system commands to copy files.

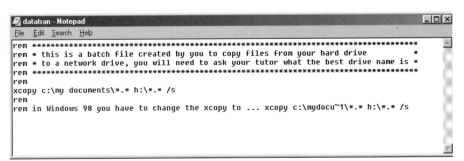

Figure 25 Datatran batch file

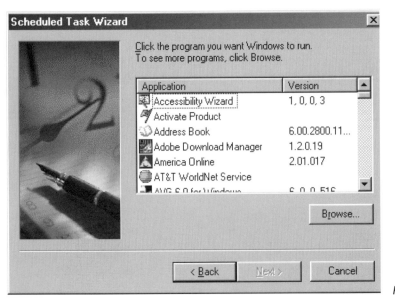

Figure 26 The Task Scheduler

Step two: Save the batch file as datatran.bat

Step three: Open Programs/ Accessories/System Tools/Scheduled Tasks and click on the Add Scheduled Task option to start the task wizard. Click on Browse and select the file datatran.bat.

Step four: Set the frequency for the data transfer, e.g. as daily for this activity.

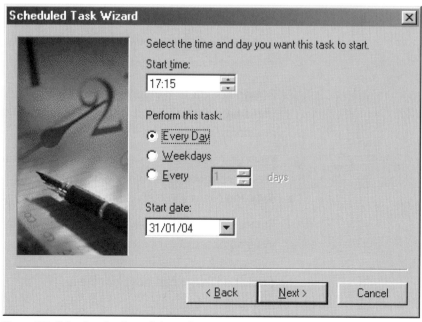

Figure 27 Selecting the frequency of the task

Step five: The backup needs to happen after you finish work. The rule of thumb is to set the time as 15 minutes after that. You can now finish the wizard, and will have successfully configured a task for data transfer.

Figure 28 Selecting the time of the task

This type of data transfer is not uncommon. Many employees back up their local hard drive to the network and the contents of the work they are doing on the system as a local copy. While network administrators are very effective in ensuring that network data is reliably backed up, no one dismisses this 'belts and braces' policy.

PRACTICAL TASK

With the permission of your tutor, complete a similar schedule that will:

◆ copy local files to a remote location

◆ copy files from a remote location to a local workstation.

4.1.3 Scheduled virus scan

You may have enabled the Task Scheduler as part of the normal configuration of an anti-virus program. It is important that you consider carefully what time you want the test to take place as well as how often. Options may be to:

◆ run a scan after work to counter any possible infections that may have been downloaded or installed during the day

◆ run a scan before the working day starts so that you are aware of any issues with your computer

◆ run a scan every four hours for paranoid security

◆ run a scan daily for tight security

◆ scan the system weekly for reasonable security

◆ scan the system monthly for lax, 'could not care what happens' security.

Remember, the anti-virus program is always resident and will alert you to any immediate detection of a virus. The purpose of scheduling a scan is to look for any dormant infections.

What you elect to do will reflect your organisation's security policy. The preferred frequency is daily. Where you have a system with large quantities of data, the overnight scan is best, as this will slow down your computer.

Before you start the scan, you must ensure that the system has the latest virus database. It is pointless scanning for the latest virus if your database is over a week old. This equates to having armed guards on all the gates, but no protection from an attack from the air.

In Unit 401, you configured the database update utility to load and install the latest database 1 hour before the test.

Configuring the scheduler for a user is easy. Right-click on the AVG icon in the bottom right-hand corner of the screen, and select the Run AVG Anti-virus option.

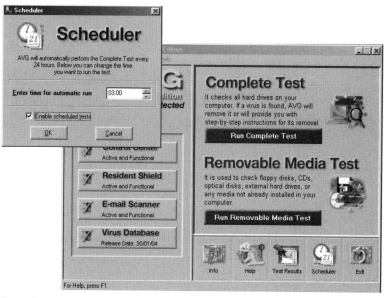

Figure 29 Scheduling an anti-virus application

The ideal time depends on the size of your hard drive or data volume you are scanning. An estimate is that 20 Gb of data takes approximately 1 hour.

If you have a virus on your system, AVG will alert you, so that when you return in the morning to the computer, you can either disinfect the drive or seek assistance from an appropriate expert.

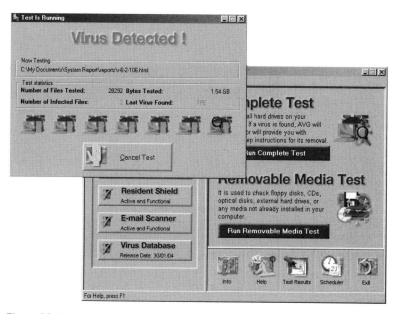

Figure 30 Detection of a virus

After the scheduled scan, you can look at the log file which is maintained by AVG, and this may be used in a report to senior management.

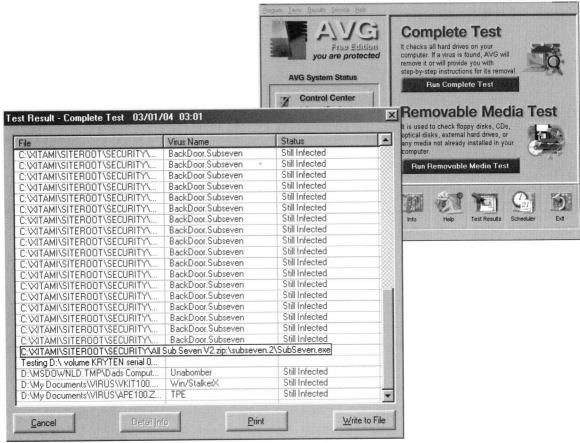

Figure 31 Test results

PRACTICAL TASK

With the permission of your tutor, install AVG on at least five computers. Ensure that AVG:

◆ is installed

◆ is set to check boot viruses, executable viruses, macro viruses

◆ will use heuristic scanning

◆ has the update manager set to complete an update every 24 hours

◆ will run a scheduled test every day during your lunch break.

Maintain a log of all the tests for a period of 15 days.

4.1.4 Scheduled maintenance

The Scheduled Maintenance wizard is a feature of only one version of Windows: Windows 98. This automated task is used to improve system performance by:

◆ running Scandisk to repair any errors on the hard drive

◆ starting the Disk Defragmentation utility to reorganise storage space and speed up the running of some applications and the operating system

◆ removing temporary (cached) Internet files

◆ removing any temporary files associated with Scandisk

◆ removing any other temporary files associated with installation of applications.

For operating systems such as Windows 2000 and XP, you are required to create your own scheduled tasks for this maintenance work. Windows 2000 and XP use a different file system by default (Windows 98 uses FAT32 and XP/2000 use NTFS), where Scandisk is no longer available.

Go out and try!

Scandisk has been superseded by CHKDSK (ironic as CHKDSK preceded Scandisk in some of the earliest versions of MS-DOS). Using the Command prompt, run the CHKDSK command and see what services it has to offer to maintain the integrity of your hard drive.

Hint: you may wish to try CHKDSK/?

One feature that is common to all operating systems is the **Disk Cleanup wizard**. This will lift from the hard drive:

◆ the contents of the recycle bin

◆ temporary files

◆ temporary Internet files

◆ offline web pages

◆ Windows components that you do not use

◆ applications that you do not use

◆ your computer's system restore history, except for the last restore point (Windows XP only and potentially very dangerous).

As can be seen, Disk Cleanup is a subset of the Maintenance wizard.

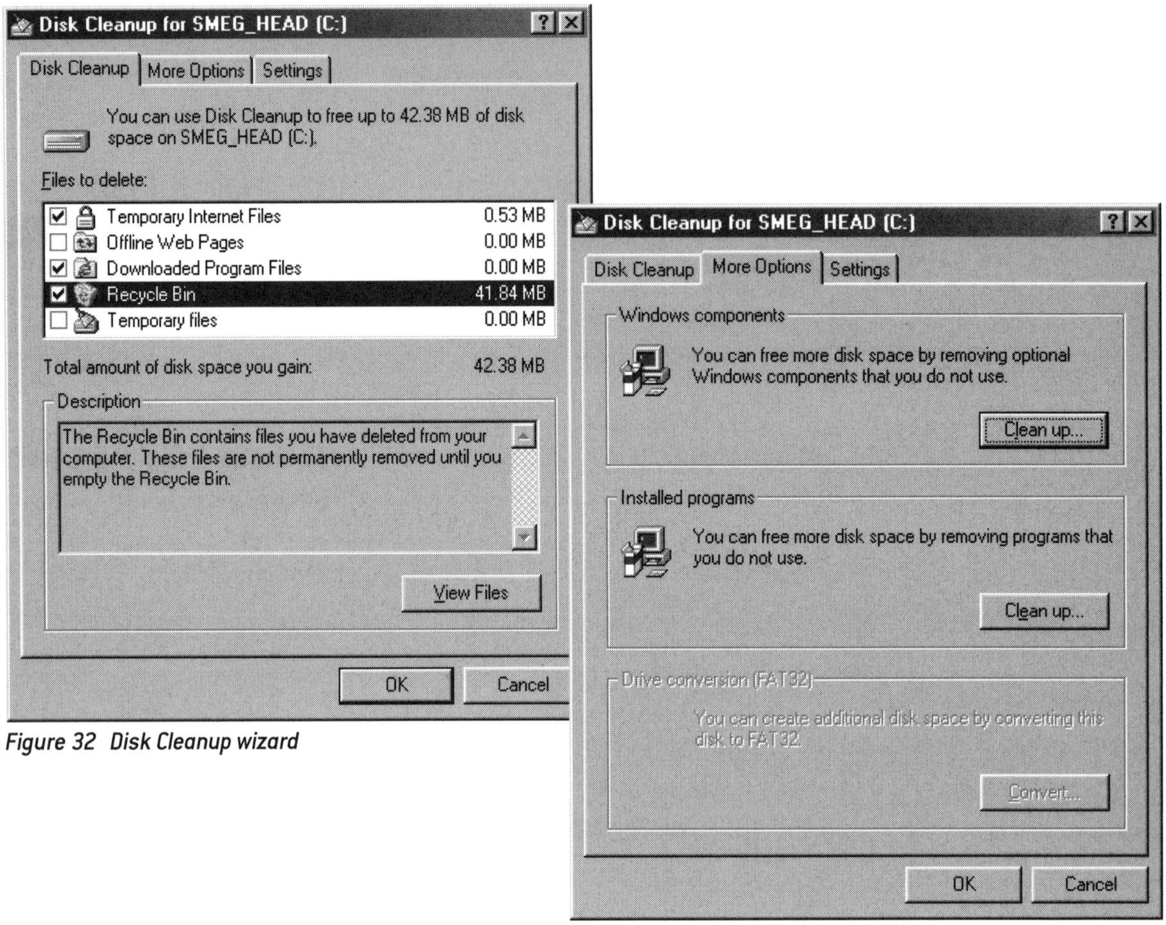

Figure 32 Disk Cleanup wizard

For disk maintenance, it is worth considering creating a weekly schedule for the task. Your computer is busy adding and removing files from your hard drive on an hourly basis, but it is unlikely that you will need to maintain the storage space less than once a week.

PRACTICAL TASK

Using the skills you have developed with the Task Scheduler, create automated tasks for:

◆ disk defragmentation on a monthly basis

◆ disk cleanup on a weekly basis.

Create a simple batch file that will use the CHKSDK command and create an automated task to run this once a month.

4.1.5 The creation of shortcuts and hyperlinks

Time is consumed traversing the Internet to find a page or website that you need on a regular basis. It is also time-consuming to hunt through myriads of folders on your hard drive for applications or files that you need.

To create a shortcut to an application, using *Explorer*, find the application that you wish to use.

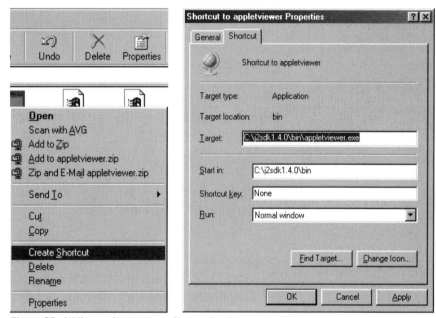

Figure 33 Adding a shortcut to a file/application

Right-click on the File icon and select the Create Shortcut option. This will create a shortcut file (called a PIF or program information file).

Type in the full address of the website you wish to access (and you must include the http://) and then give the link a name.

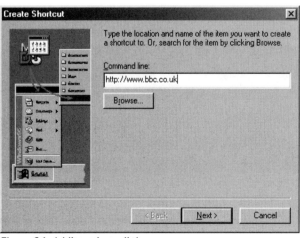
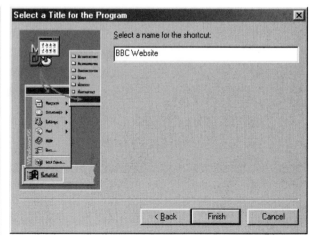

Figure 34 Adding a hyperlink

PRACTICAL TASK

Create links:

◆ to your college's or employer's website

◆ to an application in the Windows folder

◆ to a file in your My Documents folder.

4.1.6 Enabling applications to autorun

Autorun means that an application can start without manual intervention. There are three situations where you (or the computer) may need an application to autorun:

◆ on system start-up

◆ at a specific time of day, week or month

◆ in response to a system event.

Some applications, on installation, will configure the registry to enable the application, or an element of the application, to autorun on **system startup**. When you installed the anti-virus application, it installed a **TSR (terminate and stay resident)** application that starts with the computer and will always monitor for any potential virus threat.

So that the computer will load them on startup, these applications will configure:

◆ the system registry

◆ older .ini files

◆ the StartUp menu.

Go out and try!

Run msconfig or inspect the registry to look at:

◆ the registry run keys

◆ the load= lines in win.ini and system.ini

◆ any commands in autoexec.bat

What applications are being started by your computer?

You can affect the loading of applications at startup by adding your own if you wish. If you press Start/Programs/StartUp, you will see that there is a folder for any application you may wish to use. Many professionals will create a shortcut to their email application and copy it to this folder.

PRACTICAL TASK

Create a shortcut to your favourite website and copy it to the StartUp folder. Restart your computer so that you will see that this website is loaded on login.

You can enable applications to start periodically at any time of the day, week or month using the **Windows Task Scheduler**. This may be useful:

◆ when you want to initiate a backup

◆ to carry out a data transfer

◆ in starting a critical application

◆ to remind you that a specific task needs doing NOW!

PRACTICAL TASK

Using the skills you have developed with the Windows Task Scheduler, create a series of tasks to:

◆ start an email application at 10:00

◆ load a website of choice at 13:00

◆ start a backup at 17:30

◆ start *Solitaire* on the first day of every month.

Windows may autorun some applications in response to a predefined event on the system. This may be:

◆ a virus

◆ a network message

◆ a new email

◆ an error with the hard drive.

Anti-virus applications like AVG are designed to react as soon as a virus has been detected. Windows can be prompted by a network message or *Outlook* can remain dormant until the email arrives. If there is an issue with the hard drive on your computer (it's nearing its capacity), the Disk Cleanup wizard may be configured to start, so that you are alerted and it will attempt to remove files that are not required.

4.2 Implementing complex automated procedures

If you need to complete a more complex task for a user or a customer, it is important that you do some planning before you embark on the task.

The task you may embark on could be:

- the configuration of log-in script for a server that the user accesses as part of their daily use of the system
- the implementation of a complex macro that enables them to enhance their work
- a batch file that carries out a series of system tasks.

The work you do will impact upon the user and may need documentation so that a successor to the user, as well as yourself, can understand what has been done.

4.2.1 Documentation

Before the task of including a macro or configuring a login script starts, you need to look at the computer or network system. This is important because:

- you may make changes that affect the system and you will need a record of the previous state
- the application or network system version may prove to be incompatible with the changes made and you may need to restore and identify the incompatibility
- it works and this was the first time with the new version.

Information that you may need to gather includes:

- the processor specification of the hardware
- the system memory available
- the version of the operating system involved
- the version of the application involved.

PRACTICAL TASK

Look at the hardware in use by your employer or place of study. Look at the specification of at least five different computers. If you are doing this at your place of study, you may need to look at different classrooms or study areas.

4.2.2 Configuring the system

The **batch file** is a throw-back to the computer systems of the 1960s where your predecessors would create a series of system commands to carry out a variety of processes.

Batch files have existed in the Microsoft operating system since the first version of MS-DOS (the 1970s). Other operating systems like Unix and Linux also employ similar systems (often referred to as **script files**).

A batch file will employ all underlying operating system commands and programs as well as have some commands that are batch file specific.

It is worth noting that operating systems like Windows 95 and 98 are built on a DOS platform, whereas Windows 2000 and XP offer the same system as a managed command environment and is not an integral part of the system.

Commands that you may use are listed in Table 2.

Table 2 *System configuration commands*

Some operating system commands		Some operating system programs		Some batch file commands	
cls	Clears screen	**ipconfig**	Provides network settings	**goto**	Jumps to a label
dir	Lists contents of a directory	**chkdsk**	Checks disk integrity	**call**	Calls another batch file
copy	Copies files	**format**	Formats drive	**:**	Label
md	Make directory	**fdisk**	Partitions (divides) drive	**rem**	comment
rd	Remove directory	**deltree**	Remove an entire directory structure	**pause**	wait
cd	Change directory			**Echo off**	Stops system output
				Echo	Displays a message
				%1	Command line input

You can create batch files too, move files for a data transfer or copy files for a backup.

Go out and try!

Follow the links to the MS-DOS website from www.heinemann.co.uk/hotlinks and look at the commands available for the underlying operating system. You can access the system in any version of Windows by using Run/Command. With the permission of your tutor, try some of the commands.

Creating a batch file is not difficult: open *Notepad* and create a file with a .bat extension.

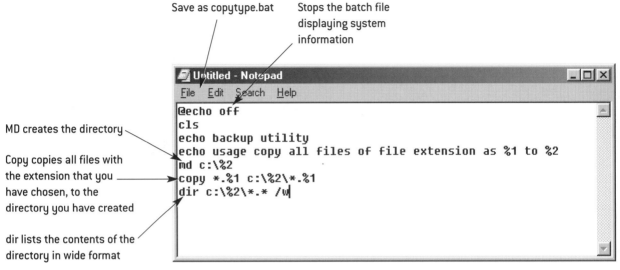

Save as copytype.bat

Stops the batch file displaying system information

MD creates the directory

Copy copies all files with the extension that you have chosen, to the directory you have created

dir lists the contents of the directory in wide format

Figure 35 A batch file

To create a batch file called copytype.bat, type in all commands listed in Figure 35. The underlying operating system allows you to run the batch file by typing the filename (which is often limited to 8 characters), where the %1 and the %2 represent options that you can enter, which in the case of this batch file is:

COPYTYPE %allfileswiththesameextension %toanewfolderthatyouhavecreated

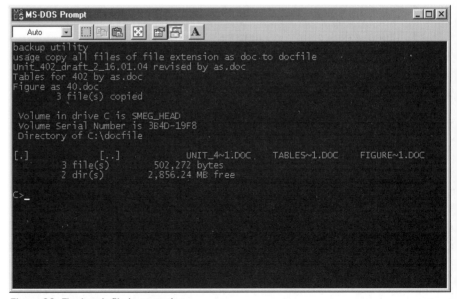

Figure 36 The batch file in operation

Use Run/Command to enter My Documents or another folder that has a collection of *Word* documents. To use your batch file enter:

COPYTYPE doc docfiles

This will create a folder on the C: drive called docfiles which will be populated with *Word* documents, i.e. files with the .doc extension.

Tip: There are many complex rules for managing DOS and batch files. You may need to copy COPYTYPE into the folder you are going to copy from for this to work.

PRACTICAL TASK

Using the COPYTYPE example, create a batch file that will create two backups, one locally as well as one in another location (a network drive).

In Windows 2000, **login scripts** are an extension of the batch file. You can configure the user profile of a local machine to run a sequence of commands on login.

Login scripts can be applied to individuals as well as groups of users and are often used:

◆ to ensure that the user is connected to a variety of network services such as server drives and printers

◆ to carry out routine system maintenance tasks such as the backing up of the user's data or the clearing of files that are not required.

Login scripts are used in a networked environment and are commonly available for Microsoft operating systems post Windows 2000; they are also supported by Unix, Linux and Netware.

To employ a login script, you need to adapt an existing user. As your place of study or employer may not give permission for this, you will need to create a temporary user profile that you can alter.

To create a user using Windows 2000, click Start/Settings/Control Panel/Administrative Tools/Computer Management.

Click on Local Users and Groups to locate the Users folder (Figure 37).

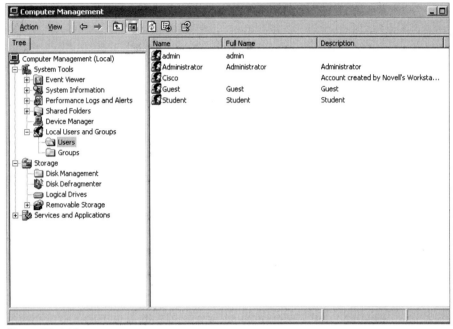

Figure 37 Adding a new user

Click on the Action button and select New User...

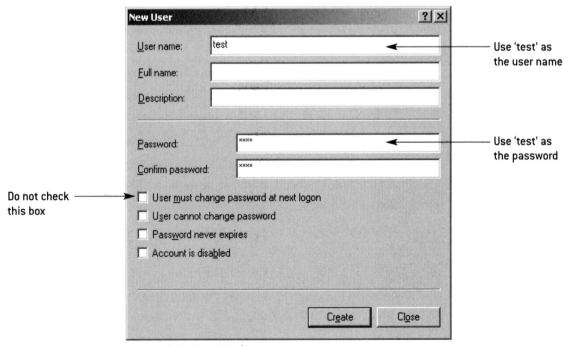

Figure 38 The individual user

Call the user test, with the password of test and ensure that the 'User must change password at next logon' tick box is *not* selected.

You will be able to see in Computer Management that the new user test has been created (Figure 39).

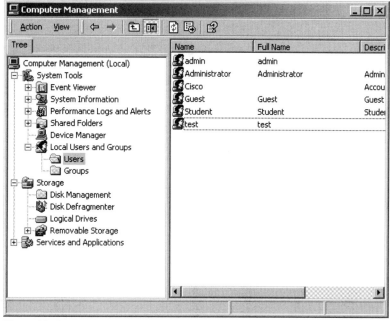

Figure 39 The new user, created

Before you can apply a login script, if you are the first user to implement this feature on your Windows 2000 workstation, you will have to create the folder in which the script file will reside. To achieve this, ensure that the following folder path is created:

C:\winnt\system32\repl\import\scripts

C:\winnt\system32 will already exist, but you must create the subsequent folders.

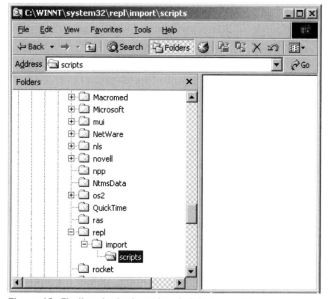

Figure 40 Finding the login scripts in Windows 2000

Once you have completed this, you can create a simple batch file. This may contain a range of commands, for example, to run chkdsk to check the integrity of the hard drive on login.

Create the batch file shown in Figure 41 and save it in *C:\winnt\system32\repl\import\scripts* as this.bat.

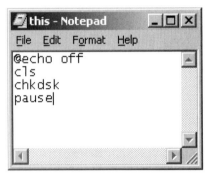

Figure 41 A possible login script

Now you can go back to the Computer Management window and double-click on the test user.

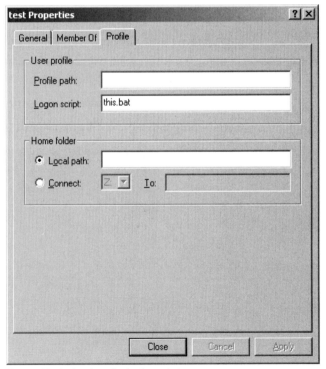

Figure 42 Activating the login script

In the User window, select the Profile tab and, into the Logon script text field, type this.bat and select Apply. Now you are ready to test the script.

Logout and make sure that you login as username test with password test.

During the login process, the window shown in Figure 4.3 should appear.

```
C:\WINNT\system32\repl\import\scripts\this.bat
The type of the file system is NTFS.

WARNING!  F parameter not specified.
Running CHKDSK in read-only mode.

CHKDSK is verifying files (stage 1 of 3)...
File verification completed.
CHKDSK is verifying indexes (stage 2 of 3)...
23 percent completed.
```

Figure 43   The login script in action

If your computer has any problems executing a script, it may be associated with the user privileges that the test login has. With the express permission of your tutor or line manager, you may need to make the test a member of the administrator's group.

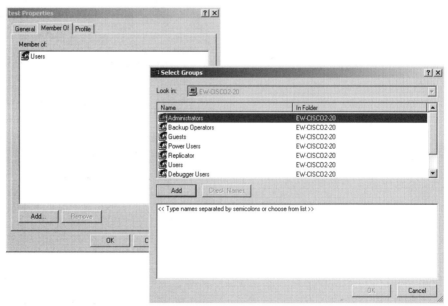

Figure 44   User groups available

PRACTICAL TASK

Create a login script that carries out a data transfer as well as a backup on the user logging into the computer.

As you are not a programmer, you will not be expected to write or configure complex macros. This does not mean that you are unable to do this, just that, for your job description, it is not yet a reasonable expectation of you.

However, it is the commonly expected standard that you may install corporate macros that have been prewritten by an external software house or another employee of your organisation.

The great news is that, for any version of *Word* beyond 97, adding a macro (so long as you follow instructions specific to the macro!) is easy.

First, ensure that your security level has been changed to normal so that *Word* will run the macro. This is due to the fact that virus creators have been known to use this language as a means to cause havoc with other people's systems.

Go out and try!

Go to the McAfee Security site from www.heinemann.co.uk/hotlinks and complete a search on *Word* macro viruses. You may find that the most famous is Melissa.

The security option can be accessed from the Tools/Macros submenu.

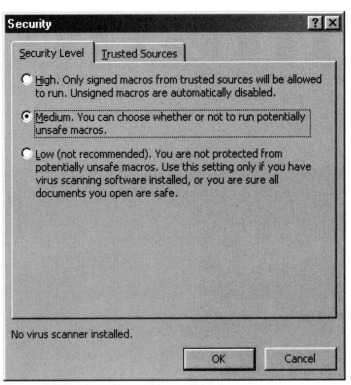

Figure 45 Macro control

As is shown in Figure 45 you have control over the degree of access unknown macros may have: high, medium or low security. For macros that have been installed or created by you, the medium option is ideal.

To create the new macro, click Tools/Macro/Macros, type in the name of the new macro and click on Create. (Note that you are not allowed spaces in the name of a macro.)

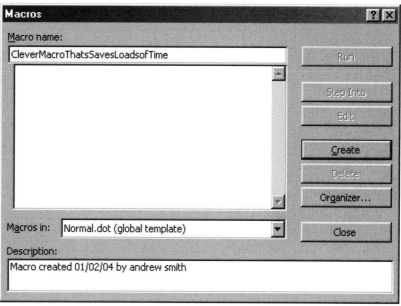

Figure 46 Starting a macro

The Visual Basic editor will start, so you can type, insert or copy/paste the macro code, and then save it and exit the editor.

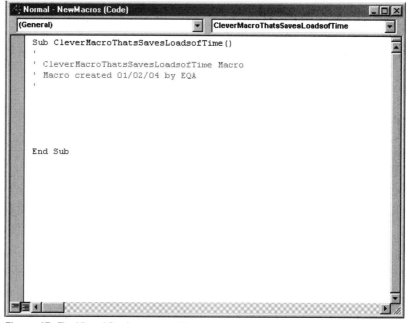

Figure 47 The Visual Basic macro editor

Now that the macro is available, you can access it any time by selecting the macro and pressing the Run button.

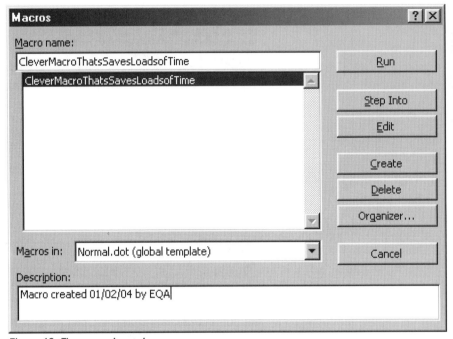

Figure 48 The macro is ready

PRACTICAL TASK

There are many 'good' macros available on the web, which can be found in Google. With the permission of your tutor and ensuring that you have virus checked the file, download and install a macro of your choice.

4.3 Check and test automated procedures

A variety of automated procedures can be installed, configured or implemented:

◆ timed backups

◆ timed data transfer

◆ scheduled virus scan

◆ scheduled maintenance

◆ shortcuts and hyperlinks

◆ autorun applications.

Once you have installed them for the user, it is essential that you check that they are working or effective:

◆ Carry out the automated procedure as a 'dry run'.

◆ Come back to the user, to witness the automated procedure.

◆ If the automated procedure is at an anti-social time, check system logs or change the timer to complete a test run at a sociable time.

◆ Restart the computer to check if any autorun applications run.

◆ Manually trigger the computer to carry out an automated procedure. (This is not advisable for a virus scanner.)

PRACTICAL TASK

Create a check sheet that would assist a computer professional in checking that the automated procedures that they have implemented are successful, with a helpful list of likely solutions if there is a problem.

Use this check list yourself on:

1 Scheduling a virus scan.

2 Scheduling an application to autorun.

3 Implementing a hyperlink.

4 Carrying out a scheduled maintenance task.

4.4 Keeping a record of automated procedures

Keeping records may not be exciting, but keeping records is incredibly important. Any automated procedure that you may create for any computer for your organisation can have an impact on the performance of a computer:

◆ the system is updated and a new application is added, and this may conflict with the automated procedure

◆ a new application or automated procedure may fail unexpectedly due to a conflict

◆ a computer's performance may be causing concern and the professional who is looking at the computer needs as much information as possible to diagnose the problem.

The record needs to be a summary of the automated procedure, the date it was installed and a description of the task it carries out and, where appropriate, a copy of any batch file or macro code.

PRACTICAL TASK

Look back at the automated procedures you have created and produce some comprehensive documentation listing:

◆ the name of the task

◆ the purpose of the task

◆ how the task is accomplished

◆ any macro/batch file code as appropriate.

Unit 403/4

Install and configure equipment, operating systems and software

Introduction

Since computers became part of commercial life in the 1950s, people employed to maintain, upgrade and fix these systems have needed to develop a comprehensive understanding of the technology.

In reading this unit you will explore the skills involved in installing, repairing and upgrading a computer system, and will develop an understanding of how the technology works with the main emphasis on personal computer systems.

This unit is divided into six sections, each looking at important aspects involved with installing hardware and software on various computer systems.

1 How would I prepare a computer for an installation/upgrade/build?

2 Installing and configuring various computer components.

3 Testing installed components.

4 Installing or upgrading an operating system.

5 How do I configure and test the installed operating system?

6 How do I successfully install any additional software?

1 How would I prepare a computer for an installation/upgrade/build?

Many professionals (yes, you're one as well) will open a box, remove the component, dismantle the system and install the component before completing a comprehensive check.

◆ Check packaging contents for any damage.

◆ Check compatibility of all components.

◆ Prepare yourself and the computer.

◆ Decide what must be done once the job is finished.

1.1 Check packaging and contents for any damage

A damaged carton that contains a computer or a component often bodes ill fortune. Whilst some components, such as a monitor or base unit, usually have polystyrene padding in the box, smaller components may be covered in bubble wrap or inserted in a plastic moulded form.

Although the component has arrived safely, the outside damage may indicate that the component has been crushed in transit. If you find a box that has been damaged you may wish to do one of the following:

◆ carefully check the internal component for damage and, if necessary, send it back

◆ if the damage is superficial (on the exterior of a monitor or computer case), negotiate a discount.

Various component boxes

Go out and try!

If possible, look at the packaging of all the computer hardware that you have. What sort of packaging is used? Compare what is used against the following list.

◆ Solid polystyrene baffle.
◆ Polystyrene chips or beans.
◆ Air bags.
◆ Bubble wrap.
◆ Shredded paper.
◆ Recycled cardboard baffle.

When you accept delivery of any equipment, check the packaging before you sign a receipt for the transit company. Then check the equipment and if you find any damage, do not attempt to use or install the equipment.

It is essential that you are aware that with the sensitive nature of computer technology, the damage to the equipment may be microscopic. This means that you cannot see the damage and the issue will only become apparent when you attempt to use the resource.

On technology such as a motherboard, minute faults may occur when:

◆ the motherboard is dropped
◆ the surface is bent through stress as someone tried to force it into a box or a computer
◆ the intricate surface tracks are scratched
◆ the motherboard has been too warm and heat expansion has caused damage (this can happen if the technology is not in an air-conditioned room at the height of summer in the United Kingdom)
◆ the motherboard has been exposed to extreme cold (which can happen in international transit) and frost/contraction has caused damage.

It is essential that you contact the supplier or the manufacturer. Under UK law you can demand a replacement to exactly the same specification. This may mean that the supplier/manufacturer will ship a new part, whilst you ship back the faulty component.

Different devices require different protection, due to the nature of their sensitivity and physical robustness. There is a need to protect the device from shock as well as providing anti-static protection from you or others that may handle the equipment.

Printed circuit boards (motherboards, memory and any additional cards) are very fragile and must not be touched apart from at the edges. They must be transported in an anti-static bag and in a protective cardboard carton.

Boxed motherboard

Disk drives and **CD/DVD/ROM/RW drives** must also be protected with an anti-static bag as they have sensitive components. Because they have small motor assemblies and sensitive read-write mechanisms, they must be transported in a foam casing to absorb any minor impact.

Hard drive in anti-static bag

The **CPU** will be transported in an anti-static bag but will also be contained in a plastic form to protect the pins that connect the CPU to the motherboard.

PHOTO 61
Close up of
CPU and
plastic form

Processor in protected packaging

So, what must you do when you receive any computer technology?

◆ You must check for any broken security seals, as the device may have been replaced, tampered with or possibly stolen.

◆ Look at the condition of the packaging. Any damage from water, frost, being dropped, crushed, etc., could indicate that there are unseen issues with the contents. It's worth noting that some expensive systems have tilt and shock indicators (small ink beads or easy to crush ceramic cylinders).

CASE STUDY

As a very busy and successful computer professional, you are promoted to a supervisory position and you are now responsible for a team of ten computer support specialists.

You recognise that they need a variety of help guides to enable them to 'be successful' in what they do, as well as learn the intricacies of the tasks that they have to perform. One of these will be a guide on the different types of anti-static packaging for:

◆ motherboards
◆ disk drives
◆ CD and DVD readers and writers
◆ various types of memory
◆ processors (CPU).

Use either Microsoft *Word* or *Publisher* – or some other software – to write this guide.

If there are any issues with the equipment or packaging being damaged in transit, you or your employer may have to contend with:

- **delays in the installation** of the system, which in turn lead to missed deadlines for which your employer may be financially liable
- **customer dissatisfaction**, which may lead to legal action, loss of future business or, worse, loss of reputation amongst other customers
- the installation of a temporary solution whilst the replacement is being sent, which will incur indirect and increased **support costs** making the work less profitable.

If you discover that any equipment has been damaged in transit or installation, it is important that you record and report what has happened.

- Write a comprehensive report on the issue including a description of the problem, so that this can be copied to a supervisor or manager who will handle the issue.
- Take photos of the damage so that your impression of the issue cannot be disputed.

There are three reasons why you record and report any damage that occurs:

1 It minimises any chance of the problem reoccurring; the organisation or, hopefully, the supplier learns from the experience.

2 Keeping an audit trail of issues allows any project supervisors to clearly identify what may have caused problems. Financial managers may also make sure that they are not charged twice for any component, and receive any discount negotiated for the inconvenience caused.

3 If there is a problem with the design of the packaging, or even the component, then the original supplier or manufacturer can also be suitably informed so that they can rectify the issue and possibly modify the design.

CASE STUDY

Widgets R'Us have recently acquired new premises in Dulton, where your employer PC Incorporated have won the contract to install 150 computers to support a variety of commercial functions.

As team leader you are responsible for the installation of the computers on delivery at Widgets R'Us along with three others.

On the day that the delivery is expected you are phoned by the manufacturer who informs you that only 90 of the 150 computers are ready, and the others will be delivered 3 days late but with a 10% discount on cost.

The other 90 computers arrive on time but the packing on the base units and monitors look like the computers have enjoyed a free rollercoaster ride at Disneyland.

Write a short report (no more than 1000 words) taking into account these points:

◆ What do you need to tell your line manager?

◆ How are you going to report this to the customer and resolve any potential customer dissatisfaction?

◆ What issues are the 60 late computers going to cause?

◆ What issues is the visible external damage going to cause (and the consequences of unseen damage)?

◆ What costs might be incurred by this problem?

Then list in a separate document:

◆ how you would check for broken security seals

◆ what checks you would make for any damaged packaging

◆ what a tilt/shock indicator would show.

1.2 Check compatibility of all components

You may have the best piece of equipment available in your hands, but if you cannot connect or install it on your system then it is completely useless. All hardware and software will list on the outer carton direct compatibilities (or obvious incompatibilities). Therefore, before you open the box and damage the contents, check whether they are suitable.

◆ Is the device's connector compatible with your system? It's no good having firewire if you do not have a firewire port.

◆ Is the hardware's configuration compatible with the technology your system is using (bus speeds etc.)?

◆ Is there a minimum processor requirement?

◆ Is there a minimum operating system requirement?

◆ Is there a minimum memory requirement?

◆ Is there a demand on hard drive resources?

◆ Does the system need any other specialist components for the one you are installing to work?

Often told as a joke in the office canteen, the purchase of 1000 keyboards that do not connect to the 1000 computers is hilarious but is a result of more serious issues. An organisation that acquires a large quantity of incorrect and incompatible equipment:

◆ experiences serious delays

◆ suffers financial loss through time or the possession of equipment that is unneeded

◆ has to endure immense embarrassment.

When ordering, specifying or receiving and installing equipment it is essential that you check the following.

◆ Is the processor compatible with the motherboard, through connector type, voltage, and clock speed?

◆ Is the power supply for the base unit compatible with the motherboard?

◆ Is your organisation's electricity supply compatible with the technology being used?

◆ Is the firmware for the BIOS or other components capable of supporting the existing technology?

◆ Are the device interfaces compatible with the system bus available? Having an AGP card is useless when your motherboard only has PCI slots.

◆ Are external interfaces compatible with externally connecting devices? Does the system have enough serial interfaces? Are they the right type for the devices that are used? For example, if your system has two USB interfaces, and you have a USB mouse, keyboard, scanner and printer, you have a 'sockets to plugs' issue that can only be resolved by purchasing a £5 USB hub. Whilst this may sound simple, imagine what will happen if this is translated to a company that has just acquired 100 such systems. The £500 in surplus cost will cause serious financial issues.

What does it mean?

Bus: A communication channel used for data.

BIOS: Basic input output system; a processor that manages the hardware and boot-up process of a computer system.

Firmware: A computer program embedded in a chip such as the BIOS.

There are two common hard drive connectors available, and between them there is total incompatibility:

◆ **(E)IDE, enhanced integrated drive electronics**, has a 40-pin connector that can support up to two drives (this includes CD/DVD readers and writers)

◆ **SCSI, small computer system interface** is a faster standard and has a variety of connectors (which are actually incompatible with each other). You may encounter the following SCSI standards.

  ◆ SCSI-1: Uses an 8-bit 25-pin connector, and supports data rates of 4 MBps.

  ◆ SCSI-2: Same as SCSI-1, but uses a 50-pin connector and supports multiple devices.

  ◆ Wide SCSI: Uses a wider cable (168 cable lines to 68 pins) to support 16-bit transfers.

  ◆ Fast SCSI: Uses an 8-bit bus, but doubles the clock rate to support data rates of 10 MBps.

◆ Fast Wide SCSI: Uses a 16-bit bus and supports data rates of 20 MBps.

◆ Ultra SCSI: Uses an 8-bit bus and supports data rates of 20 MBps.

◆ SCSI-3: Uses a 16-bit bus and supports data rates of 40 MBps. Also called Ultra Wide SCSI.

◆ Ultra2 SCSI: Uses an 8-bit bus and supports data rates of 40 MBps.

◆ Wide Ultra2 SCSI: Uses a 16-bit bus and supports data rates of 80 MBps.

What does it mean?

Bit: An individual unit of computer data, represented as a 0 or 1. If you know that a device is 8-bit then all you have to do is calculate 2 to the power of 8 (2^8) which will give you 256 combinations.

Clock rate: The speed of the electronic circuit based on the physics involved with the frequency of the signal and how much data can be sent.

MBps: Mega bytes per second. A byte is eight bits, a kilobyte is 1024 bytes and a megabyte is 1024 kilobytes. MBps represents how much data can be sent every second across a bus.

The only check that can be made for compatibility is 'does it fit?', as each connector for SCSI and (E)IDE are different.

On the rear of your computer you will notice a variety of connectors.

A **DB9** is the 9-pin connector for serial devices (mouse, connections to network management devices etc.).

A **DB25** is the 25-pin connector, found on older computer systems and used to connect to external modems and other communications devices (sometimes referred to as a RS232-C or EIA/TIA232-C).

A **PS/2 connector** is for the keyboard and mouse (yes, different connections can be used for the same devices).

One or more **USB connectors** are used to connect network devices, printers, mice, keyboards and many other USB devices.

A **parallel connector** (or Centronics connector, named after its manufacturer) is designed for the high data rates needed with printers.

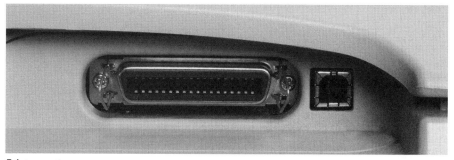

Printer port

What does it mean?

MODEM means **mod**ulator **dem**odulator and describes the technology used to convert computer data (which is digital) to the physical (analogue) form that telephone systems use, and vice versa.

PS/2 is an old system developed by IBM, but the connector has been retained as a technological standard.

USB stands for universal serial bus, a common standard that can support up to 128 devices per connector.

Serial is a form of data communication where one bit of data is sent at a time (in series).

Parallel is a faster method of data communication where there are many lines of data, so that the whole byte of information can be sent at once.

Whilst it seems unlikely, you should also check the compatibility of the BIOS. The BIOS has an inbuilt computer program (often referred to as **firmware**) designed to manage a range of technologies that are available at the time the system was built and this will manage a limited range of upgrades.

In some rare instances you might purchase a system and need to make an upgrade to the hard drive within a short time, but your new hard drive is at a capacity beyond the recognition of the BIOS. To enable the BIOS to 'handle' the new equipment, you need to go to the manufacturer's website to download the software to **flash** (upgrade the firmware) the BIOS.

Go out and try!

Visit your local computer game retailer and visit the PC games section. Look at the back of some cases and identify system compatibilities. For five chart topping games list:

◆ minimum processor specification

◆ operating system required

◆ memory required

◆ hard drive space needed

◆ type of graphics card required.

CASE STUDY

The finance director of your company Camborio Inc, in a fit of cost saving, has purchased a wide range of computer systems and components at a heavily discounted price as they are 'end of line' stock.

When the equipment is delivered, you discover that the technology order is, on the whole, incompatible with existing systems and that the contract for purchase prevents you from returning the equipment.

The problem has reached senior management and they are reviewing what can be done. You have been instructed to compose a short report (no more than 500 words) to assist their decision:

◆ What checks were made to ensure that the serial, USB, parallel and sound connectors where compatible?

◆ What checks were made to ensure that the hard drive connectors were compatible?

◆ How did you know the current version of the firmware for the BIOS?

◆ How did you check the compatibility of the power supply?

(You may wish to use images or diagrams.)

1.3 Prepare yourself and the computer

Before fitting a hardware component to a computer, you need to make sure that you are prepared. Apart from the obvious considerations, i.e. having the right component and software, you must:

◆ ensure that you have an ESD wrist strap
◆ check that you have all the correct tools
◆ make sure that you are working in an area that is not too dusty
◆ check that the area is well lit.

1.4 What must be done once the job is finished?

Fitting components does not mean that the job is over. Your software may be installed and working, that extra piece of hardware is operational and the customer is happy but, inevitably, you may have to come back to work on the computer in the future when there is a problem or a new component to install.

Conventional wisdom is that you keep all packaging, manuals, software/driver CDs and any licensing information in a safe place. You will never know if:

◆ the technology will fail
◆ there is a software audit to check the validity of all licences
◆ you will eventually remove the component to replace it and need the packaging
◆ you need to consult the manual over an unexplained issue
◆ it's not you that is going to work on the problem and the incumbent has to obtain as much information as possible.

2 Installing and configuring various computer components

Being able to understand how each component of a computer system operates and interacts will improve your ability to solve problems when out in the field. Computer technology is constantly changing. The systems described in this section were current in 2004.

In this section you will:

◆ develop an understanding of a computer system

◆ learn how to configure a wide range of computer components

◆ gain an ability to check that the equipment meets suitable safety requirements

◆ learn how to identify any problems with installation

◆ learn how to configure hardware and equipment

◆ maintain records of the installation process.

2.1 An overall view of a computer system

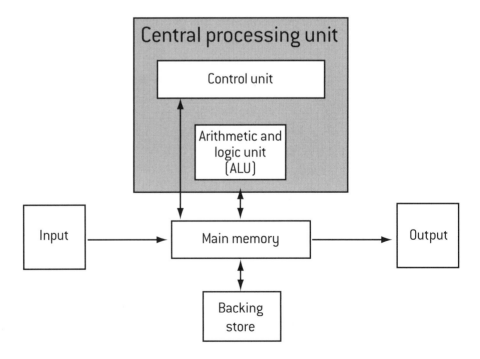

Figure 1 The structure of a computer system

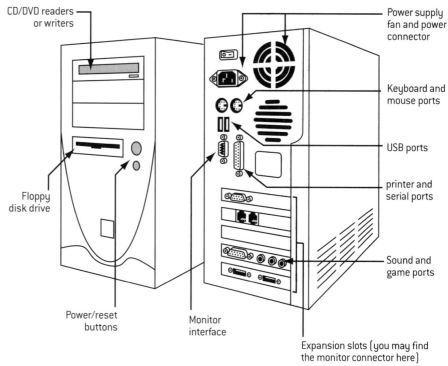

Figure 2 Outside a computer

The computer is the **base unit**. The monitor, keyboard and mouse are external devices that enable the user to use and interact with the computer system. Modern computer systems have a standard case called an ATX **form factor** (see Unit 401).

The rear of a computer will have the following connectors.

◆ **Power:** Connecting to a normal 240 V mains. You can also have a **parasite cable** which provides power for the monitor.

◆ **Fan:** Cools the power supply.

◆ **Keyboard and mouse ports:** Uses the PS2 standard to connect these user devices directly to the system.

◆ **USB (universal serial bus) ports:** While always at the back, you may find additional connectors on the front of some computer cases.

◆ **Printer and serial ports:** Used to connect various devices that can send and receive data to the computer system.

◆ **Monitor interface:** Depending on the motherboard, you may have an inbuilt video system or an additional board to manage the signal being sent to the monitor.

◆ **Sound and game ports:** Connectors for your speakers and joystick/wheel if you need them.

◆ **Case screws:** Don't lose them!

Rear of computer

2.2 What a computer looks like from the inside

Not everyone's computer is the same, especially when you look inside. Figure 3 provides an example.

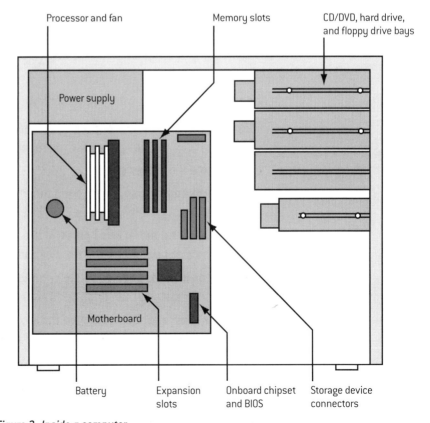

Figure 3 Inside a computer

When you open the case, you are likely to encounter:

◆ the **power supply** which serves power to the motherboard, drives and other devices you may have connected inside your computer

◆ **memory slots** for the cards that provide the systems main memory

◆ **drive bays** and device connectors for CD/DVD as well as hard and floppy drive systems, which provide the backing store

◆ the **motherboard** with **onboard chips** along with the **BIOS** and **battery**

◆ the **processor**, which will be connected to a **cooling fan**

◆ a variety of **expansion slots**, providing connections to various additional boards, video, USB, keyboard, mouse, serial and printer connectors.

Go out and try!

Read Unit 401 to discover how important it is to wear anti-static protection. Once protected, by wearing an anti-static wristband and with appropriate permission, open the computer you are using and compare the external and internal structure to Figures 2 and 3.

2.3 Installing and configuring various computer components

You may have had the opportunity to install a computer system at home, work or college. For most people this has been done by others; if incorrect assumptions are made, without knowledge of what is required, this can cause problems for the computer as well as the user.

2.3.1 Position of equipment

The placing of computer equipment is important. Poor placement can have a harmful effect on the user, or cause a major inconvenience in the use of the computer system.

When installing a computer system you must consider these factors:

◆ Are the monitor, mouse and keyboard accessible?

◆ Is the layout ergonomic?

◆ Is there too much glare on the monitor?

◆ Can the monitor be seen by all of those who need to? And no one else?

What does it mean?

Ergonomics: The applied science of equipment design and layout to improve our comfort through use.

It is no good having a computer that cannot be reached. Making sure that someone can gain access to a computer and have room to use the keyboard and mouse is very important. If there is too little space for the mouse, it becomes almost impossible to use Windows successfully.

Having the monitor at the right height and distance from the user when they are seated, combined with the keyboard at the correct height, creates an environment that is comfortable to use. So long as the seating is comfortable, and there is reasonable desk space, then the user is protected from RSI, joint issues or back injury.

What does it mean?

RSI: Repetitive strain injury, which is caused by poor use of keyboards when completing repetitive tasks.

Using **ergonomics**, you can carefully position a computer to suit the user.

When installing a computer at someone's desk, you must consider these factors (Figure 4).

◆ Ensure that the user's head has a comfortable line of sight with the monitor.

◆ Ensure that the keyboard/mouse is in a comfortable position.

◆ Ensure that the seating is comfortable and provides appropriate back support.

Figure 4 Ergonomics

Monitor glare is the single greatest cause of frustration and eye strain. Ensuring that the monitor screen is positioned away from windows or a strong light source makes the screen easier to read and therefore easier to use.

Many monitors are not for solo use. They may be part of a public access terminal, a demonstration station or in an environment where it is likely that more than one person may wish to view the screen at any given time. Having the monitor cramped in a corner is of no use, nor is having it turned away from the viewer. When installing any computer equipment, enquire as to how many people may be using the system and discuss with the user where the ideal position would be.

2.3.2 Supply of electricity

All computers need electricity. The position of the computer is totally dependent on distance and accessibility to a power outlet.

When fitting a computer, and connecting it to a power supply, you cannot:

◆ leave trailing wires, as this will pose a trip hazard

◆ overload a single socket, as this is an electrical and fire hazard.

2.3.3 Environmental conditions

Long gone are the days when computer technology was restricted to air-conditioned environments. We have computers in our offices, living areas, bedrooms and anywhere else that is convenient.

But this does not mean that the technology is happy about the conditions that we subject it to. When installing computer systems we cannot place a computer in an environment that is hostile:

◆ Too **dusty**. Fine dust can compromise a wide range of systems.

◆ Too **hot**. The heat will damage the processing capability of the computer as well as affect the storage media.

◆ Too **cold**. Any moisture that forms on the computer circuitry due to the low temperatures will immediately damage the system when the temperature goes up.

◆ Too **magnetic**! High voltage equipment such as electricity generators will affect the entire computer system.

2.3.4 Failure to remove shipping protection devices

Printers have many moving parts that have to be protected in transit. Most protection comes in the form of tapes and small plastic baffles. When fitting this type of equipment you will find that the manufacturer has provided a guide to the removal of such protection. If you forget to remove any you will find that your printer may:

◆ not print

◆ print rubbish

◆ break as the shipping protection has caused an inappropriate jam in the system.

2.3.5 Faulty connecting cables

Brute force and ignorance are the common causes of cable damage. Occasionally you may find that the manufacturer has provided either the wrong cable or one that has become damaged in some way.

Check that plug A will fit comfortably into slot A without any force. If the connector does not fit, gently check the connection and look at any pins for possible damage.

2.4 Specific safety factors to consider

If there is a dangerous way to do it, then be sure that someone will manage to do it that way!

Refer to Unit 401 for the section on **manual handling**. Lifting computers, especially monitors, can be hazardous to you (or others if you drop the monitor). If you don't adopt a safe lifting position, you can cause back, shoulder or arm injury.

All computers pose an **electrical hazard**. The power supply, if handled inappropriately, can produce an electric shock. Do not use damaged cables or faulty sockets and do not overload an electrical outlet. Also, never attempt to open a monitor or tamper with a laser printer as the potential voltage is lethal. An electrical surge is more likely to damage the computer but, for some people, a shock of as little as 12 volts can induce a heart attack. This also applies to **electrostatic hazards**. You have to ensure that anyone handing the equipment is suitably grounded and is using electrostatic bags to store any components.

The **position of equipment** can be very dangerous. If a monitor or a base unit is precariously balanced or the support is not strong enough to maintain the weight of the equipment, accidents will happen. Unless the support is a professional office desk or one that has been specifically designed to hold a computer or monitor, do not use it.

If the **routing of cables** has been done badly, e.g. if they are running across the floor or walkways, then every health and safety legislation imaginable has been broken. Ensure the cable is:

◆ running behind work areas
◆ inserted into cable trays or conduits
◆ running under the floor
◆ inserted into cable mats
◆ if temporary, stuck down with sufficient gaffer tape.

Keeping equipment ventilated ensures that you can enjoy the maximum working life available. At the back of current computers are gaps for two fans:

one for the power supply and the other for the base unit. These fans are used to cool the system, which means that if the back is blocked in any way then the computer system will overheat. If you have to set up a system where the base unit is locked in a cupboard (common for Internet cafes), it is worth advising the customer that the cupboard needs a ventilation hole, with an extraction fan (if possible).

Check your understanding

Using the environment that you work or study in, identify an area where there are more than 15 computers in use.

◆ What cabling hazards are apparent? If there are none, what has been done to prevent this?
◆ What issues may there be with ventilation of the computers?
◆ Are there any electrical hazards? How are they dangerous?
◆ Are any computers or monitors badly positioned? Are there any health and safety issues with respect to this?

Now, stop and think!

◆ How could you improve this area?
◆ What changes could you make without incurring any costs (or as few as possible)?

Working with computers, you may encounter three-phase power. Three-phase power has many uses from devices such as computers to welders, transformers, technical applications, ovens, fridges, and just about anything else you can imagine being powered by electricity.

Three-phase is a much more smooth form of electricity than normal mains. It is this more consistent electrical power that allows the machines that use it to run more efficiently and last many years longer than machines running on the other phases.

This is achieved by your employer ensuring that the mains supply to your server/communications room has a different power supply from the ordinary mains system.

2.5 Step-by-step guide to building a computer

Building a computer has become a routine task. With the correct preparation and experience, a professional can assemble a complete system in less than twenty minutes. As this is not a race and the components you are installing will be costly, take your time! No one will be thanked for breaking equipment.

The first task is to source the components and make sure that you can buy the best for the best price.

This will be completed as an exercise. You will use the shopping list in Table 1, which reflects the array of computer technology described in Section 4 of this unit.

PRACTICAL TASK

Shopping for a computer

Follow the links to an online computer parts store from www.heinemann.co.uk/hotlinks, using Table 1 as a shopping list (this is normally referred to as a check list of components). Source appropriate components at the lowest possible price so that you can specify an entry level system. You must ensure that the motherboard and processor are compatible and that the motherboard supports the memory you have acquired.

Table 1 Computer components shopping list

Component	Specification	Cost	Manufacturer
ATX case	Must cost no more than £20		
Motherboard	Must support an AMD processor and have onboard AGP, MODEM, sound and network card		
Processor	With an AMD Athlon or Duron (or whatever the current equivalent product is) at the lowest possible speed		
Memory	Must be at least 256 Mb and be compatible with the motherboard		
DVD-ROM	Obtain the lowest cost device		
CD writer	Obtain the lowest cost device		
Floppy disk drive	Must cost less than £6		
Hard disk drive	Must be IDE and cost less than £60. (What is the largest capacity you can obtain?)		
Monitor	Must be a 17-inch CRT and cost less than £80		
Speakers or headphones	Must cost no more than £5		
Mouse	Must be a standard ball mouse and have a scrolling wheel and cost less than £2		
Keyboard	Standard 105 keys and cost less than £4		
		TOTAL	

Once completed, total the cost of your specification.

◆ Did it cost less than £300? If so, by how much?

◆ Could you have made a greater saving?

Go back to the online store and look at the cost of Windows XP as an operating system. How does this affect the price? What benefits would there be in installing Linux instead?

2.5.1 Preparation

Now that you have a check list, do you have the tools? The process of building (installing) computer systems is generally the same. Here you will be using standard tools.

- ☑ Size 1 Phillips screwdriver (the crosshead variety)
- ☑ Anti-static mat and wristband earthed
- ☑ A torx screwdriver (six spokes, rarely used but sometimes required)

2.5.2 Stages of building

You have the tools; you have the components; now you can build the system. Building a computer is a step-by-step process. Any failure means that you may need to replace the component.

It will be assumed that, at all stages, you are wearing an anti-static wristband and that the computer is on an anti-static mat. You will need to test the system, and this will be explored in more detail in Section 6 of this unit.

Step one

Remove the computer case from the box and remove the outer cover. You will find at least three screws on the back. Make sure that you have safely stored the screws.

Step two

Connect the motherboard to the computer. Be careful to ensure that the support struts are correctly installed, and that you do not overtighten the screws on the motherboard.

Most causes of motherboard failure at this stage are from motherboards making contact with the case and screws being so tight that the motherboard has bent, causing damage to the printed circuit board.

Connect the motherboard

Step three

Remove the processor's packaging and carefully insert the processor in the ZIF socket. Remember: no force must be used at any time and you must check that the pins are correctly lined up before inserting the processor.

What does it mean?

ZIF: Zero insertion force is the socket used to connect the processor to the motherboard.

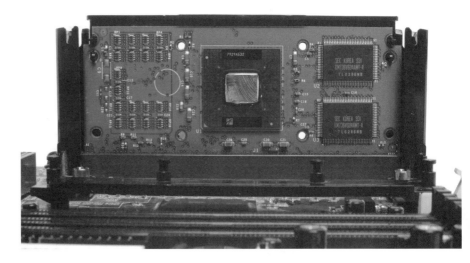

Processor being inserted

The motherboard manual will tell you what jumpers need to be set, according to the processor that you have installed (voltage and clock speed).

Step four

Add the memory to the motherboard. The number of slots you need to use will depend on the quantity purchased. The motherboard manual will tell you which slot is zero, and which is the first that you must use.

Step five

If you do not have an onboard graphics card, and you have elected to have an independent AGP card, add the card now.

Now you need to make your first check that the system is fine. Connect the ATX power plug from the power supply to the motherboard. Connect the monitor to the graphics card and connect all the external power cables.

Start the computer. You will now complete a simple **POST** (**power on self-test**) of the computer, and everything should be working if you:

◆ have a display

◆ the computer has completed a memory test.

Normally the boot process will stop at either keyboard or hard drive failure. This is fine as you haven't installed them yet!

There are two likely issues:

◆ No display caused by motherboard, graphics card or processor problems.

◆ No memory check because there are memory problems.

An important function that the BIOS carries out is to **boot up the system**. When the PC is first turned on, its main system memory is empty, and it needs to find instructions immediately to tell it what to run to start up the computer. These are found within the BIOS.

This process is referred to as **POST**. The BIOS will check all essential system components during boot up before handing over control to the processor.

As soon as you switch on your computer, a typical **boot sequence** involves these steps:

1 First the power from the power supply is checked. The power supply handles multiple voltages and so, if there is a problem, the system will be reset.

2 When the processor first starts up, it has no information. Therefore, it is configured to look for the BIOS software from the chip to start the POST. If there are any fatal errors, the boot process stops. If this happens, the computer will beep to let you know what is wrong (see Table 2).

3 The BIOS looks for the video card. In particular, it looks for the video card built-in BIOS program and runs it. The system BIOS executes the video card BIOS, which initialises the video card. Most cards will display information on the screen about the video card, and this can be seen at the very start of the boot up process.

4 The BIOS then looks for other devices' ROMs to see if any of them have BIOSs. This includes the hard drive.

5 The BIOS displays its start-up screen.

6 The BIOS completes more tests on the system, including the memory count-up test which can be seen on the screen.

7 The BIOS performs a 'system inventory', doing more tests to determine what sort of hardware is in the system. Modern BIOSs have many automatic settings and will determine memory timing (for example) based on what kind of memory it finds. Many BIOSs can also dynamically set hard drive parameters and access modes, and will determine these at

Table 2 *BIOS beep codes*	
American megatrends	
Number of beeps	**Issue**
1	Fault with system memory
2	Parity checking (fault checking) failure
3	Base memory issue
4	System timer failure
5	Processor failure
6	Keyboard controller
7	Mode failure
8	Display memory error
9	BIOS error
10	CMOS fault
11	Processor cache memory error
Continuous	Memory or video issue
Award/Phoenix	
Number of beeps	**Issue**
1 long beep	Memory issues
1 long then 2 short	Video error
Continuous	Memory or video issue

Please note that this varies through time and model and that you need to refer to the manufacturer's website for accurate information.

around this time. Some will display a message on the screen for each drive they detect and configure this way.

8 The BIOS will also now search for and label **logical devices** (serial and printer ports).

9 The BIOS now detects and configures **Plug and Play devices** and displays a message on the screen for each one it finds.

10 The BIOS will display a summary screen about your system's configuration. Reading this page of data can be helpful in diagnosing setup problems, although it can be hard to see because it may flash on the screen very quickly before scrolling off the top.

11 The BIOS begins the search for a drive to boot from. Most modern BIOSs contain a setting that controls if the system should first try to boot from the floppy disk (A:) or from the hard disk (C:). Also BIOSs will let you boot from your CD-ROM, ZIP drive, network card or flash memory.

12 Having identified its target boot drive, the BIOS looks for boot information to start the operating system boot process. If it is searching a hard disk, it looks for a master boot record at cylinder 0, head 0, sector 0 (the first sector on the disk); if it is searching a floppy disk, it looks at the same address on the floppy disk for a volume boot sector.

13 If it finds what it is looking for, the BIOS starts the process of booting the operating system, using the information in the boot sector. At this point, the operating system in the boot sector takes over from the BIOS.

14 If no boot device at all can be found, the system will display an error message and then freeze up the system.

Step six

You now need to connect the storage devices. Each has a supporting slot in the case and a connection in the motherboard. The primary hard drive from where you will boot the operating system is normally the master on the primary IDE. The BIOS will auto detect these devices (if you are using resources that are over three years old, you can get older BIOS to search for the hard drives).

When installing storage devices, you will need to follow nine possible steps.

1 Install the floppy disk drive in the case.

2 Connect the floppy disk drive to the 34-pin connector on the motherboard and the drive, ensuring that the red stripe is at pin 1.

3 Connect the power supply to the floppy disk drive.

4 Check that the jumper on the hard drive is set to master before installing it into the case.

5 Connect the primary hard drive to IDE 1 (or 0) ensuring that the red stripe is at pin 1.

6 Connect the power supply to the hard drive.

7 Connect the DVD/CD-ROM or CD-RW drives to the case.

8 If you have more than one, then the first will be the slave on IDE 1 (or 0) and the next the master on IDE 2 (or 1) and so on.

9 Connect the power supply to the DVD/CD-ROM or CD-RW drives.

Storage devices in computer case

Storage devices are constantly being improved and density and speed increase at almost the same speed as processor technology. For example, CD/DVD readers are getting faster and CD/DVD writers are also increasing their speeds. When CD technology started you could store 650 Mb; now a DVD has the potential of retaining 17 Gb of data.

It is the PC's **hard disk** (and floppy disk as well) that provides a **non-volatile**, mass storage medium and is the repository of a user's documents, files and applications. It's hard to comprehend that not so long ago 100 Mb of hard disk space was considered generous. Today, this would be totally inadequate, and hardly enough to install the operating system, let alone an application such as Microsoft *Office* XP.

The hard disk is a magnetic platter that is sealed in a semi-vacuum and read at high speeds by a head that floats microns above the surface of the platter.

Hard disks are rigid platters, made of aluminium alloy or a mixture of glass and ceramic, covered with a magnetic coating. The trend is towards glass technology; this has the better heat resistance properties and allows platters to be made thinner than aluminium ones. The inside of a hard disk drive must be kept as dust-free as the factory where it was built. To eliminate internal contamination, the platters are sealed in a case with the interior kept in a partial vacuum.

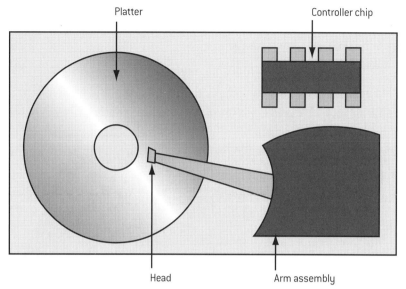

Platter

Controller chip

Head

Arm assembly

Figure 5 Inside a hard drive

A typical hard drive will have two or three or more platters stacked on top of each other with a common spindle that turns the whole assembly at several thousand revolutions per minute (5400, 7200 or 10,000). There is a small gap between the platters, making room for a read/write head, mounted on the end of an arm. This is so close to the platters that it's only the rush of air pulled round by the rotation of the platters that keeps the head away from the surface of the disk – it flies a fraction of a millimetre above the disk, landing gently on it when the drive is powered down (this is called the **Bernoulli effect**). A small particle of dirt could cause a head to 'crash', touching the disk and scraping off the magnetic coating, creating irrecoverable damage.

There's a read/write head for each side of each platter, mounted on arms which can move them towards the central spindle or towards the edge.

Each platter is double-sided and divided into tracks, which are concentric circles around the central spindle. Tracks physically above each other, and the platters are grouped together into cylinders which are then further subdivided into sectors (like slices of a cake).

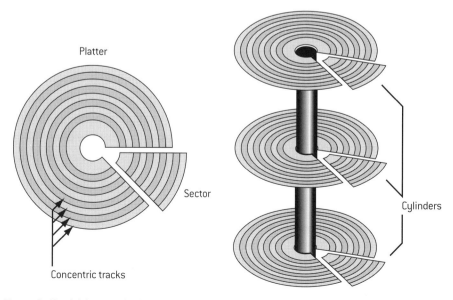

Platter

Sector

Concentric tracks

Cylinders

Figure 6 Hard drive terminology

A floppy disk is basically a junior hard disk drive, working on similar principles. It is a soft magnetic disk. It is called floppy because it 'flops' if you wave it (at least, the old $5\frac{1}{4}$-inch variety did).

Unlike hard disks, floppy disks (often called floppies or diskettes) are portable. Floppy disks have slower access than hard disks and have less storage capacity (1.44 Mb and 2 Mb max), but they are much less expensive.

Floppy disk and CD-ROM drive on a laptop

CD/DVD devices use very similar technology. The only differences are density and sensitivity. Compact disc-read-only memory is an optical disc capable of storing large amounts of data from mini-CDs with 210 Mb of data up to 800 Mb on a normal size disc. CD-ROMs are a 'write once, read many' (WORM) technology.

Apart from far more sophisticated error-checking techniques, the mechanism of a CD-ROM drive is the same as CD audio players. Data is stored in the same way on all CDs. Information is stored in sequential 2 Kb sectors that form a single spiral track that starts at the centre of the disc and wraps around many times until it reaches the outer edge of the disc.

A player reads information from the CD's spiral track, starting from the centre of the disc and moving to the outer edge. It does this by firing an infrared laser, 780 nanometres wide and generated by a small semiconductor. Although it's of very low power (laser class 1), it's strong enough to damage the eye if shined directly into it.

The media operates by the laser reading the light reflected off the disc. There are two areas called **pits** (1s) and **lands** (0s). The binary digits are measured based on the time taken for light to return to the reader from the original light being sent out (the speed of light is a constant).

CD technology has built-in error correction systems which are able to suppress most of the errors that arise from physical particles on the surface of a disc. Every CD-ROM drive and CD player in the world uses Cross Interleaved Reed-Solomon Code (CIRC) detection.

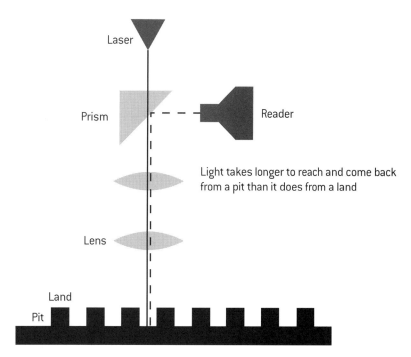

Figure 7 CD reading

CD-RW (CD-ReWritable) discs are a type of CD disc that enable you to write on to it in multiple sessions. One of the problems with CD-R discs is that you can only write to them once. With CD-RW drives and discs, you can treat the optical disc just like a floppy or hard disk, writing data onto it many times.

CD-writers operate at slower speeds than the readers. The medium is designed to retain the 'image' burnt onto it by a more intense laser beam.

DVD (digital versatile disc) is a more compact optical disc technology that is rapidly replacing the CD-ROM. The DVD holds 4.7 Gb of information on one of its two sides, or enough for a 133-minute movie. With two layers on each of its two sides, it will hold up to 17 gigabytes of video, audio, or other information. (Compare this to the current CD-ROM disc of the same physical size, holding 650 Mb. The DVD can hold more than 28 times as much information!)

Step seven

Do you have anything else to do? It is at this point you:

◆ connect the enclosure connectors according to the motherboard manual

◆ add any other cards you have chosen to install on your computer.

On the front of your computer, there is a hard drive activity light, a power status light and often a reset button. The motherboard has a series of pins that provide a connection between the case and the system.

A **jumper** is a small switch that allows you to configure the motherboard for the resources that are attached to it. A jumper is a series of pins that are connected by a small bridge, and the position of the bridge will indicate the type of system configuration you require.

A common use for jumpers is in the management of the processor. A motherboard can deal with a range of processors (from 1.4 GHz to 3.2 GHz) and various manufacturers' products (AMD or Intel). Each processor has a different bus speed and voltage, so you will configure the jumper to indicate which processor is on the motherboard.

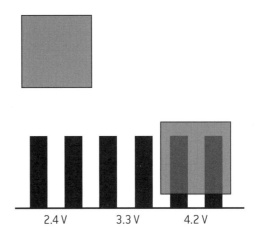

| 2.4 V | 3.3 V | 4.2 V |

Figure 8 Jumper settings

Go out and try!

With appropriate permission, open up your computer and establish what make of motherboard you have. Go to heinemann.co.uk/hotlinks and follow the links to a site that will help you to search for the guide for that motherboard and identify the various jumper settings on your system.

Step eight

Check that it all works, connect all the computer components to the mains and connect the keyboard and mouse. Then switch the computer on. If all is well, then the computer will go through the entire POST boot process until it discovers that there is no operating system installed.

If there are any problems at this point, check whether any storage devices from step six are faulty or connected incorrectly.

Step nine

Now for the operating system! Depending on your organisation's policies, you may connect the computer to a network port and use a ghost (or image cast) boot disc and download the operating system from a network server; or you may install the operating system from CD.

To install from CD, you will need to set the boot features in the BIOS. In the advanced menu, the boot order is normally hard drive then floppy drive then CD.

Change this so that the CD is the first device. (You will need to restore this setting on completion of this step.) Insert the CD and restart the computer.

For Microsoft products, as well as any other operating system, you will be provided with comprehensive instructions on the installation of the operating system. To ensure that this is completed successfully you will need to have:

◆ the serial number

◆ the name of the workstation that will be used by your organisation

◆ any workgroup or network addressing details. (You must get this from someone in a supervisor position though, normally, these will be in the guidance documentation.)

The operating system will detect all hardware and, where appropriate, will ask for the manufacturer's driver disc.

The computer will reboot, and the operating system will start. You will need to localise the system and configure:

◆ screen resolution

◆ colour depth

◆ keyboard locale

◆ local time

◆ local language.

Figure 9 Fully connected PC

2.5.3 Installing a computer that came in a box (or from elsewhere)

Building a computer system from 'scratch' is seldom done nowadays. Most organisations can obtain computers at a low cost because they buy the systems in bulk. They will often buy over 100 computers at a time to replace computers that have become out of date (over 3–4 years old). Companies can obtain new computers at 25% less than the retail price by using this purchasing process.

When presented with a pre-built computer system for installation, you will have:

◆ a monitor
◆ a keyboard
◆ a mouse
◆ power cables

- the processor base unit
- speakers and/or sound cables.

You will need to connect up the peripherals and test the system. This will be explored in more detail in Section 6 of this unit.

If the computer has come to you boxed, you will need to remove all the packaging, polystyrenes baffles and any bags. The safe process is to open the top of the box and turn the box upside down. The computer or monitor will slide out of the box easily using its own weight. Ensure that the waste is disposed of appropriately. Most organisations require that you keep the packaging until the computer is installed and then you dispose of the waste in an environmentally sound manner.

Using the guidance in Section 2.1 (position of equipment), you can then assemble the computer:

1 Seat the base unit in an appropriate location. If it is a tower unit, you could position this on the floor. If you have a desktop unit, you must ensure that wherever you place the unit, there is adequate space for the keyboard and comfort for the user viewing the monitor. The base unit must be near any network ports and in easy reach of a mains outlet. Also, the rear of the base unit must have adequate ventilation space so that the system can be kept as cool as possible.

2 The monitor must be at eye level height for the comfort of the user, and connected to the mains as well as to the base unit. If the monitor is a CRT system, the back must not be covered; this will cause the monitor to overheat.

3 Connect the keyboard and mouse, checking that they are in easy reach of the user. Don't forget the user may be left handed; make sure that they are comfortable. This will mean that you should ask the user to sit at the system and to advise you.

4 Configure the operating system. You may need to:
   - calibrate the mouse
   - set the keyboard speed
   - adjust the screen resolution/colour depth
   - set locale
   - install any applications that the user requires
   - configure any additional user features (disability settings, etc.)
   - apply the organisation's security policies, user login etc.

2.5.4 Why do I need to keep a record of the installation process?

When building a computer or simply installing it for the customer, you need to keep an accurate record of the installation process:

◆ as a reference for the future. If the computer system has any faults, this record can be used to prove (or disprove) the case

◆ as documentation that a supervisor/manager can refer to if you encounter a problem for which you need assistance.

A normal record will contain:

◆ each of the steps in installation

◆ the hardware and software installed

◆ any issues encountered and solutions rendered

◆ any settings implemented for the user

◆ all software installed

◆ any configuration of the hardware or the operating system.

PRACTICAL TASK

Using the steps in building and installing a computer system, create a suitable check list that will provide you with an accurate record of the process involved. Make sure that the check list is comprehensive and covers every task in detail.

Then use your check list on at least three installations.

◆ Did you find that this check list helped you?

◆ What could you do to improve the check list so that it is easier to use?

---

3 Testing installed components

To solve any problem during any installation, or during the lifecycle of a computer system, you will need to test a variety of components to ensure that they are working to specification or troubleshoot a perceived issue.

This is done to ensure that the computer system is working correctly and as a quality control process to prove to the customer that the system they are using or purchasing is satisfactory.

3.1 **Test plans and reports**

Professionals may work with two important documents when testing computer hardware and software:

◆ The test plan.
◆ The test report.

The **test plan** outlines the strategy that you will take when approaching a problem or when you are testing a computer for performance. (This is often seen as **preventive maintenance**; see Section 4 of Unit 401.)

Many problems or performances tests involving computer systems are commonplace, so you may find that there are already test plans in place that you can follow.

A test plan will contain information on:

◆ the problem or test type
◆ any other possible symptoms and other tests that may need to be performed
◆ possible causes
◆ tools and other resources that may be required
◆ steps that must be taken to identify causes with possible solutions.

Below is a sample test plan for benchmarking a computer during a routine annual check. This is followed by a test plan to use if the display of a computer system stops responding.

Widgets R'Us Systems Support Division TEST PLAN No. 104 **Benchmarking** Step	
1.	Shut down all applications and utilities that may be running on the computer system.
2.	Start benchmarking application.
3.	Select comprehensive test.
4.	Allow test to run to completion.
5.	Save copy of report on floppy disk and print a copy of the report for records.
6.	Compare report to previous report on record.
7.	List all differences below and report to line supervisor.

A test plan for benchmarking a computer

Widgets R'Us Systems Support Division TEST PLAN No. 28

Troubleshooting

Step

1.	Is there a light on the front of the monitor?	YES/NO
2.	Is the monitor connected to the mains and is the mains switched on (remember that there is normally an on/off switch on the monitor itself)?	YES/NO
3.	Is the monitor signal cable connected to the computer?	YES/NO
4.	Do the horizontal and vertical controls on the display require adjusting?	YES/NO
5.	Is the computer switched on?	YES/NO
6.	Is the brightness or contrast on the monitor turned down?	YES/NO
7.	Does another monitor work on the computer?	YES/NO
8.	Will the POST screen display?	YES/NO
9.	If Windows boots a. Is the display distorted? b. Is the colour density adequate?	YES/NO YES/NO

A test plan for troubleshooting the display

PRACTICAL TASK

Looking at the examples above, create test plans for:

◆ identifying whether a computer has a virus infection (use the section on preventive maintenance in Unit 401)

◆ checking hard drive performance

◆ dealing with a possible keyboard fault.

Your test plans must be comprehensive and be able to guide someone else in your class to carry out the test without your personal intervention.

The **test report** provides you, your successor (the person who takes over the job from you), the customer (the user in most cases) and your supervisor with a comprehensive breakdown of the work you have completed and the outcomes you have discovered.

Most organisations use test reports to:

◆ communicate issues or, sometimes, the lack of issues (everything is fine)
◆ identify common faults that may be reoccurring
◆ provide evidence in the case of legal action, pursuit of warranty (where a supplier has to provide a replacement) or provision of support for a user who may be causing the issue.

As the test report is read by many and can be used in legal proceedings, you have to be careful about what you write. If there is an issue, you must try to make the negative a positive, and all problems seem like opportunities.

So statements like these may appear:

◆ the user may appreciate some specialist training and support on the use of the system
◆ the equipment is faulty and may need to be referred to the manufacturer
◆ the equipment appears to be incompatible with a specific element of our system
◆ the technology has now been superseded and a suitable replacement is required.

The test report for most organisations will include important information:

◆ What the test was and why it was required.
◆ Any faults found.
◆ Solution provided, if required.
◆ Resources used.
◆ Constructive feedback to user.
◆ Constructive feedback to manager/supervisor.
◆ Date/time of test.

Below is a sample test report.

Computer /System tested	Finance/Ms Jayne Parr
Date	30/01/2004
Time	14:50
Name of tester	Will S Spear
Signature	WillSpear
Fault/issue as reported by customer	
Computer not starting	
Tests carried out	
POST check Power check Monitor check	
Results and likely outcomes	
Monitor faulty, no power, no display	
Recommendations/solution	
Monitor replaced, faulty monitor sent for warranty repair	
Reported to	Mr Marr
Resources required	
Monitor taken from stores	

A test report

PRACTICAL TASK

Looking at the example above, create test reports for:

◆ identifying whether a computer has a virus infection (use the section on preventive maintenance in Unit 401)

◆ checking hard drive performance

◆ dealing with a possible keyboard fault.

Your test reports must be comprehensive and provide someone else with an understanding of the work you have done.

Missing a test can be the weak link in the system that eventually leads to failure. Being prepared to be systematic and methodical is routine but essential.

In testing any new installation you will need to do lots of tests:

◆ Are all connectors correctly connected, internally and externally? Check each device is connected and that there is a mains connection to the computer system.

◆ Is the display working correctly, and the resolution adequate for the monitor and the applications that are going to be used on the system? Also check that the colour depth is correct as some systems may need 32-bit rather than 24-bit colour quality.

◆ Are the processor and memory performing adequately? Is all the memory available (apart from that which is reserved for system tasks) and is the processor able to offer optimal performance?

◆ Is the hard drive performing adequately? Are there no issues with the storage media?

◆ Is the operating system performing as expected? Are there no issues that prevent the user from being able to use the system successfully?

◆ Are all applications installed working as expected? Is the user able to carry out work as required on the system?

An **installation check list** (sometimes called a **check sheet**) is used for you to carry out this task as a guarantee that the system is performing properly. Below is an example of such a check list.

Task	Completed ✔
Components checked and appear to be in good working order	
Tools checked and appear to be in good working order	
Base unit for installation checked and appears to be in good working order	
No damage to packaging or protective wrapping	
Anti-static wristband and mat earthed and in good working order	
After system is installed (this may be operating system, computer build or the installation of hardware component) the computer successfully completes the POST boot-up process	

Installation check list

PRACTICAL TASK

Using a copy of the installation check list, carry out at least three installations and complete the check list to prove that the systems are working as expected. Ask your tutor or supervisor to confirm that the tasks are completed as expected.

3.2 Use various tools and applications to check your installation

There are many methods that can be employed to check that the system you have installed is working correctly. This is another area where the disciplines of preventive maintenance and installation overlap (see Unit 401, Section 4).

Likely tasks that you may have to complete on installation include:

◆ file check
◆ registry check
◆ anti-virus scan
◆ disk scan
◆ system tune up or benchmarking.

The **file check** can be a misnomer in that it implies that you have to check that all important system files are in place before the system is used. Most operating systems have an annoying habit of 'not working' if any important files are missing.

Many organisations require that you install system-special files that allow the system to work effectively within the organisation. This may be document templates, system files, small applications or utilities, etc. To ensure that all is in order with an operating system such as Microsoft Windows, it is worthwhile using *Explorer* to check the following folders:

◆ C:\Windows
◆ C:\Windows\system
◆ C:\I386 (for Windows 2000 and XP)
◆ C:\program files.

PRACTICAL TASK

With appropriate permission, complete a file check on at least three computers.

As described in Unit 401, the registry is a database (of sorts) used by Windows to record the settings for all system hardware and software. Once the system is installed to your satisfaction, you can perform a simple test called the **registry check** to see that the registry is intact.

Click on Start/Run
Enter 'scanregw'

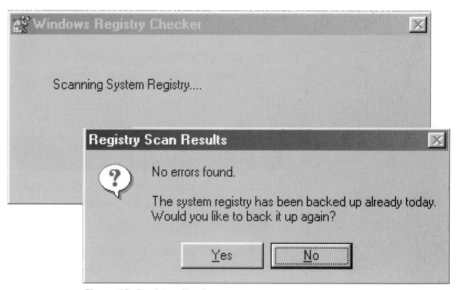

Figure 10 Registry Checker

If there are any faults with the registry, the utility will notify you and then attempt to repair the registry keys.

PRACTICAL TASK

With appropriate permission, complete a registry check on at least three computers.

Also in Unit 401 you had the opportunity to install anti-virus software and complete a comprehensive scan of the system. Completing an **anti-virus scan** on installation and on the installation media is not as ridiculous as it seems.

◆ Many operating systems are adapted to an organisation's needs and the process of creating an adapted version could have allowed a virus in.

◆ As soon as a new operating system installation is connected to a network, it will 'broadcast' its presence. This is an open invitation for network-based

Trojans and worms to infect your unprotected system. It happened with a DCOM vulnerability in late 2003.

To protect your computer adequately on installation, you must ensure that it has a **firewall** to stop attacks taking place, before you install and run an anti-virus system.

PRACTICAL TASK

Revisit the practical tasks in Unit 401. Ensure that the firewall and anti-virus software are suitably installed and complete a full virus scan of the system after you have updated your anti-virus database.

Write a test plan for these tasks and complete a test report for the work you have done.

Running a **hard disk scan** at installation will not improve the performance of your computer. As there is little software on the system, and because the system has not been extensively used, there will be no fragmentation issues with the hard drive due to prolonged use, in comparison to what you are likely to find when you are completing preventive maintenance on your computer system.

The sole reason for completing a disk scan at installation is to identify if there are any faults with the surface of the hard drive. To achieve, this you need to use both Scandisk and Defrag.

PRACTICAL TASK

Following the practical task on page 127, complete a comprehensive Scandisk and Defrag on the system you have installed. Write a test plan for this and complete a test report for the work you have done.

For older systems, such as Windows 98, you needed to perform a regular **system tune up** or **benchmarking** to ensure that the system was running at ideal performance. This was done by using the Hardware Maintenance Wizard.

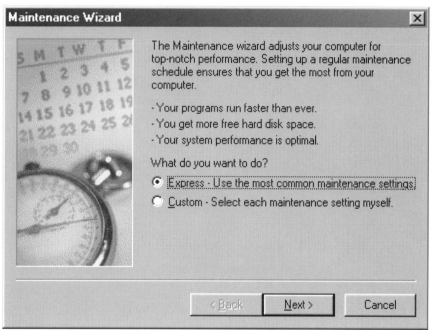

Figure 11 *The Windows 98 Hardware Maintenance Wizard*

In operating systems like Windows 2000 and XP, the system tune-up is continuous and it is completed by the system on boot as well as during operation. The best hardware maintenance you can complete is to use a benchmarking tool such as *FreshDiagnose* to measure the performance of your computer system (see Unit 401, Section 4, page 69).

PRACTICAL TASK

Following the practical task on page 69, complete a comprehensive benchmark for the system you have installed. Write a test plan for this and complete a test report for the work you have done.

Go out and try!

Windows XP will tidy away unused desktop items for you as part of the continuous system tune-up. Create a shortcut on your desktop (right-click on your desktop as in Figure 12) and make sure that you do not use it.

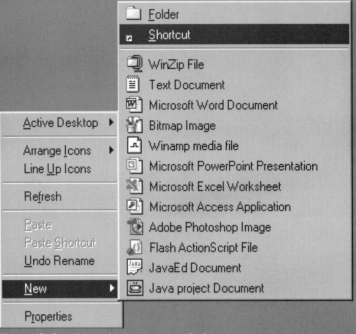

Figure 12 Creating a shortcut on your desktop

How many days elapse before Windows XP removes the icon and places it in a folder called Unused desktop items?

CASE STUDY

You have been working at Widgets R' Us for over 18 months and have the opportunity for promotion to team leader. With this role comes the responsibility for system testing and quality assurance.

The interview goes well and you are now short-listed with one other candidate. As a 'decider', the interviewing panel ask you to create a 15-minute presentation using *PowerPoint*, which will address these topics:

◆ The purpose behind testing hardware after installation.

◆ The purpose behind testing hardware in response to a customer problem.

◆ What would be done if the results obtained from testing were different from those expected?

◆ What are common hardware issues with a personal computer system?

◆ What are the benefits of maintaining test reports and providing test plans?

Tips for a good *PowerPoint* presentation

◆ Prepare no more than two slides on any one subject.

◆ Use sentences, not paragraphs.

◆ Remember: if the subject bores you, it will most certainly bore the audience. Without being silly, try to liven it up.

◆ Make sure your voice is clear and easy to understand (speak to the back of the room).

◆ Do not read from the screen. Maintain eye contact and connect with the audience.

◆ Use understated colours. Bright, garish presentations tend to annoy an audience.

◆ Practise beforehand and time the presentation.

◆ Print out the slides as a handout. (Some people may not be able to see the screen for various reasons.)

---

4 Installing or upgrading an operating system

4.1 What is an operating system and how does it work?

The operating system provides the connection between you, the user, and the technology.

4.1.1 Types of operating systems

The type of operating system depends on the technology and the purpose.

◆ Windows is a **disk operating system,** whose primary purpose is file and device management.

◆ **Real-time operating systems** are used for defence and control-based systems.

◆ **Network operating systems** provide services to many other computers or users across a network.

◆ **Cluster operating systems** concentrate on sharing processing power.

◆ **Multi-user operating** systems focus on many users sharing the processing power of one resource.

◆ **Dedicated operating systems** are used on PDAs (personal digital assistants), etc.

Microsoft Windows is not the only operating system product available. There are many systems and many versions available (and many of them are free):

◆ Windows XP for home or professional use
◆ Windows 2000 and 2003 server products
◆ Windows CE for PDAs
◆ The Novell, Netware server product family
◆ Linux (there are many flavours, each with its own advantages)
◆ Unix for multi-user systems
◆ Sun Microsystems, Solaris 9
◆ Mac OS X, for the Apple platform
◆ QNX for dedicated real-time systems
◆ Free-BSD.

Go out and try!

Follow the links from www.heinemann.co.uk/hotlinks to help you find this information:

1 How many versions of Linux are available? What does each of them offer?
2 Compare the NetWare system to Windows 2003.
3 Download a copy of the Knoppix operating system and follow the instructions to burn it onto a CD and boot your computer up using Knoppix. You will find that Knoppix has in a CD image all the same software as Windows.

4.1.2 The structure of a modern operating system

Each operating system is structured differently. This section gives an informal overview as to what you may expect to encounter in an operating system's components.

Table 3 **Operating system components**

You the user			
Graphical user interface			
Connection to underlying operating system, using system administrative tools	Applications and utilities		
	Clipboard	Application program interface	Object linking and embedding control
	System database (Registry)	Device drivers	Dynamic link libraries
	Drive and file management via *Explorer*	Hardware management	Communication management via kernel
PC hardware			

As you are the user, the operating system has to be designed to work with you. Apart from the **GUI (graphical user interface)**, this will include the mouse, monitor and keyboard.

Connection to underlying operating systems, using **system administrative tools,** is provided through the Settings menu in Windows, allowing you to configure the operating system as well as manage the hardware and other resources.

While you use **applications** and **utilities**, such as *Office* and anti-virus software, they provide **services** that depend on the operating system and sometimes (like anti-virus software) support the operating system, thus providing an essential additional service.

Moving data between applications is an essential resource. The **clipboard** is an area of memory managed by your operating system so that you can copy and paste material from one application to another.

Each application uses common system resources, like Save, Open File and Print; the **application program interface (API)** provides the code so that programmers working for the software house writing the application software do not need to know how to control the file system or device and communication management for the printer.

No single application sits alone any more. **Object linking and embedding control** allows the applications that you are using to link with other applications resources. This enables you to:

◆ use *Word* to create hyperlinks to websites

◆ include an *Excel* spreadsheet in a *Word* document

◆ import an MP3 into a *Flash* multimedia movie.

and much more!

To maintain a record of all system configurations, hardware, device resources etc the operating system keeps a **system database** which is called the **registry** in Microsoft Windows.

No operating system could possibly contain every possible instruction to manage every possible device that may be added to the system. On installation, a hardware manufacturer provides the operating system with an unique series of commands called a **device driver** that provides Windows with the resources to manage the component. Windows has many default drivers contained in **dynamic link libraries (DLLs)**, of which there are many in use.

Windows *Explorer* is a core element of the Windows operating system for **hard drive and file management**. In other operating systems, like Linux, this is KDE or Gnome. *Explorer* provides an interface between the hard drive's own management system and keeps control over the movement or deletion of files.

Hardware management is done as part of the operating system **kernel** which manages communication between all the different elements of the computer system. This links all the higher layers which can be accessed by the user to the underlying PC hardware.

4.2 Installing/upgrading an operating system

In Section 4.1 of this unit you had the opportunity to discover the structure and processes involved in the operation of an operating system. Whilst operating systems serve many purposes, the installation process for them all tends to be very similar, with minor refinements according to the task specified for the operating system or a local organisational variation.

Like computer hardware, operating systems are under continuous development. As you are reading this section, Microsoft is working on their latest product and the Linux community are enhancing their own operating systems.

You normally need to upgrade your operating system every three years to remain current and be able to access the latest developments. There are two principal reasons why you may need to update your operating system:

◆ you have installed new hardware that is incompatible with your current operating system

◆ you need to run an application that will not work with your current operating system.

As operating systems are developed, newer systems need more resources than their predecessors. You must consider and confirm the following issues before any installation or upgrade:

◆ Does the system have enough memory (RAM)? The new operating system will occupy more system memory space.

◆ Is there adequate storage space on the hard drive? Remember that you have the operating system, space for applications, space for files/data and space for any virtual memory.

◆ Can the processor cope? Newer operating systems, in their quest for new resources, crave greater processing power.

◆ Can it manage the various devices that are connected to the computer or part of the system bus on the motherboard? Technologies such as USB and firewire, as well as different processors and printers, can cause operating system problems.

Normally, when you install an upgraded operating system, this is done on a new computer as the incompatibility between hardware and software is problematic.

What does it mean?

Virtual memory: A file that acts as a temporary memory area on your computer's hard drive.

PRACTICAL TASK

On your computer, find out the size of space occupied by the Windows directory. This can be done by right-clicking on the icon and selecting Properties as in Figure 13.

Figure 13 Size of the Windows directory

Find out how system resources are being used by your current operating system. (Use Start/Run, and then type in MSINFO32.)

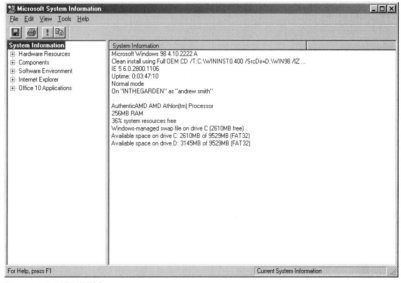

Figure 14 MSINFO32

Go out and try!

Operating systems have a lowest processor speed at which they can operate, and this is openly declared by the manufacturers. Using the Internet as your research tool (or ask your tutor) find out the lowest specification for:

◆ Windows 95

◆ Windows 98

◆ Windows 2000

◆ Windows XP

◆ Red Hat Linux.

Before you complete the installation of the operating system, you may wish to **back up** the contents of the hard drive. Why is this?

◆ The installation may go wrong and you may be forced to wipe the installation and roll back to the previous operating system.

◆ The system contains valuable corporate or personal data that will be lost on installation of an operating system.

PRACTICAL TASK

In Unit 401, creating backups was discussed as a measure used in preventive maintenance. Using the skills that you learnt in this section, create essentials backups of:

◆ the Windows directory

◆ the Program files directory

◆ the Document and Settings folder (or My Documents).

It is common practice in many schools, colleges, organisations and homes to repeatedly install the operating system using one copy of the installation media. Unless you are in possession of appropriate software licensing, this is illegal.

Infringement of software licensing is an infringement of copyright in UK Law and can incur penalties:

◆ imprisonment, when it is proved that you have made criminal gain from software duplication

◆ fine, for the multiple use of a single licence as well as the legal costs of the software manufacturer that has brought the claim

◆ removal of all equipment that has been involved in the process of copyright infringement, i.e. your computer, the network server or in extreme cases the entire system at work or your place of study.

Large software manufacturers employ aggressive legal teams dedicated to tackling companies, organisations and individuals that breach copyright.

Go out and try!

Visit www.bbc.co.uk and search on the term 'Software Copyright'. Read what the news service has to report about software copyright.

There are many types of software licensing available for operating systems, applications and utilities. You must decide which is appropriate for your installation.

- **Freeware** is software that is completely free. Most of this software can be acquired from sites such as downloads.com, or from the creator's website. Freeware is normally for personal, not corporate, use and rarely comes with any support. Linux is an example of a freeware operating system. Winamp is an example of a freeware application.

- **Shareware** has many definitions but, for the purpose of this course, it is where an application is distributed freely for a limited trial period or is shared with features missing (i.e. the user cannot print any product created with an application). Shareware is often a vehicle used by software manufacturers to promote their products. An example is Macromedia who offer their applications on a 30-day trial.

- **Single user** is a version of software for installation on a single machine. A common misconception is that single user allows you to install it on more than one computer. You can only use one instance of the software at any given time; to use it on several single machines requires a **concurrent licence**.

- **Multi-user** means having enough licences for more than one user. For example, an organisation could have multi-user licences for 50 users of Microsoft *Office* to cover all employees. Multi-user can also refer to server systems; then there is a limit on the number of people that can simultaneously access a system.

- **Corporate**, **campus** or **site licence** are dependent on the software manufacturer and the organisation that requires the licence. Corporate licensing requires that a company pays an annual fee to the software manufacturer so that they can use as many copies of the software as required (without being concerned that they are infringing copyright) and be able to obtain the latest version of the software.

To ensure that the software house or manufacturer does not send the unfriendly legal team, it is important that you complete the appropriate **software registration card** or corporate documentation and submit this information to the software house/manufacturer or to your supervisor.

BUSINESS REPLY SERVICE
Licence No: SW23296

2

SOFTWARE MEDIA INC

PO Box 123
Bedford
MK45 7AL

Thank you for buying this application. To ensure that we can provide comprehensive warranty support, please complete this card and return it to Software Media Inc. (No stamp required if posted within the UK.)

Title   Name

Job title

Company

Address

                                                         Postcode

Country

Email

Date of purchase/installation

Figure 15 Example software registration card

In many cases, you can **register online** by visiting the manufacturer's website, phone a **registration free phone hot line** or send your organisational information to a specialist email address.

Some manufacturers will prevent you from using the software until you send them your personal information. They will then issue an application serial number or email you a piece of software that will unlock the application or operating system.

PRACTICAL TASK

Design a form that keeps a record of all instances of Microsoft *Office* installed at your centre. On this form, ensure that you include:

◆ date installed

◆ version of application

◆ serial number or identity of computer upon which the software is installed

◆ location of computer.

When installing operating system software you must consider system security. Most systems have predefined security policies that you must adhere to when you add a new system:

◆ preventing the user from having local administrative rights, thus preventing them from being able to install software on the computer or changing various system settings

◆ ensuring that the computer has a client that synchronises with a network server so that system access policies are sent to the local computer

◆ applying workgroup and addressing policies that provide the computer with access to network and Internet resources.

All of this information will be provided by your supervisor and is not left to your own personal decision.

4.2.1 Installing an operating system

To install an operating system, you must ensure that you have the following resources:

◆ a licensed CD of the operating system (such as Windows 2000 Professional)

◆ a computer with a working CD/DVD-ROM drive

◆ a copy of the licence key.

Here we will install Windows 2000 Professional.

What does it mean?

Licence key is the serial number used to install the software. This is normally a mathematically generated number that will only work with your operating system disk. A licence key for Windows 2000 could be QWASD-2YBGH-WERD2-JG6GH-22BCD.

Your employer may require you to install the operating system from a pre-configured image using applications like Norton *Ghost*. This involves downloading from the network the completed configuration.

Go out and try!

Follow the links from www.heinemann.co.uk/hotlinks and identify what advantages using an application like Norton *Ghost* could offer a large computer manufacturer.

Before you install the operating system, you will need to reboot the computer and during the first 10 seconds of the boot process, enter the BIOS configuration utility. This will depend on the version of BIOS and may require you to press F2 or Del.

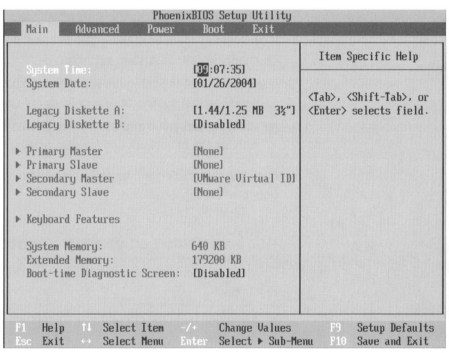

Figure 16 The BIOS

Once you are in the BIOS you need to change the boot settings to make sure that the CD-ROM is the first device in the boot sequence. Then the BIOS will not attempt to load any existing operating system(s) that may be on the hard drive.

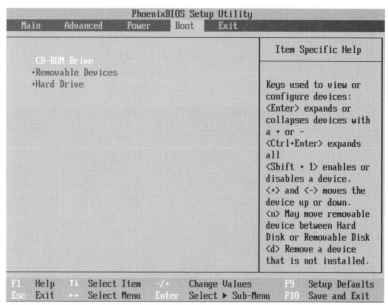

Figure 17 Setting the CD-ROM to boot

After you have completed this you need to make sure that the BIOS has saved the new settings.

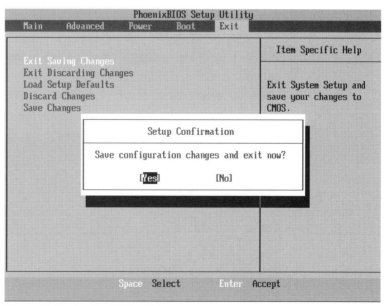

Figure 18 Saving the BIOS settings

Now the computer should restart and the BIOS POST process will load the installation system from the CD-ROM. Make sure that the CD is in the CD Drive!

The Windows 2000 setup system will automatically start and may spend three minutes loading a variety of applications from the CD. Once this has been completed you will be presented with a choice.

◆ To repair a damaged installation: Windows 2000 will replace any lost or damaged key files but it is worth noting that this can be unreliable

◆ or to install a new operating system from scratch.

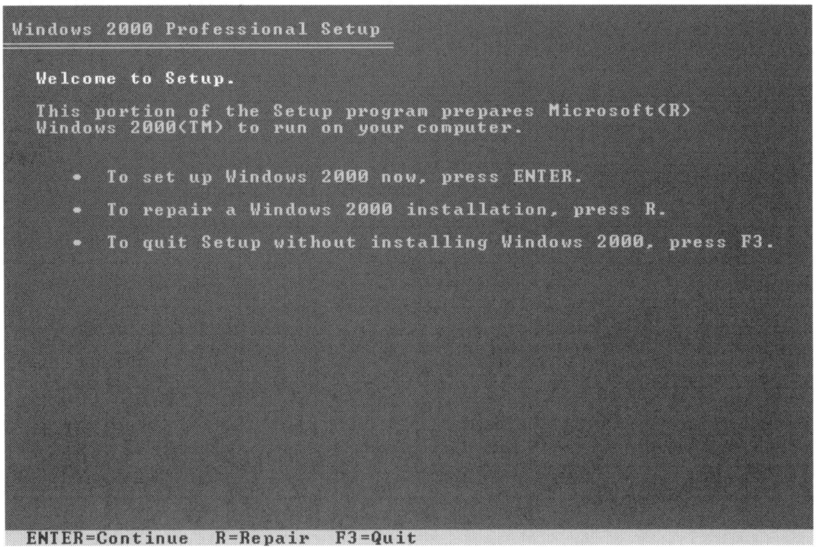

Figure 19 Install or repair

For this exercise, press Enter to install.

The next screen to appear is the **EULA** (**end-user licence agreement**). You cannot avoid this and must press F8 to acknowledge that you have no intention of copying or distributing Windows 2000. This means that Microsoft can sue you for breach of copyright if you make copies.

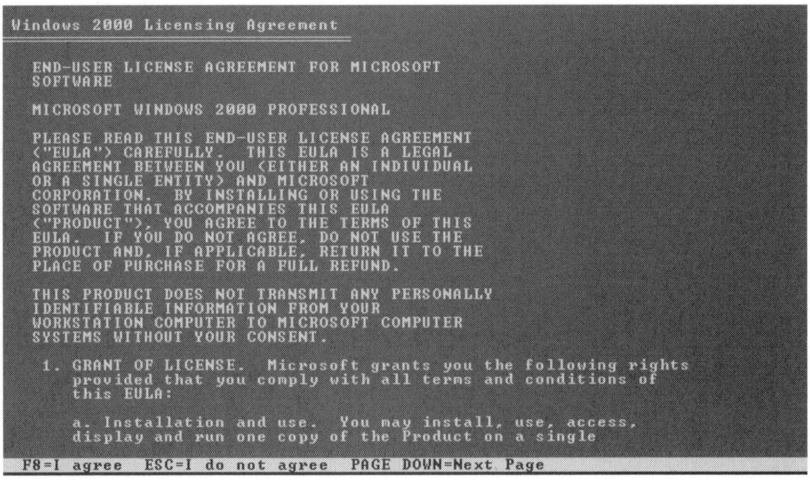

Figure 20 EULA

Press F8 to continue.

Next, you are presented with the opportunity to partition your hard drive.

Partitioning is a technique where you can split your hard drive into smaller units that act as if they are separate hard drives. This allows you to have more than one operating system in existence on one hard drive.

Normally you would not partition a hard drive unless you are installing Windows 2000 on a computer whose hard drive has never been used before (or has been repartitioned to remove data etc.).

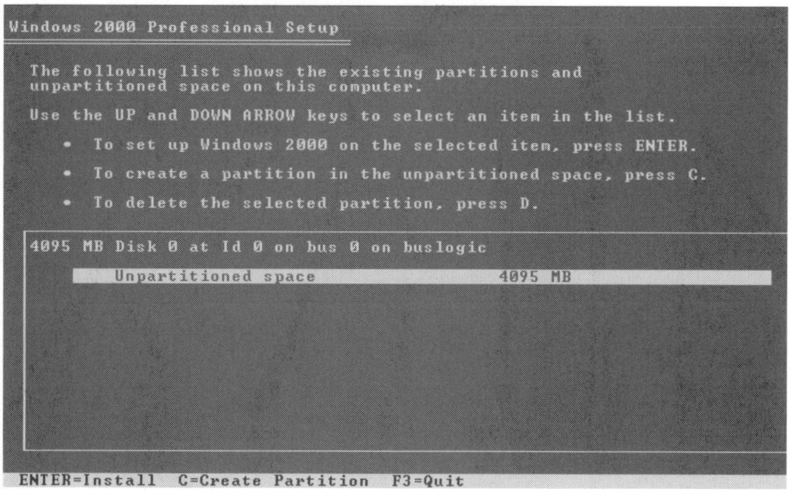

Figure 21 Partitioning

For this task, press Enter.

The installation CD needs to create an appropriate file system for the hard drive that the operating system is going to reside in. You have two choices to format the hard drive partition:

- **FAT32 (file allocation table 32)** is an older hard drive management system popular with Windows 98.
- **NTFS (new technologies file system)** is a newer file management system and is used on a file server because it more efficiently manages the storage.

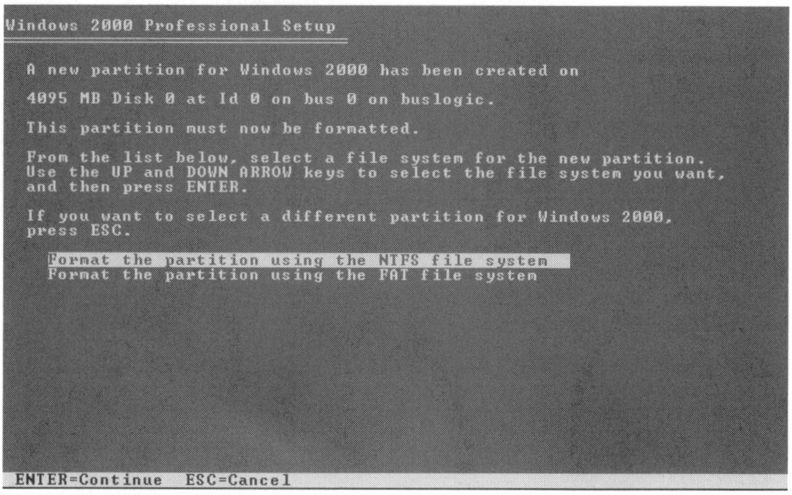

Figure 22 FAT32 or NTFS

285

Choose NTFS as your file management system, unless your tutor/supervisor advises otherwise.

The Windows 2000 installation will now automatically format the hard drive, and copy essential files to the hard drive.

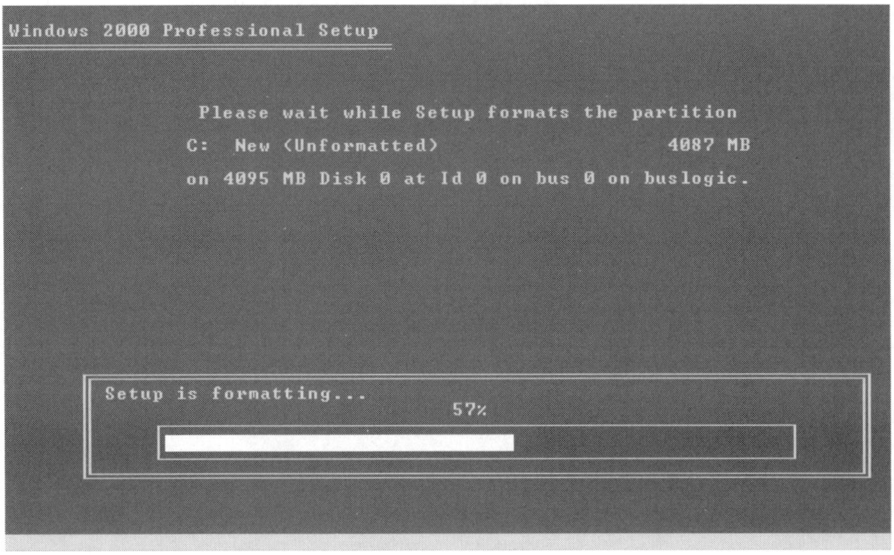

```
Windows 2000 Professional Setup



              Please wait while Setup formats the partition
              C:   New (Unformatted)                    4087 MB
              on 4095 MB Disk 0 at Id 0 on bus 0 on buslogic.








          Setup is formatting...
                                        57%
            ┌──────────────────────────────────────────────┐
            │██████████████████████████                    │
            └──────────────────────────────────────────────┘
```

Figure 23 Formatting

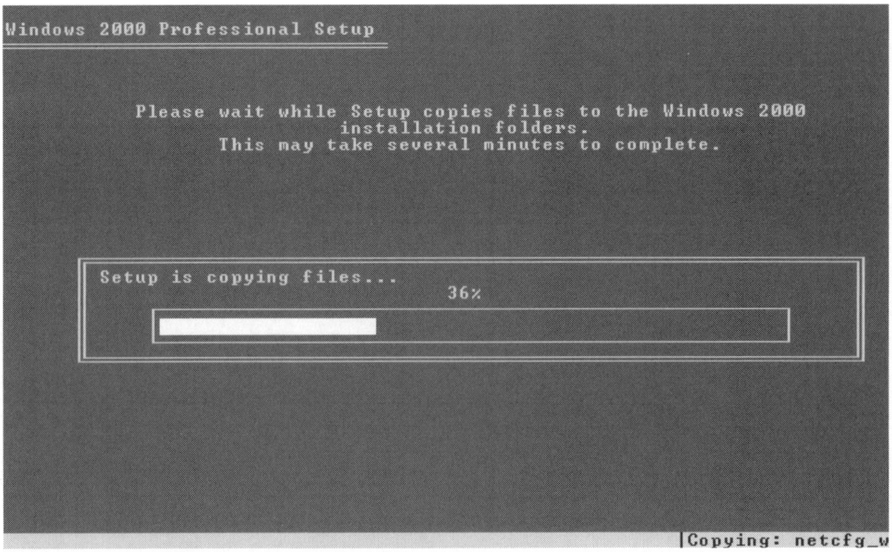

```
Windows 2000 Professional Setup



            Please wait while Setup copies files to the Windows 2000
                            installation folders.
                 This may take several minutes to complete.






          Setup is copying files...
                                     36%
            ┌──────────────────────────────────────────────┐
            │████████████████                              │
            └──────────────────────────────────────────────┘




                                                    |Copying: netcfg_w
```

Figure 24 Copying files from CD to hard drive

It will then prompt a restart. You must eject the CD so that it does not attempt to reinstall.

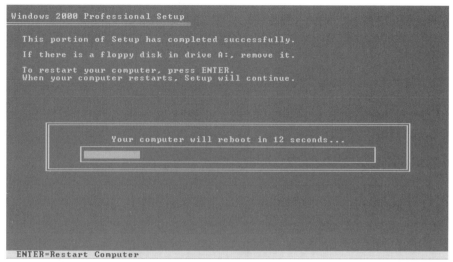

Figure 25 Restart

On restart you will be greeted with the Windows 2000 Startup screen.

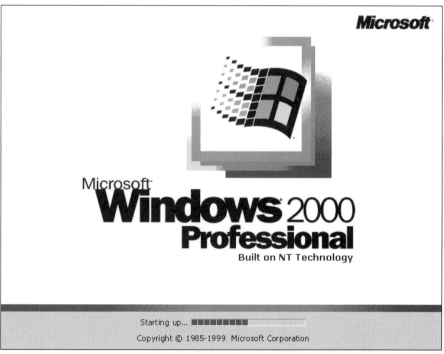

Figure 26 Startup of new installation

Once this screen has been displayed, reinsert the CD so that Windows can carry on with the installation. When the operating system is ready, it will wait and tell you to press Next so that it can detect various devices on your system (keyboard, mouse, drives, graphic adapter, monitor etc.). The screen will flicker; this is normal.

Figure 27 Press Next to detect devices

You are going to have to configure the locale for the computer (unless you are reading this book in the USA). You need to set UK keyboard (symbols like £@"# are all in different places), as well as currency and the way we display the time and the date.

You will need to customise the locale for each option.

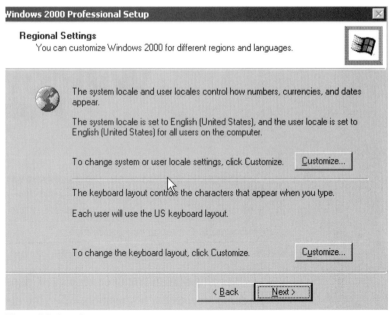

Figure 28 Locale

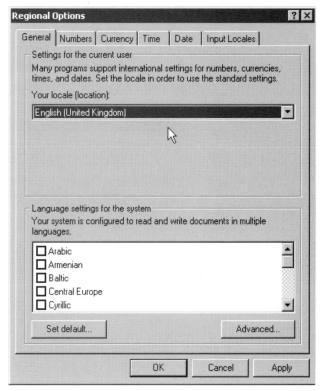

Figure 29 Setting the locale

Next, you will need to personalise the computer. You might put the user's name, designation (the job they do) as well as the company for whom you are installing the operating system.

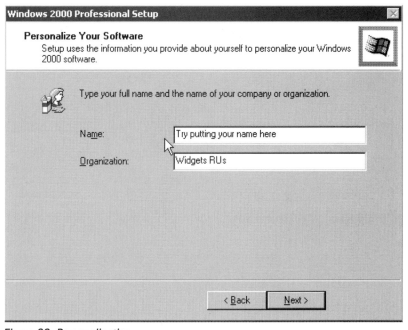

Figure 30 Personalisation

You will need to provide the computer with a unique identity which is used for asset management as well as possible network identification. The 'administrator' password is used to control the workstation. When anyone uses the login 'administrator', they will be able to install additional software and reconfigure the computer; anyone else is prevented from doing this.

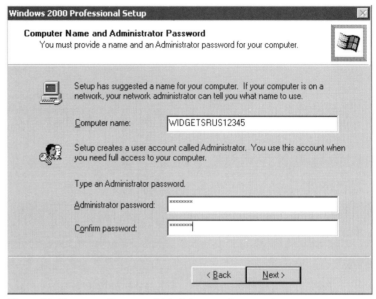

Figure 31 Computer Name and Administrator Password

This is followed by a simple screen in which you can set the correct time, date and time zone. The default time zone includes Seattle, which is the head office of the Microsoft Corporation!

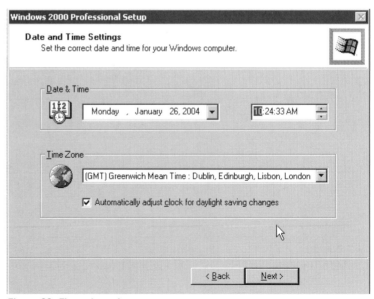

Figure 32 Time, date, time zone

Windows will install networking components and various other resources. For the purposes of this exercise, it is recommended that you select the Typical settings, as Custom settings need to be configured by an experienced networking professional (which you may become).

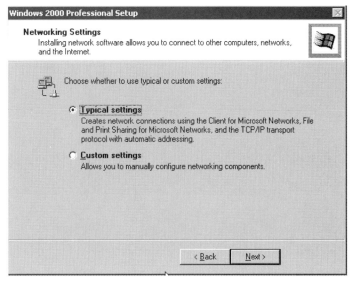

Figure 33 Network Settings

A **workgroup** is a collection of computers in a peer-based network system. Make the computer that you are configuring part of the group WIDGETSADMIN.

What does it mean?

*A **peer-based network** is one where each device in the workgroup is an equal and all parts of the system can share the same resources.*

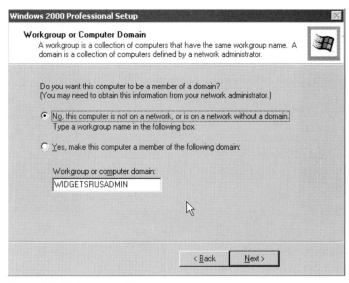

Figure 34 Workgroup settings

Based on the choices you have made, Windows 2000 will install the required operating system components. The process becomes very automated, and may take up to twenty minutes depending on the speed of the computer.

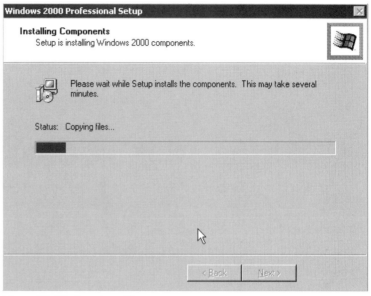

Figure 35 Windows installing components

Once this has been completed, you will be asked to remove the CD and Windows 2000 will restart the computer. On restart you will be presented with the Network Identification Wizard. This will allow your computer to access any network that has been connected. (You may need to check that the network card is connected to the wall socket.)

Figure 36 Restart

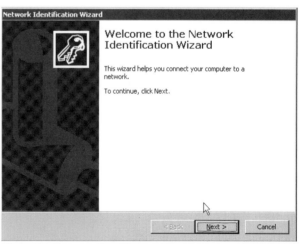

Figure 37 Network Identification Wizard

You will be asked to enter the administrator details and the password.

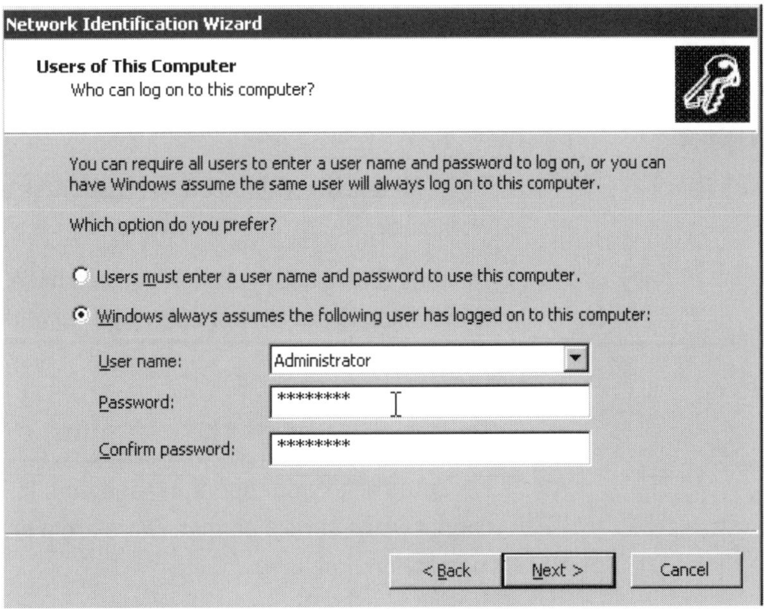

Figure 38 User access

Finally, the operating system will install and you are 'up and running'.

Figure 39 The end: one happy operating system

You may need to finely configure the operating system now that it is installed. It may require:

- motherboard, printer or USB device drivers
- the display adapting
- network settings finalised.

This will depend entirely on the resources available at your school, college or workplace.

The most likely configuration you will have to do, once the operating system is installed, is the network settings. All of the above are covered in greater detail in Section 5.

4.2.2 Issues with installing an operating system

We would all like our operating systems to install without hitch, but alas life cannot be as simple as that. There are a few common operating system installation problems.

- If the monitor is incompatible with the display size and properties required by the operating system, you will need to replace the monitor or install compatible drivers after setting the operating system to 640 × 480 with 16 colours.
- If the operating system lacks the drivers for various system components, you will have to install each individual driver.
- If you have forgotten, lost or misplaced the serial number, form a search team to find it! Unless you have this information before you start the install process, all is lost.
- You might not have carried out the checks as required and now find that the system has run out of memory. The operating system will be too slow as the processor cannot cope or the operating system will not fit on the hard drive partition as it is too small.
- An unlikely but possible fault includes the failure of the hard drive or corrupt media during installation.

5 How do I configure and test the installed operating system?

Now that you have successfully installed the operating system (as in Section 4) you now have to adjust the system to suit:

◆ your personal preferences

◆ the requirements of your employer

◆ the needs of the main user of the computer.

Therefore no installation is the same as any other (well, almost). Some of the configuration is done during the installation process, but you may have to return to ensure that the system is configured correctly.

The likely common settings for a computer that you will have to configure include:

◆ default and other printers

◆ time/date

◆ screen definition

◆ language (regional settings)

◆ user profiles

◆ network access and drives

◆ screen saver

◆ accessibility.

5.1 Configuring an installed operating system

If a printer is plugged in, recent versions of Windows (guaranteed from XP) will use **Plug and Play technology** to automatically detect any printer that is connected via the parallel lead or USB cable. Install the drivers and, if it is the only printer, it will make it the default.

Figure 40 Adding a printer

So long as you are in possession of the correct drivers, installation of a printer is simple in any version of Windows. Using Start/Settings/Printers and faxes, you can use the Add Printer Wizard.

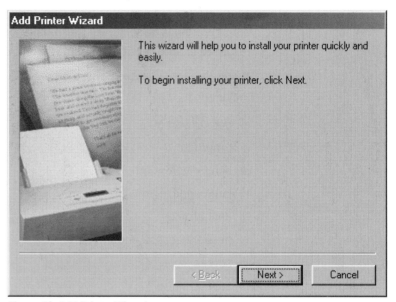

Figure 41 Add Printer Wizard

You can choose between a locally connected printer and one that is connected via the network. (You will need the address or network name of the printer for installation.)

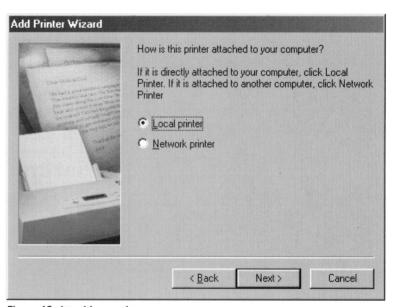

Figure 42 Attaching a printer

Choose Local port and click Next. You will be presented with a wide range of default drivers that Windows retains for common manufacturers and printers. If your printer is not in this list, then you will have to use the driver provided by the manufacturer.

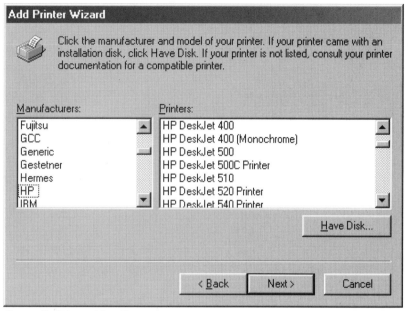

Figure 43 Printer driver list

You will then have the choice of confirming this installation as the default printer.

PRACTICAL TASK

Look back to the practical task on page 129, where you configured the printer driver. Go to the manufacturer's website and download the drivers for the same model. Plug in a printer to your computer using the parallel cable, and install the printer.

Setting the **time/date** for desktop computers should only need doing once, unless there has been a problem with the clock on the motherboard. Windows will make automatic changes to daylight savings in March and October.

You may need to regularly change the time/date settings for a laptop if the user is a frequent international traveller. Figures 44 and 45 show that you can set the time and date, as well as the local time zone of the computer.

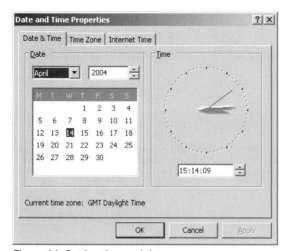

Figure 44 Setting time and date

Figure 45 Setting the time zone

With Windows XP and 2003, you can set the workstation or server to calibrate the local time with a remote time server, either provided by Microsoft or on your network.

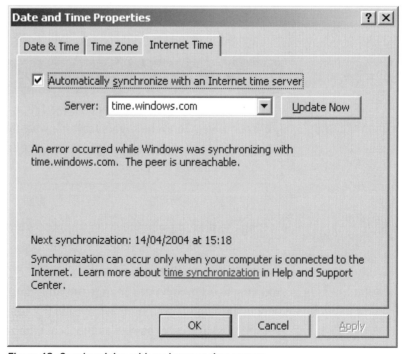

Figure 46 Synchronising with an Internet time server

PRACTICAL TASK

Changing the date and time is a mundane task so, instead, change the date to find out:

◆ the highest year possible

◆ the earliest year possible.

Try to explain these values.

The **screen definition** depends on:

◆ the size and quality (resolution) of the monitor

◆ the number of colours (quality) required for the applications being used (imaging and design require higher quality than word processing)

◆ the type of application (CAD (computer aided design) for engineering requires a large desktop area for the size of the designs).

Setting the screen in Windows can be done by right-clicking on the Desktop, selecting Properties and then selecting the Settings tab.

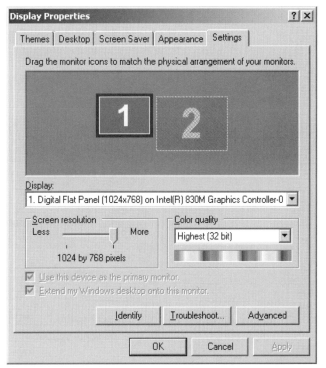

Figure 47 Setting the screen definition

Making the screen settings too high can prove problematic for the monitor. Note that Windows has a 15-second fail-safe in case of the display corrupting.

PRACTICAL TASK

Use the screen settings to see how high the resolution can be tuned before the monitor is unable to display the desktop.

The **language or regional settings** of a computer system can affect:

◆ the way the date is displayed (month/day/year instead of day/month/year)

◆ keyboard settings (different countries use different keyboard profiles; in the United States the @ is above the 2)

◆ how currency is managed ($ instead of £).

These can easily be changed using Control Panel/Regional Options.

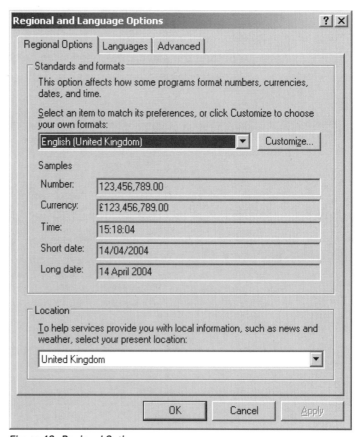

Figure 48 Regional Options

In Unit 401 you changed the keyboard's language settings. This was to overcome issues with the keyboard as the user was having difficulties with the system: the keys they pressed did not represent the characters displayed on the keyboard.

PRACTICAL TASK

◆ Make sure the computer you are using has the correct regional settings.

◆ Make sure that you have made a note of all the local settings on the computer that you are using.

◆ Then configure the system with incorrect regional settings to discover what happens with the wrong settings. Change the keyboard settings, first, to Spanish, then to Russian and finally to Afrikaans.

◆ For each keyboard setting, experiment with the keyboard.

User profiles are used when there is more than one permanent user for an individual computer. This may be:

◆ a family computer at home

◆ a computer that is used in an area where staff operate in shifts

◆ a public access system

◆ a work station that a predefined set of personnel may use, e.g. in a shop or a production area.

User profiles can also be configured to:

◆ be restrictive in what particular users can or, more likely, cannot do, i.e. restricting their access to files, folders and preventing them from being able to change settings or add any more software

◆ provide some users with more **access rights**, allowing them access to folders and files and some system settings

◆ provide a limited selection of users with overall rights (called **administrative rights**) which allows full access to all files, folders, settings and the ability to install any applications.

This feature has been available since the development of Windows 95. Unfortunately, user profiles in Windows 95 and 98 have no effective security restrictions unless you purchase additional software from third party suppliers. To find user profile management in Windows 98, go to Control Panel and select the Users icon (see Figure 49).

What does it mean?

Third party is, in legal terms, a company or person that has no direct contact with you and another company or person.

Figure 49 Windows 98 User Settings

As you can see from Figures 49 and 50, you can create a new user by following the wizard provided. You have to provide the local user name and password and any personal profile information as required.

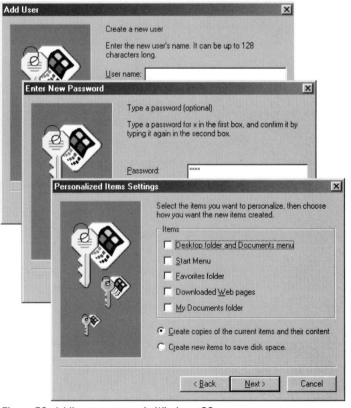

Figure 50 Adding a new user in Windows 98

PRACTICAL TASK

With the permission of someone in authority, gain access to a Windows 98 computer with no restrictions. Following the steps shown in Figure 50, create a new user with the user name of TEST and password of TEST, and then apply local settings of your own choice.

Windows 2000 and XP are very good at providing comprehensive and secure user profiles, improving on the inadequacies of Windows 98. Windows 2000 and XP are based on an older system devised for Windows NT (Version 4). In Windows NT, the local user profile can be associated with network access and this allows remote management of the user profile by a network administrator.

To access user profiles in Windows 2000, select Start, then Control Panel, and then select the Users and Passwords utility.

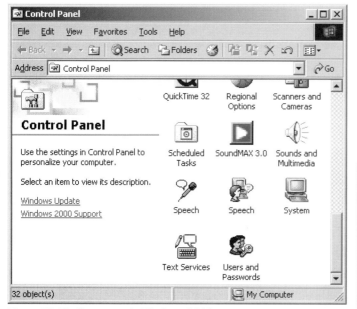

Figure 51 Finding a user in Windows 2000

Figure 52 Adding a user

To add a user, click on the Add option and you will be introduced to a simple wizard. Create a user of choice and provide a simple name and description.

Figure 53 Setting the user name

This will be followed by a **password**, which you are required to double-enter.

Figure 54 Setting the user password

Passwords are powerful mechanisms designed to prevent others from accessing personal and sensitive information. There are many 'dictionary' and 'brute force' tools available to 'hack!' into your password.

◆ Do not use a word that is easy to remember or easy to associate with you. The name of your cat, home town, favourite football team, pop/rock group or family cat is a poor choice.

◆ Instead, choose something obscure, like the name of the actor who walked on in the third sequel of *Terminator*.

◆ Or mix your password with letters and numbers. Instead of Mississippi you can have m1551551pp1, or hippopotamus can be h1pp0p0tamu5.

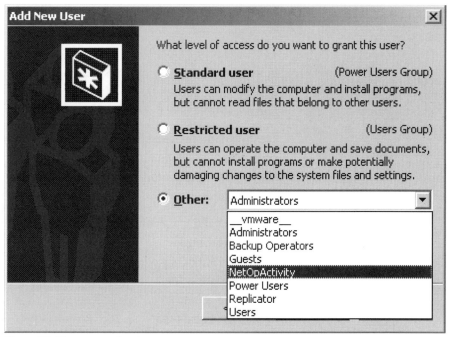

Figure 55 User access level

There are many types of users, according to privilege.

◆ The **standard user** type allows the user to add, remove and modify applications in their own profile but not to access the work or resources of any other user on the computer. This is ideal for a system where the user has a degree of technical trust.

◆ A **restricted user** cannot see the work of others and cannot modify the system. This type is often used in public access environments, or where there is no trust involved with the user. (This may be used in some schools or colleges.)

The remaining options are from administrators (who have comprehensive rights) through to administrator configured profiles (where you can restrict what the user can or cannot do).

For this example, use a standard user.

Restart (or log out) the computer you are using and you will find that you are able to login using the profile you have created.

PRACTICAL TASK

On a computer where you have appropriate rights and permission from your tutor/supervisor, create:

◆ a restricted user

◆ an administrator.

In a corporate system, or a small office or home network, providing the user with **network access** to share an Internet connection, and/or access to drives and printers, is now becoming commonplace.

Creating appropriate **network settings** for a computer on a corporate or college network does not mean that you have to be an expert in networking, but it is part of the process required to enable the computer to access a network drive.

First, you need to right-click on Network Neighborhood or My Network Places. Then you will be able to access the Local Area Connection Properties.

Figure 56 Local Area Connection Properties

You will then need to click on the TCP/IP settings.

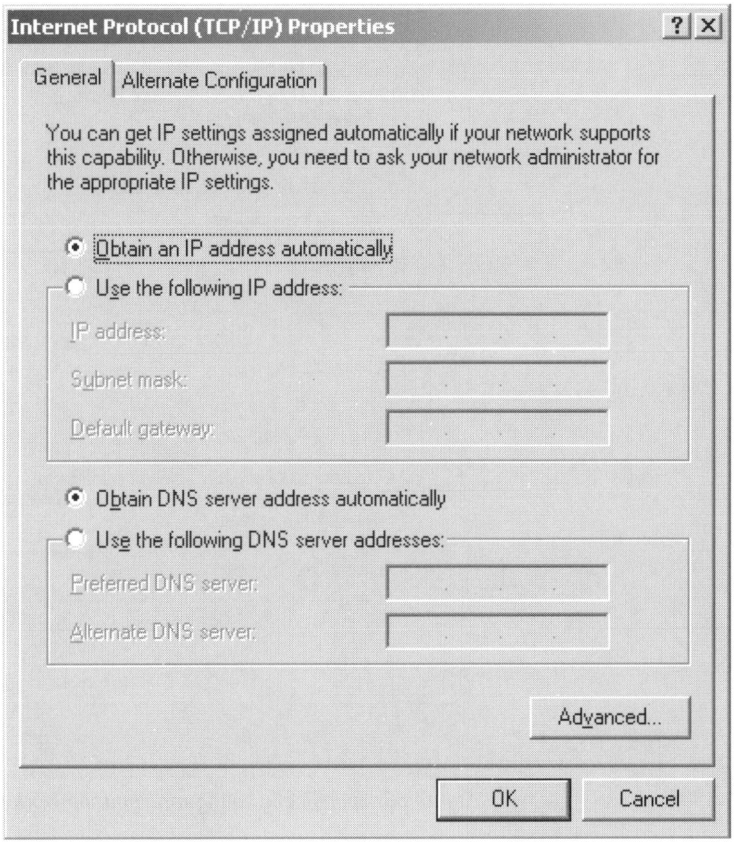

Internet Protocol (TCP/IP) Properties ? X

General | Alternate Configuration |

You can get IP settings assigned automatically if your network supports this capability. Otherwise, you need to ask your network administrator for the appropriate IP settings.

⦿ Obtain an IP address automatically

○ Use the following IP address:

IP address:

Subnet mask:

Default gateway:

⦿ Obtain DNS server address automatically

○ Use the following DNS server addresses:

Preferred DNS server:

Alternate DNS server:

Advanced...

OK   Cancel

Figure 57 TCP/IP settings

What does it mean?

TCP/IP (transmission control protocol/Internet protocol) is a technology used to enable computers to communicate with each other across a network or the Internet.

As you can see, your network administrator may have configured your network so that there is a DHCP server providing your computer with an address in order that it can communicate on the network.

What does it mean?

*DHCP (dynamic host configuration protocol) allows a server to give all the computers on a network a unique identity called an **address**.*

However, you may have to configure an address directly into your computer. Unfortunately, you cannot pick random numbers. There are some very specific rules on what constitutes a valid network address.

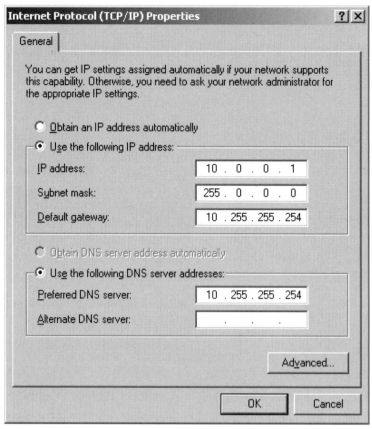

Figure 58 Specifically configuring your network address

Your network administrator or subject tutor may provide you with appropriate information to complete the address. Otherwise you could use addresses similar to those in Figure 58.

- 10.0.0.1 is known as a **private address** (which means that it can be used on your LAN). If you configure another computer, you will need to use 10.0.0.2 and above; you cannot use the same address on more than one device.

- 255.0.0.0 is the **subnetwork mask** and is a mathematical way of splitting your network into smaller systems. 255.0.0.0 means that there is only one network.

- 10.255.255.254 may not be the correct address. This is the default **gateway**, i.e. the way out of your network. This may be a proxy server or a network communication device like a **switch** or a **router**. If you have one of these devices, use this address on this system.

- The **DNS** (**domain name system**) server is used to match logical addresses to TCP/IP addresses. So the BBC website would be matched to an address like 210.23.12.56. This enables your computer to access the Internet and find other network services, like printers and network drives.

PRACTICAL TASK

Obtain appropriate permission and configure two computers with:

◆ IP addresses of 10.0.0.1 and 10.0.0.2
◆ a subnetwork mask of 255.0.0.0

Connect both computers to the same switch or hub (these are network communication devices) using the DOS command prompt and test the connection by using the following commands:

◆ on 10.0.0.1, type ping 10.0.0.2
◆ on 10.0.0.2, type ping 10.0.0.1

If the mini-network is working, you will see the messages shown in Figure 59.

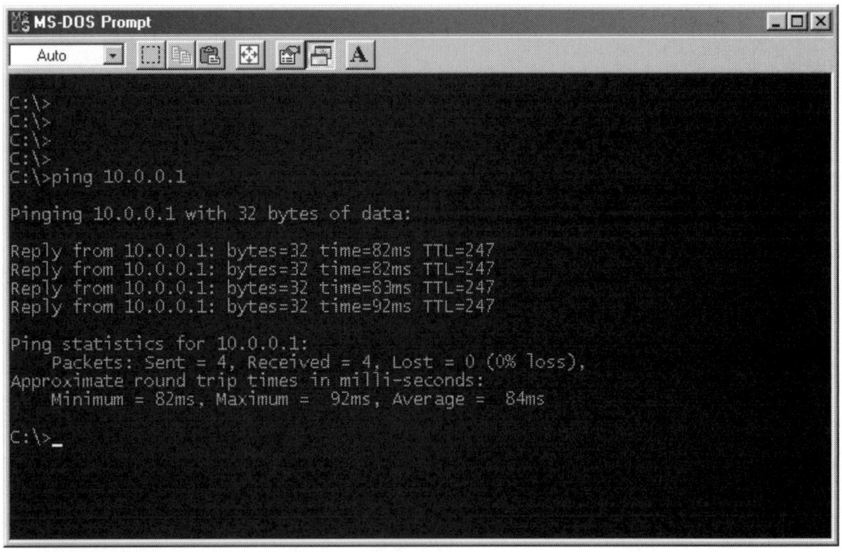

Figure 59 Using ping to test your mini network

If you have done the previous practical task, you will have created a small network, so you can now share the drives and provide network access for each computer across this network. This takes three stages:

◆ ensuring that your computer is in the same network workgroup as the other computer(s)
◆ sharing a network resource which, in this case, will be part of the hard drive but could be the CD-ROM or the printer
◆ accessing the remote network drive from your local computer.

Each version of Windows approaches this slightly differently. A computer with Windows 98 can be accessed by a computer with Windows XP, but the reverse is not true. Therefore for the benefit of this exercise you will be provided with examples of Windows XP, which are very similar to Windows 2000.

To make your computer(s) a member (or members) of the same workgroup you need to right-click on My Computer and select Properties. In the System Properties window, select the Computer Name tab.

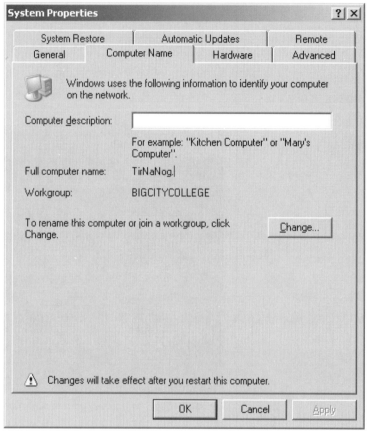

Figure 60 Workgroup settings

The workgroup name must be exactly the same for each computer, whereas the full computer name must be unique. When you elect to change the workgroup name you will have to restart the computer.

To share a hard drive or a folder for network access follow these steps:

◆ Select the folder or hard drive that you wish to share.

◆ Right-click on the resource and select the Sharing option.

For Windows XP, you can activate sharing by using a wizard.

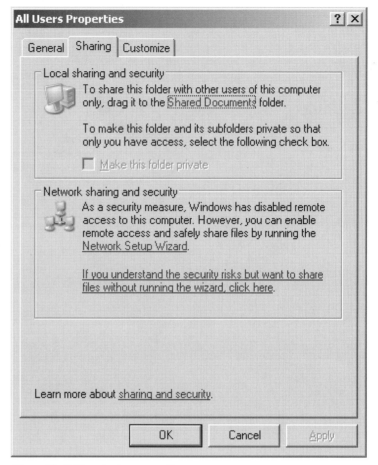

Figure 61   Folder sharing properties

Note: For Windows 2000 and 98, you can share a variety of folders. A hand icon will appear on the folder and you have to activate File and Printer Sharing in Network Properties.

Once sharing is activated, you can share the folder by selecting the share option and providing a **share name**: a logical name which will be seen by other computers. You can set the area as read only or with read/write access depending on whether you select the 'Allow network users to change my files'.

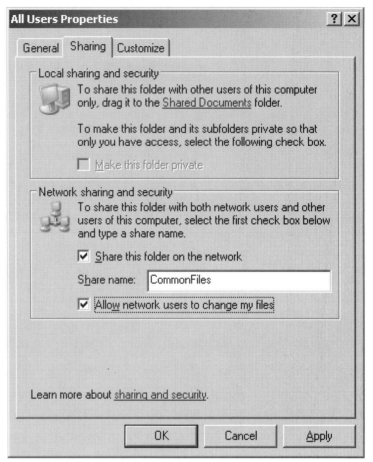

Figure 62 Network sharing properties

Figure 63 A shared folder

To access the network drive on the other computer, open My Network Places (or this could be Network Neighborhood). Select the option to View Microsoft Windows Network (called Entire Network in Windows 98) and open the BigCityCollege workgroup.

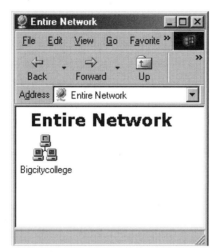

Figure 64 Network icon

Figure 65 Computer icon

You will find that all the computers are available on the network and that you can open any of the icons that relate to the computers. Once opened, the window will display all the shared folders that you can access. Each can be opened and used accordingly.

Figure 66 Network accessible folders

Figure 67 Network accessible subfolders

If the network connection is reliable, you can permanently map a drive to the network folder. This means that when you restart your computer, it will connect to the network drive each time and will be available in My Computer.

PRACTICAL TASK

Using the two computers that you have connected together in your mini-network, create a workgroup called MYWORK on each computer and name the computers Comp1 and Comp2. Share a folder of your choice from each system.

Current monitor technology has improved to such an extent that the original need for a **screen saver** has been surpassed. In the past, if you left the same screen on a monitor for a considerable period of time, the monitor would burn the image on the phosphor coating. Since then screen savers have found a new role as:

◆ a way that employees make their own personal mark on a computer

◆ a privacy mechanism, in that they stop people casually looking at work on the computer while you are away from your desk

◆ a security mechanism, wherein a password is required to stop the screen saver.

To set the screen saver on your computer, access it by right-clicking on Desktop and selecting Properties and then choosing the Screen Saver tab.

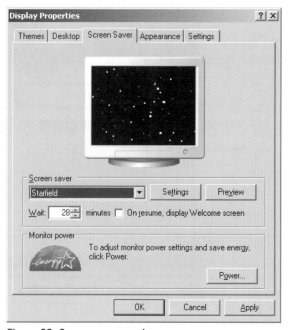

Figure 68 Screen saver settings

Most screen savers are configurable in that you can provide a password (in Windows 98) or the screen saver will use the password of the user profile in use on the computer (Windows 2000 and XP).

PRACTICAL TASK

With the permission of the person responsible for the computer that you are using, follow the links from www.heinemann.co.uk/hotlinks and search for free screen savers (at the last check there were over 600).

Install, configure and use the screen saver that you have selected.

Go out and try!

Windows XP home edition has an inbuilt screen saver. You can fill the My Pictures folder with images of your choice and it will use them in a personal screen saver.

You may need to configure the computer to make it more accessible. **Accessibility** is a feature that is available in all graphical operating systems; you can adapt the appearance and behaviour of the system to support a wide range of user needs.

◆ You can **change the size of the cursor** so that it is large and visible.

◆ You can **add motion trails** to the cursor so that people who are visually impaired can locate the cursor on a visually complex screen.

◆ Similarly, you can **change the contrast of the screen** and the colours used.

◆ You can **add voice-based support.** Microsoft provide excellent voice-based support in American, British and many other accents. This comes as standard with Office XP and is available for download for free from their corporate website. This is supported by many other applications.

◆ You can **reconfigure the keyboard with sticky keys.** Many people cannot use both their hands or all their fingers. There are keyboards, mice and voice recognition software available for this, but this does not help such people when they are using someone else's computer. If you hold down Shift for more than 5 seconds, sticky keys will activate, allowing the user to 'one finger' access all shift options. The same is true with Alt and Ctrl.

All of the above can be configured using the Control Panel/Accessibility option. As you can see from Figure 69, Accessibility Options provides keyboard, sound, mouse and display access.

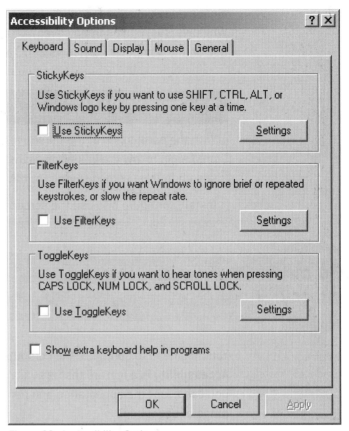

Figure 69 Accessibility Options

PRACTICAL TASK

With the permission of the person who is responsible for the computer that you are using, adapt the Accessibility settings. Change the keyboard, mouse, sound and display settings.

Before you make any changes to the operating system to adapt it to the user's or organisation's needs, you need to make a **backup of the registry** so that you can **restore any system settings** that you may have made.

Backing up the registry is a relatively simple process since the Windows 98 operating system makes automatic regular images of the registry. In Windows XP, you can find the System Restore feature in Control Panel/System Properties, System Restore tab.

For older operating systems, the process of backing up the registry is manual and needs to be done:

◆ on initial installation

◆ before any critical change to the system (such as adding a new component or replacing an application).

To access the registry, use Start/Run and type in REGEDIT.

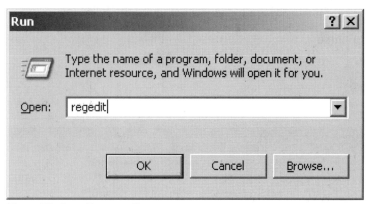

Figure 70 Start/Run regedit

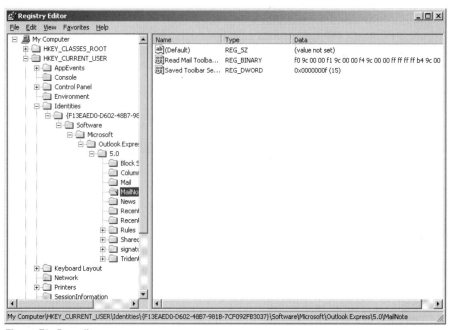

Figure 71 Regedit

The backup process is achieved by selecting File/Export Registry and exporting the entire registry as a .reg file. This file contains the entire registry database and can be re-imported to supersede any new settings. You can therefore recover the computer from any issues with a change that may have taken place. The registry is always saved on system shutdown, so restart the computer to ensure that the changes are permanent.

PRACTICAL TASK

Make a backup of your computer's registry. Open the saved .reg file in *WordPad*. You will notice that the database is in plain text format and contains all the keys described in Unit 401.

Use the Find utility to locate information using the following terms:

◆ your name

◆ Run

◆ Word

◆ Sol

Figure 72 The registry database

5.2 Testing an installed operating system

The process involved in the installation and testing of an operating system is, in principle, the same as the installation and testing of any hardware component or system.

When you have successfully (or maybe unsuccessfully) installed an operating system, there are a variety of elements that will benefit from being tested. You need to identify if any of the following problems occur.

◆ Does the operating system have any device conflicts?

◆ Is the operating system compatible with the hardware platform on which it is installed?

◆ Is the boot process slower than expected?

◆ Does the boot process stop (or hang) for any reason?

◆ Does the system crash or freeze for any unexplained reason?

◆ Is the user able to carry out their work without any problems?

◆ Is there enough hard drive storage space?

◆ Is there enough system memory for the applications that are being used?

◆ Do error messages appear?

◆ Is the display providing an adequate image?

◆ Has someone already managed to delete/relocate system files? (You will be surprised how adept users are at doing this.)

Go out and try!

Making sure that you have suitable permission, find a computer that is not needed by anyone at your place of study (or workplace). Go into the Windows directory and either:

◆ delete all the files with the .exe extension, or

◆ rename all the files with the .exe extension.

What happens when you restart the computer?

Testing your system can be done in a relatively simple manner.

◆ On installation, benchmark the computer to set the base standard. (This is the best performance of the system, upon which all other benchmarks will be measured.)

◆ Go into System Properties and Display Properties to check all device and driver settings.

◆ Use MSINFO32 to find out what resources are being used.

Any changes that you make to an operating system can be restored at a later date/time. This is especially useful if the change did not work, was not required or you were required to ensure that the user adhered to software licensing.

Windows XP has a System Restore facility which allows you to 'roll back' the operating system to an earlier state.

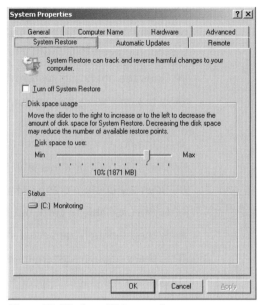

Figure 73 Windows XP System Restore

The Windows XP System Restore facility can be accessed from the System Properties dialogue (right-click My Computer, Properties or Control Panel/System).

With Windows 2000 and 98 you may wish to take a regular backup of the registry using REGEDIT. The Add/Remove Programs feature, which can be found in the Control Panel, is designed to completely remove a program/application and restore the operating system to the state prior to its installation.

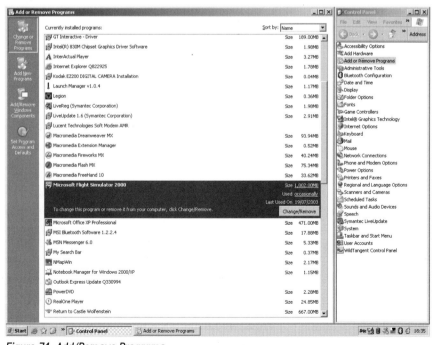

Figure 74 Add/Remove Programs

This is done by:

◆ removing applications files and associated directories

◆ ensuring that elements of the application which may be shared by other applications or system resources remain

◆ removing any drivers or system libraries that relate only to the application

◆ removing any references to the application in the system registry.

PRACTICAL TASK

Using the guidance on test plans and reports in Section 3, compose a plan for testing an operating system on installation. You will need to create tasks for these checks:

◆ Device conflicts: how they may be resolved?

◆ Hardware compatibility: what are the issues and possible solutions?

◆ Checking whether the boot process is slower than expected: what needs to be removed or upgraded to improve this?

◆ Identifying whether the boot process stops: what can be done?

◆ Checking whether the system is crashing or freezing: what can be done?

◆ Checking whether there is adequate hard drive storage space and freeing up used space.

◆ Checking whether there is enough system memory for the applications that are being used.

◆ The appearance of error messages: what are the likely solutions?

◆ Checking whether the display is providing an adequate image: how could this be improved?

◆ Checking how lost or relocated files can be replaced or repaired.

Then use this test plan on at least three computers and compile a comprehensive test report.

6 How do I successfully install any additional software?

Have you ever installed an application or game, only to find that your computer was incapable of running the software? Applications and games vary in complexity and the resources that they require. Checking system resources is essential as you or your employer may invest considerable quantities of money to find that:

◆ the money is wasted

◆ new computers need to be purchased at considerable expense

◆ existing computers need to be upgraded at some expense.

Heads may roll!

Therefore it is important that, before an application is installed or purchased, you check the availability of the resources recommended in the software installation instructions, which can be found:

◆ on the side of the box or disk case

◆ on the manufacturer's website

◆ in promotional literature provided by the manufacturer

◆ by contacting the company and liaising with an appropriate representative.

For most systems the following need to be checked.

◆ The *speed of the CD/DVD-ROM*, especially if the application uses resources from this media during operation
A slow CD-ROM can affect the performance of a game.

◆ *How much RAM is required* to run the application
Be aware that this is normally described as the minimum requirement and does not take into account that you may need to run other applications at the same time. An excellent rule of thumb is that you need to have twice as much RAM as that recommended by any application!

◆ The *speed and capacity of the processor* is paramount
It is very unlikely that you can run the application on a processor that is slower than the specification recommended by the manufacturer. Some applications demand extra processor resources, especially if the application relies on the processor carrying out mathematic functions. For example, *Flight Simulator* by Microsoft is heavily dependent on the Maths capability of any processor.

◆ How much *storage* is available on your hard drive, even in these times of extensive hard drive space
You need to be mindful of the capacity of the application as, through time, you are likely to absorb hard drive space.

◆ The *licence* will restrict what you can do with the software
You may find that you have limited the desired use of the application, as seen in Section 4.2.

PRACTICAL TASK

Search on the Internet to identify what the system requirements are for:

◆ the current version of Microsoft *Office*

◆ the latest version of Microsoft *Flight Simulator*

◆ the number-one ranking game at your local games retailer.

It is important that you back up and virus check the system prior to the installation as well as when you have completed installation. No application from any manufacturer can be guaranteed as virus or Trojan free, and it is considered wisdom that you ensure the integrity of your system (see Unit 401).

There are many applications that you can install. To develop comprehensive skills you will install:

◆ a device driver for a printer

◆ a web-installable application

◆ a comprehensive Office suite

◆ a utility or resource.

Each of these needs to be done by reading the manufacturer's installation plans or instructions. You can also create your own.

PRACTICAL TASK

Based on a computer game that you have or like, create a simple plan (this could be done as a diagram) listing all the stages involved in installing the software.

Installing a **device driver for a printer** has already been explored in Section 5.6.13 of Unit 401. The principles behind installing this as a service (a resource for an application) are the same as when you have to install or repair hardware (and operating systems).

Web-installable applications are a recent development. The software vendor does not want you to have the software so that you cannot be tempted to resell or pirate their hard work.

Applications that are installed from the vendor via the web tend to be:

◆ small applications such as games or utilities

◆ add-on components to an application that you have already purchased

◆ patches and system updates where the application requires modification.

Go out and try!

Visit the Macromedia website by following the links from www.heinemann.co.uk/hotlinks. If your computer's web browser is not up to date with the latest plug-in, they will offer to install the resource for you.

What does it mean?

Plug-in. An additional software component.

Microsoft distribute their web browser, Internet *Explorer*, by this method because they need to revise and update the application as new web attacks occur. To obtain this application, follow the links from www.heinemann.co.uk/hotlinks and search in downloads for **Internet Explorer 6 service pack 1**.

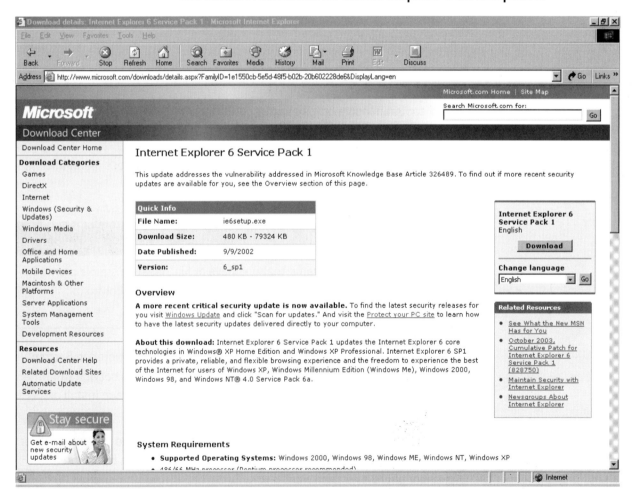

Figure 75 Adding a service pack

When you select the download option on the right-hand side of the screen, you will be able to download and run an installer application that is only 450 K in size.

On starting the installer you will have to accept the EULA.

Figure 76 Accepting the service pack

You may wish to choose to customise the browser on installation.

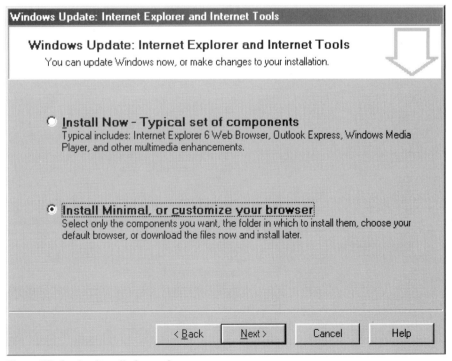

Figure 77 Setting installation options

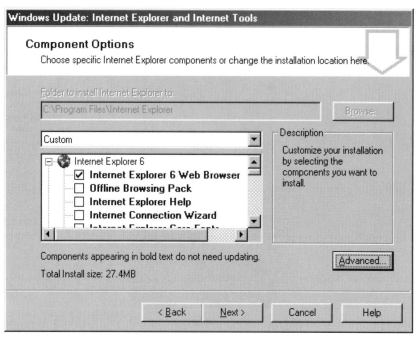

Figure 78 Selecting the components to install

As you can see from Figure 78, Internet *Explorer* provides a wide range of components that can be included (or excluded). If you click the Advanced button, you can download the entire application for installation on another computer (common on some secure systems).

Internet *Explorer* will download and install like any other application.

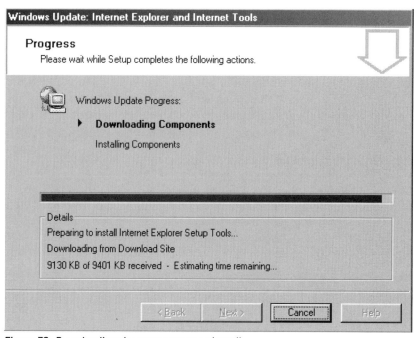

Figure 79 Downloading the components to install

Go out and try!

Follow the links from www.heinemann.co.uk/hotlinks to two sites with fun downloadable applications (real audio player and web tangent). Install either of these applications as applicable and either listen to the web radio or play the web games on the shockwave website.

Microsoft *Office* is a very popular and comprehensive office suite, containing:

◆ a word processor

◆ a database

◆ presentation software

◆ a spreadsheet

◆ an email application

◆ many utilities.

There have been many other high standard Office applications and Microsoft *Office* is not the only one available on the market.

Go out and try!

Microsoft *Office* is not alone as an Office application. Complete research on:

◆ openoffice.org

◆ Star office

Installing Microsoft *Office* is very straightforward. Once you have obtained the installation CD and the licensed serial number, make sure that you have a computer that will successfully install your version of *Office*. For this example, you will install *Office* XP. It is suggested that you have at least:

◆ 400 Mb of hard drive space (if everything is installed)

◆ a 400 MHz processor

◆ at least 128 Mb of RAM.

Once the CD has loaded and started, you will be greeted by the licence screen. You must enter your details (or those of the user) and the product serial number (note that the example provided in Figure 80 is invalid and you must use one provided with a licensed CD).

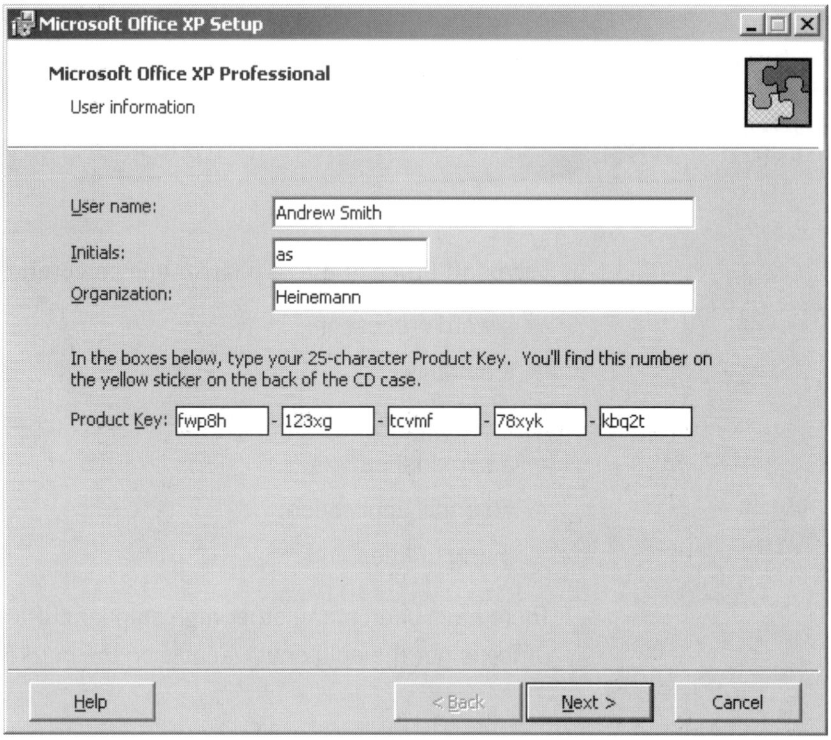

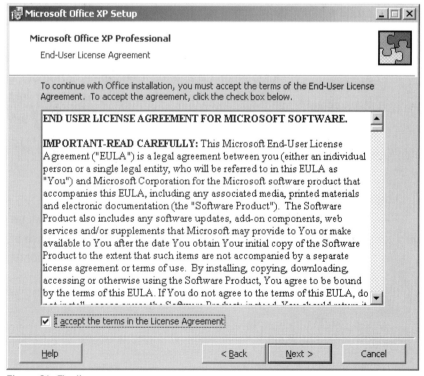

Figure 80 Providing the user details and licensed serial number

If the product serial number is valid, you will be taken to the EULA, which you must tick to proceed.

Figure 81 The licence agreement

Choose the custom installation option.

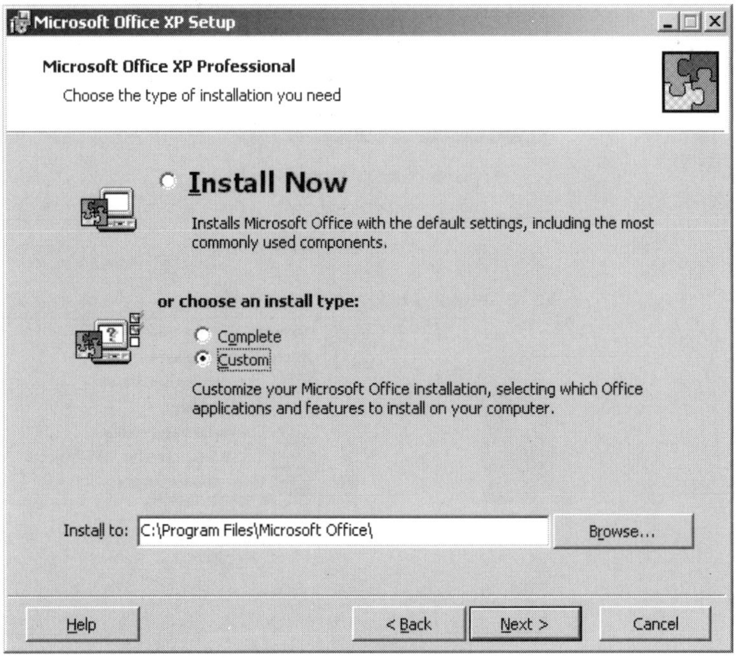

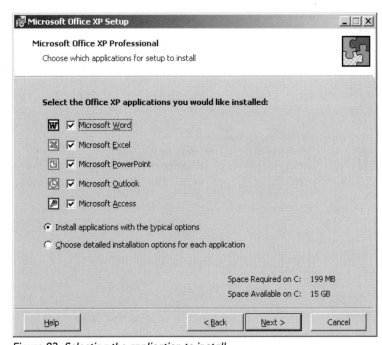

Figure 82 Selecting the custom installation options

Now you can select the type of application(s) you wish to install. It is important to remember that some users do not need every feature that Microsoft *Office* has to offer.

Figure 83 Selecting the application to install

Select the Choose Detailed Installation option.

As you will see from the menu that is offered, you can 'drill down' the options and elect to add or remove specialised components. Using Figure 84, find the Office Assistant and select the option to prevent installation.

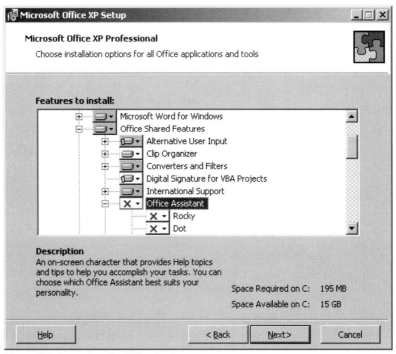

Figure 84 Removing the Office Assistant

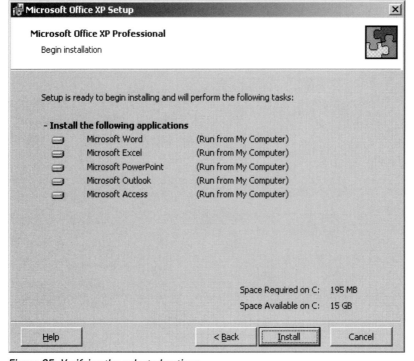

Figure 85 Verifying the selected options

Figure 86 The paper clip Office Assistant

Once you click Next, the application will install itself. Depending on the speed of your system and CD-ROM drive, this could take up to ten minutes.

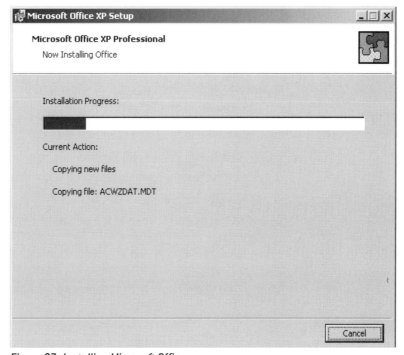

Figure 87 Installing Microsoft Office

Now that you have managed to install Microsoft *Office*, you (or the user) will be able to use it.

It is important that you check system functions after the installation of software as you may find that:

◆ the software conflicts with another application, i.e. the installation has overwritten some system files or re-associated files that you normally used another application to run

◆ the computer is unable to successfully operate the application due to the lack of memory or processor capability.

Go out and try!

There are many very good MP3 players that are freely available. The three that are commonly used are:

◆ Windows Media Player

◆ Winamp

◆ RealPlayer.

Each will try to associate the MP3 file format with their player.

Therefore, install each one (one at a time) and attempt to play an MP3. You will notice that the last application installed will be the one that plays the MP3, whilst the others are still installed on the computer.

As you saw in Figure 15 (page 280), once you have installed an application for yourself of a user, you need to complete a registration card or ensure that installation records are updated for your employer. Remember that companies are limited by various licences. If they exceed these they can incur legal action from the manufacturer.

Whilst it is unlikely that you will have problems with the installation of an application, if this does occur it is important that you make some record of this. Your experience of this problem may:

◆ provide evidence of a greater problem with the software or hardware system in use at your workplace

◆ support action that will be taken by your employer to get a refund or support from the manufacturer/supplier

◆ assist the manufacturer of the software (or the hardware) in rectifying the issue.

Once you have installed an application, it can be modified. This is normally a feature that is available with complex applications such as Microsoft *Office*.

You may wish to:

◆ add or remove a component
◆ repair an installation
◆ remove the application.

With Microsoft *Office* XP, you can reuse the installation CD to carry out all the previous items.

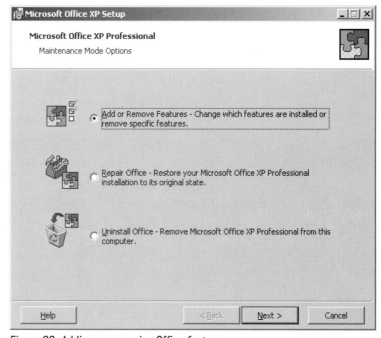

Figure 88 Adding or removing Office *features*

Adding or removing software is the same as the specialist installation of components of an application.

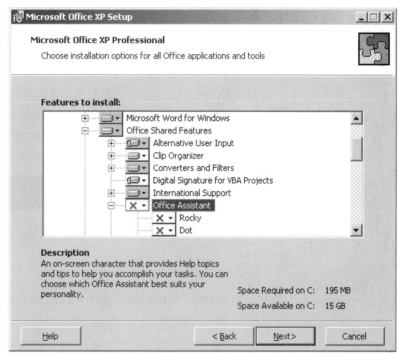

Figure 89 Selecting the specialist component to add or remove

Repairing *Office* means that you can completely reinstall the application or allow the software to run a diagnostic for you.

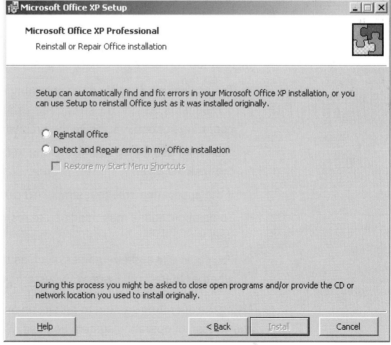

Figure 90 Allowing the application to repair or reinstall itself

Uninstall will remove the software, which means that:

◆ files and folders
◆ applications libraries
◆ registry entries

will be removed.

Testing an application is no different from the testing of the installation of hardware or an operating system. It is important that you look at how the application performs under extremes as well as with 'normal' work.

PRACTICAL TASK

Create a test plan for the comprehensive testing of your Microsoft *Office* XP installation.

Look in detail at:

◆ the size of the Word document and the number of images/drawings it can support
◆ the complexity of spreadsheet and formulae
◆ the size and complexity of the database.

If you want to produce an active test, remember that you can copy and paste information to extend the size of application files.

It is worth noting that problems with applications not working properly after installation can be resolved in one of several ways:

◆ The application may need the operating system to load specialist components on startup, so correctly shutting down and restarting the operating system may solve the problem.
◆ You might use the operating system to close software applications, using the Task Manager.
◆ If the application 'freezes', simply try closing and restarting.
◆ Some applications may need you to restore the application to 'factory set' defaults.
◆ You could use system utilities, such as the system monitor, to check whether there is an issue with system performance.

Using the operating system to restart an application can differ depending on the version of operating system you use. Windows XP and 2000 are the same, and Windows 98 is the same as its predecessor Windows 95.

In Windows XP or 2000, press Ctrl, Alt and Delete simultaneously and a window will appear called Windows Task Manager. This provides you with a degree of control of the underlying operating system and the applications that are running.

Figure 91 Windows Task Manager

The Windows Task Manager allows you to see:

◆ applications that are running

◆ processes (independent activities, which may be utility programs) that are being run by Windows

◆ current processor and memory performance

◆ networking throughput (the amount of data the network card or modem is handling)

◆ who is logged into your computer.

As you can see in Figure 91, you can prompt Windows to terminate an application by using the End Task option. This will prematurely terminate the application and you are very likely to lose any unsaved work.

You can also start a New Task. This is like the Start menu/Run option except you can start tasks that can be added to the Processes tab.

Your system is running many processes at any given time. These are the elements that ensure that Windows is able to provide you with the resources that you expect. Each time you start an application or install a utility you may start another process which can degrade the memory and processor performance of your computer. As can be seen in Figure 92, having many users increases the number of processes that will be operational.

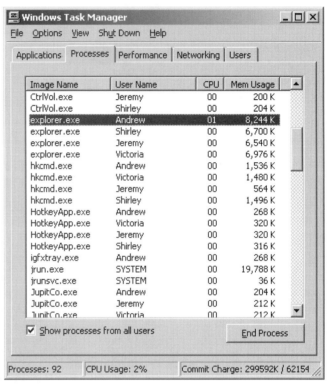

Figure 92 Processes in use by Windows

It is also worth noting that *Explorer* is an integral system process that provides control for all the file and desktop management.

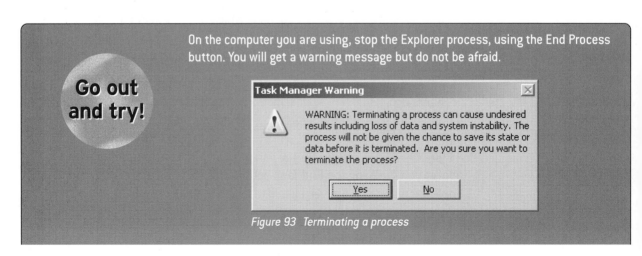

On the computer you are using, stop the Explorer process, using the End Process button. You will get a warning message but do not be afraid.

Go out and try!

Figure 93 Terminating a process

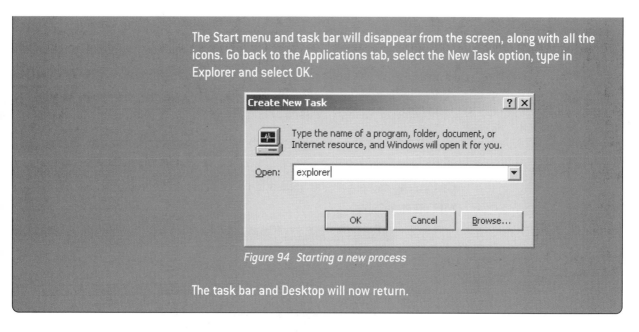

The Start menu and task bar will disappear from the screen, along with all the icons. Go back to the Applications tab, select the New Task option, type in Explorer and select OK.

Figure 94 *Starting a new process*

The task bar and Desktop will now return.

The Performance Monitor allows you to look at how the system is coping with the load that it is being given. This is particularly useful if you have a computer that is struggling with an application (or applications).

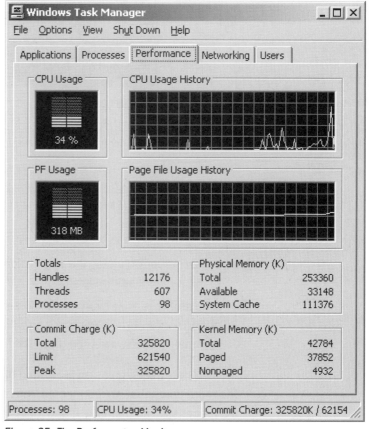

Figure 95 *The Performance Monitor*

The Performance Monitor provides you with information on:

◆ how the processor is being used at this moment and over the last five seconds

◆ page file usage (this is memory management through the use of virtual memory, which is an area on the hard drive)

◆ how much memory is used and is available

◆ how many tasks the processor and operating system are managing.

Whilst not a remit of your studies, looking at how the network connection is performing can provide an indication of the reason behind possible problems with an application.

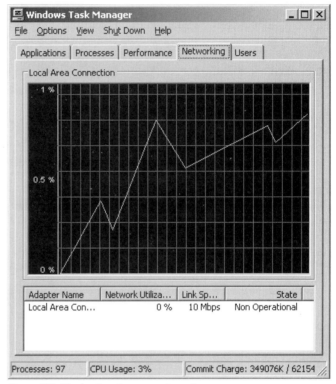

Figure 96 *Monitoring the network performance*

A busy network connection could be an indication of:

◆ a slow server providing the application or data, which needs to be reported to the network administrator

◆ a Trojan, virus or network denial of service attack that is affecting the performance of the computer and which may need you to install a firewall or anti-virus software (see Unit 401).

The final tab, Users, gives an indication of who is logged into the computer. The more users that are connected, the more processes are being used by the processor and memory. If you login as administrator you can warn, disconnect or logoff another user.

Figure 97 Monitoring connected users

Using Uninstall, you can add and remove components. Using the application's own ability to repair itself is an important part of the daily management of a computer system. It is important that, once this is completed, you report to either the user or management the outcome of the repair procedures that you have carried out. This is important because:

◆ the result may affect the customer

◆ there may need to be an analysis of why the problem originally occurred

◆ your organisation may need to look at the problem if this is a recurring issue.

This is best done by producing a report of any repairs that are carried out along with any tests that you may have carried out on the software.

PRACTICAL TASK

Install, use and remove Microsoft *Office* XP. Whilst you are doing this:

◆ back up data and test the system using a benchmark tool before installation

◆ test the system using the benchmark tool whilst the application is installed and running (open *Word*, *Excel* and *Access*)

◆ uninstall the software and run a benchmark on completion.

Create a test report that explains the changes in performance.

6.1 Using applications

The City and Guilds 7262/24 *ICT System Support* qualification is related to another City and Guilds qualification for *IT users*. This is an excellent opportunity to explore your ability to use the resource that you are installing for your customer.

It is important that you develop skills in:

◆ producing word processed documents with informative graphics using applications such as *Word*

◆ creating spreadsheets that carry out simple and complex calculations on data

◆ developing a simple database that could hold details of all users that have various software installed

◆ the manipulation of images using a graphics package such as *PhotoShop* or *Fireworks*

◆ the sending and receiving of emails as well as the use of the Internet.

Index

Page numbers shown in **bold** refer to definitions of the term in a What Does It Mean? box.